SHAKESPEARE STUDIES

EDITORIAL BOARD

Harry Berger Jr.
  The University of California, Santa Cruz

David M. Bevington
  The University of Chicago

Catherine Belsey
  University of Wales College of Cardiff

Michael Bristol
  McGill University

S. P. Cerasano
  Colgate University

Jonathan Dollimore
  The University of York

Barry Gaines
  The University of New Mexico

Jean E. Howard
  The University of Pennsylvania

Lena Cowen Orlin
  University of Maryland, Baltimore County

John Pitcher
  St. Johns College, Oxford

Maureen Quilligan
  Duke University

Alan Sinfield
  The University of Sussex

Peter Stallybrass
  The University of Pennsylvania

SHAKESPEARE STUDIES VOLUME XXIX

EDITED BY
LEEDS BARROLL

BOOK-REVIEW EDITOR
Susan Zimmerman

Madison • Teaneck
Fairleigh Dickinson University Press
London: Associated University Presses

© 2001 by Rosemont Publishing & Printing Corp.

All rights reserved. Authorization to photocopy items for internal or personal use, or the internal or personal use of specific clients, is granted by the copyright owner, provided that a base fee of $10.00, plus eight cents per page, per copy is paid directly to the Copyright Clearance Center, 222 Rosewood Drive, Danvers, Massachusetts 01923. [0-8386-3922-4/01 $10.00 + 8¢ pp, pc.]

Associated University Presses
440 Forsgate Drive
Cranbury, NJ 08512

Associated University Presses
16 Barter Street
London WC1A 2AH, England

Associated University Presses
P.O. Box 338, Port Credit
Mississauga, Ontario
Canada L5G 4L8

The paper used in this publication meets the requirements of the American National Standard for Permanence of Paper for Printed Library Materials Z39.48-1984.

International Standard Book Number: 0-8386-3922-4 (vol. XXIX)
International Standard Serial Number: 0-0582-9399

All editorial correspondence concerning *Shakespeare Studies* should be addressed to the Editorial Office, *Shakespeare Studies,* English Dept., Fine Arts, University of Maryland (Baltimore County), Baltimore, Maryland 21250. Manuscripts submitted without appropriate postage will not be returned. Orders and subscriptions should be directed to Associated University Presses, 440 Forsgate Drive, Cranbury, New Jersey 08512.

Shakespeare Studies disclaims responsibility for statements, either of fact or opinion, made by contributors.

PRINTED IN THE UNITED STATES OF AMERICA

Contents

Foreword	9
Contributors	11

Forum: Body Work

Introduction BRUCE R. SMITH	19
The Body of Stage Directions ALAN C. DESSEN	27
Between the Lines: Bodies/Languages/Times JAMES R. SIEMON	36
The Body and Its Passions GAIL KERN PASTER	44
Bodies in the Audience CYNTHIA MARSHALL	51
The Body and Geography JOHN GILLIES	57
Whose Body? JYOTSNA G. SINGH	63
Body Problems DYMPNA CALLAGHAN	68

Articles

The Need for Lavinia's Voice: *Titus Andronicus* and the Telling of Rape EMILY DETMER-GOEBEL	75
Controlling Clothes, Manipulating Mates: Petruchio's Griselda MARGARET ROSE JASTER	93

More or Less: Editing the Collaborative JEFFREY MASTEN	109
Assessing "Cultural Influence": James I as Patron of the Arts LEEDS BARROLL	132

Reviews

Judith H. Anderson, *Words that Matter: Linguistic Perception in Renaissance English* ANNE LECERCLE	165
Catherine Belsey, *Shakespeare and the Loss of Eden: The Construction of Family Values in Early Modern Culture* HELEN COOPER	169
David M. Bergeron, *King James and Letters of Homoerotic Desire* NICHOLAS F. RADEL	173
Philippa Berry, *Shakespeare's Feminine Endings: Disfiguring Death in the Tragedies* CYNTHIA MARSHALL	180
Takashi Sasayama, J. R. Mulryne, and Margaret Shewring, eds., *Shakespeare and the Japanese Stage* John Russell Brown, *New Sites for Shakespeare: Theatre, the Audience, and Asia* LOIS POTTER	184
Dympna Callaghan, *Shakespeare Without Women: Representing Gender and Race on the Renaissance Stage* NORA JOHNSON	190
Alan C. Dessen and Leslie Thomson, *A Dictionary of Stage Directions in English Drama, 1580–1642* BARRY GAINES	196
Heather Dubrow, *Shakespeare and Domestic Loss: Forms of Deprivation, Mourning, and Recuperation* GORDON TESKEY	199
Raphael Falco, *Charismatic Authority in Early Modern English Tragedy* MICHAEL D. BRISTOL	203
Susan Frye and Karen Robertson, eds., *Maids and Mistresses, Cousins and Queens: Women's Alliances in Early Modern England* LISA HOPKINS	207

Contents

Andrew Hadfield, *Literature, Travel, and Colonial Writing in the English Renaissance, 1545–1625*
Thomas J. Scanlon, *Colonial Writing and the New World 1583–1671: Allegories of Desire*
    ANIA LOOMBA   209

Paul E. J. Hammer, *The Polarisation of Elizabethan Politics: The Political Career of Robert Devereux, 2nd Earl of Essex, 1585–1597*
    PAULINE CROFT   223

Joan Pong Linton, *The Romance of the New World: Gender and the Literary Formations of English Colonialism*
    KIM F. HALL   225

Lynne Magnusson, *Shakespeare and Social Dialogue: Dramatic Language and Elizabethan Letters*
    WILLIAM H. SHERMAN   232

Nabil Matar, *Islam in Britain 1558–1685*
Turks, Moors, and Englishmen in the Age of Discovery
    CHARLES BURNETT   236

Georges Minois, *History of Suicide: Voluntary Death in Western Culture*, tr. Lydia G. Cochrane
    JONATHAN DOLLIMORE   240

Richard L. Nochimson, General Editor, *Pegasus Shakespeare Bibliographies*
    TANYA POLLARD   245

Eve Rachele Sanders, *Gender and Literacy on Stage in Early Modern England*
    MARGO HENDRICKS   249

Michael C. Schoenfeldt, *Bodies and Selves in Early Modern England: Physiology and Inwardness in Spenser, Shakespeare, Herbert, and Milton*
    JONATHAN GIL HARRIS   252

Garrett A. Sullivan, *The Drama of Landscape: Land, Property, and Social Relations on the Early Modern Stage*
    JOHN GILLIES   258

Alison Shell, *Catholicism, Controversy, and the English Literary Imagination, 1558–1660*
    LOWELL GALLAGHER   265

Index   274

Foreword

*S*HAKESPEARE STUDIES is very pleased to offer in Volume XXIX its fifth Forum, organized by Bruce Smith. "Body Work" confronts a topic which has, in the last ten years, become an object of study in its own right. This is the matter of the social constructedness of physiological knowledge, a subject pioneered in the work of Laqueur, Siraisi (1990), Butler, and Paster (1993). "Body Work" presents the thinking of eight scholars, each of whom has been asked to write out his or her thoughts on the relationship between the body and some other entity. The result, as Smith indicates, is by no means a kind of united manifesto. Rather, we observe here the raising of very large questions about the relationship between the seen and the unseen, between body and consciousness, and even between material evidence and subjectivity.

In addition to the Forum, Volume XXIX features four essays contributed by Leeds Barroll, Emily Detmer-Goebel, Margaret Rose Jaster, and Jeffrey Masten. They range in subject from a reconsideration of King James I's patronage of the arts, to practical and theoretical issues implicit in editing multi-authored texts, to theorizing the connection between clothes and matrimonial dominion in early modern England, to a study of the construction of the idea of rape in *Titus Andronicus*. The balance of Volume XXIX, as is our custom, is devoted to (twenty-one) substantial reviews of important new scholarly work.

Plans for Volume XXX, to appear in Fall 2002, include a Symposium styled as "Theatre History Updates" which will carry the contributions of ten theatrical scholars and be directed by S. P. Cerasano; and a Forum, "Ideas of History in Renaissance Study," to be directed by Dympna Callaghan. This issue will also include new essays by Philippa Berry and Gustav Ungerer.

On another front, *Shakespeare Studies* is very pleased to announce the appointment of Jonathan Dollimore of the University of York as a member of our Editorial Board. Finally, I would like to inform our readership that while the editorial offices of *Shakespeare Studies* remain at the University of Maryland (Baltimore County), I have myself become a Scholar in Residence at the Folger Shakespeare Library, effective May 2000.

The Editor

Contributors

MICHAEL D. BRISTOL is Professor of English at McGill University. His most recent book is *Big Time Shakespeare.*

CHARLES BURNETT is a lecturer at the Warburg Institute, University of London.

DYMPNA CALLAGHAN is William P. Tolley Professor in the Humanities at Syracuse University. Her books include *Shakespeare Without Women, The Feminist Companion to Shakespeare,* and *Women and Gender in Renaissance Tragedy.*

HELEN COOPER is Professor of English Language and Literature at the University of Oxford, and a Tutorial Fellow of University College, Oxford. She is currently writing a book on the Elizabethan reading of medieval romances.

PAULINE CROFT is Reader in Early Modern History, University of London.

ALAN C. DESSEN is Peter G. Phialas Professor of English at the University of North Carolina, Chapel Hill, and the author of seven books on English Renaissance drama, most recently *Recovering Shakespeare's Theatrical Vocabulary* (1995), and *A Dictionary of Stage Directions in English Drama 1580–1642,* co-authored with Leslie Thomson.

EMILY DETMER-GOEBEL is Assistant Professor of English at Millikin University. She is currently completing a book on representations of rape and consent in early modern English drama.

JONATHAN DOLLIMORE is Professor of English at the University of York.

BARRY GAINES is Professor of English at the University of New Mexico. He is coeditor of the Revels Plays edition of *A Yorkshire*

Tragedy; coeditor, with Jill Levenson, of the Malone Society edition of the First Quarto of *Romeo and Juliet*; and editor of the forthcoming Applause Shakespeare *Antony and Cleopatra,* with performance notes by Janet Suzman.

LOWELL GALLAGHER is Associate Professor of English at the University of California, Los Angeles. He is currently completing a critical history of the figure of Lot's wife in patristic, early modern, and postmodern theological and literary cultures.

JOHN GILLIES is Professor in Literature at the University of Essex. He has written extensively on early modern theater and spatial poetics.

KIM F. HALL holds the Thomas F. X. Mullarkey Chair in Literature at Fordham University. She is currently working on a teaching edition of *Othello* and a book tentatively titled *The Sweet Taste of Empire: Sugar, Gender and Material Culture.*

JONATHAN GIL HARRIS is Associate Professor of English at Ithaca College. The author of *Foreign Bodies and the Body Politic: Discourses of Social Pathology in Early Modern England,* he is currently completing a book on points of connection between discourses of disease and national economy in early modern English drama.

MARGO HENDRICKS teaches at the University of California, Santa Cruz. She is completing a book on Shakespeare and race.

LISA HOPKINS is Reader in English at Sheffield Hallam University. She is currently working on a book on female heroes in English Renaissance drama.

MARGARET ROSE JASTER is an Assistant Professor at the Pennsylvania State University, Capital College, at Harrisburg. She has published on the relationship between England and Ireland in early modern history, Shakespeare and popular culture, and other topics. She is presently working on a book-length study of clothing and conduct literature in early modern society.

NORA JOHNSON is Associate Professor of English at Swarthmore College. She is currently completing a book on actors as authors in early modern England.

Contributors

ANNE LECERCLE, Professor of English Literature at the University of Paris 10-Nanterre and Shakespeare Lecturer at the École Normale Superieure (Paris), has published widely in French and English on Renaissance and contemporary theater. Forthcoming: a book in French on the writings of Harold Pinter. In preparation: a book on the language of Renaissance drama; also, a study of Holbein.

ANIA LOOMBA is Professor of English at the University of Illinois (Urbana-Champaign). She is currently writing a book on Shakespeare and race.

CYNTHIA MARSHALL is Professor and Chair of English at Rhodes College. She is currently preparing a stage history of *As You Like It* for the Shakespeare in Production series. Her book, *The Shattering of the Self: Violence, Subjectivity, and Early Modern Texts,* is forthcoming.

JEFFREY MASTEN is Associate Professor of English at Northwestern University. He is currently completing a book called *Spelling Shakespeare, and Other Essays in Queer Philology*; with Wendy Wall, he edits *Renaissance Drama.*

GAIL KERN PASTER is Professor of English at George Washington University and Editor of *Shakespeare Quarterly.*

TANYA POLLARD is Assistant Professor of English at Macalester College. She is currently completing a book on preoccupations with poison and drugs in early modern English theater and medicine.

LOIS POTTER is Ned B. Allen Professor of English at the University of Delaware. She recently completed a book on *Othello* for the Shakespeare in Performance series.

NICHOLAS F. RADEL is Professor of English at Furman University. He has written articles on queer theory, Shakespeare, and his contemporaries for such journals as *Shakespeare Quarterly, MaRDiE,* and *Renaissance Drama.*

WILLIAM H. SHERMAN is Associate Professor of English at the University of Maryland. He is author of *John Dee: The Politics of*

Reading and Writing in the English Renaissance and coeditor (with Peter Hulme) of *'The Tempest' and Its Travels*.

JAMES R. SIEMON is Professor of English at Boston University. He is the author of *Shakespearean Iconoclasm* (1985), and *Word Against Word: Shakespearean Utterance* (forthcoming). He is editing the Arden edition of *Richard III*.

JYOTSNA G. SINGH is an Associate Professor of English at Michigan State University. She is co-author of *The Weyward Sisters: Shakespeare and Feminist Politics* (1995), and author of *Colonial Narratives/Cultural Dialogues: 'Discoveries' of India in the Language of Colonialism* (1996). She is also co-editor of *Travel Knowledge: European 'Discoveries' in the Early Modern Period* (2000).

BRUCE R. SMITH, Professor of English at Georgetown University, is the author of *The Acoustic World of Early Modern England* (1999), and *Shakespeare and Masculinity* (2000).

GORDON TESKEY teaches at Cornell University. He is author of *Allegory and Violence* (1996) and is presently writing on Milton.

SHAKESPEARE STUDIES

FORUM: BODY WORK

Introduction

Bruce R. Smith

I WILL BE FORGIVEN, I hope, the first-person new-historicist anecdote. (If your patience for this topos is exhausted, you may want to begin with the next paragraph.) Several years ago in the Old Reading Room of the Folger Shakespeare Library I was poring over a book—I'd like to think it was Sir William Cornwallis's *Essays,* printed by Edmund Mattes in 1600, but at this distance I can't be sure—when I turned the page and happened on something that literally took my breath away. What arrested my attention was not something signified by the letters printed on the page—though Cornwallis's essay "Of Experience" gave me plenty to think about—but a hair. A single hair. About three inches long. Brown in hue. It was affixed to the page by the ink. I could not resist the impulse to touch the hair, an action, delicate as I tried to be, that ended up detaching the hair from the text in which it had been impressed and made me feel a little like Pope's Lord Petre. One of Mattes's workmen had lost this hair while working the press, and here I was, nearly four hundred years later, touching it, holding it between my fingers. The clew was so very slight, but at that moment I felt a sense of connection with the past far more substantial than anything Cornwallis's text could inspire. Why should that be so? Why should contact with a vestige of this long-dead printer's body so excite my imagination? The writers assembled in these pages suggest several answers to that question as they trace approaches to the early modern body in current Shakespeare scholarship. In different ways, all of these writers are concerned with *finding* the early modern body amid the texts that inscribe it.

The body has stood in markedly different relationships to each of the dominant critical methodologies of the past thirty years. As long ago as 1932, J. B. Bamborough in *The Little World of Man* was reminding modern readers that Shakespeare's contemporaries entertained ideas about their bodies that differed markedly from the ideas of twentieth-century men and women. By and large, however, such knowledge was relegated to footnotes while the universal humanist subject continued to hold center page. The "theory" of the humors—a "theory" because so patently fallacious by the standards of modern medicine and modern psychoanalysis—might be useful in reading comedies like Jonson's *Everyman In His Humor* and *Everyman Out,* but to consider Hamlet a victim of too much black bile seemed strangely anachronistic—if anachronism can be said to work backwards from the present. Such a statement seemed to represent a diminution of that timeless entity known as tragedy.

In formalist criticism, the body is taken to be a trope. It can signify a wide range of meanings, to be sure, but on the surface of the well-wrought urn the human body occupies the same ontological status as pipes and timbrels, forest branches, trodden weeds, and lowing heifers. Even T. S. Eliot's description of the sensibility of early seventeenth-century poets like Donne, able to "feel their thought as immediately as the odor of a rose," assumes that the body and its experiences are simply *there,* waiting for the poet's mimesis.[1] If formalist criticism is indifferent to the human body, psychoanalytic criticism is obsessed with it. In psychoanalytic criticism, Keats's fair youth breaks free of the surface of the urn: he demands to be considered a thinking, feeling, above all *desiring* subject. The body in both Freud's theory of the psyche and Lacan's emerges as the site of desire, in three dimensions. It is through the erogenous body that the subject in the text is imagined to experience desire. The object of his or her desire is another erogenous body—or a fictional substitute for that body. And the reading subject is likewise assumed to be an embodied person whose reading of the text is an indulgence in desire. Mouth, anus, genitals, and their displacements in Freud become in Lacan *objets a,* openings into the interiority of the always desired never possessed Other.[2] In Freudian theory, the body in question shapes up as no less a timeless, ahistorical entity than it is in formalist criticism. Even Lacan, who allows for cultural differences via the distinct languages that inculcate the body into the Symbolic Order, nonetheless assumes a universal body as he insists on the same frustration of desire, the same existential discomfort, in all human beings, regardless of their specific cultural circumstances.

If we now find ourselves ready to confront, not *the* body, but the *early modern* body, it is surely new historicism, with its belief in the social constructedness of everything, that has brought us to this pass. After self, woman, sodomy, nation, and race it was inevitable that the body would become an object of study in its own right. The body has, of course, been implicated in all these other constructions. In fact, "self-fashioning"—the concept with which new historicism began—would have struck early modern readers as an oxymoron, since the word "self," for them, carried physical, indeed physiological force.[3] "Self" was fundamentally a place marker, a way of specifying "that very one" (*Oxford English Dictionary, s.v.* "self," A.1), as when Caesar says that Antony's death-wound has been made by "that self hand / Which writ his honor in the acts it did."[4] *Nosce teipsum*: the emphasis in that humanistic imperative fell as much on the *ipsum* as on the *te*. To know one's "self" was to know a soul-in-a-body. According to Philippe de Mornay and his English translator Anthony Munday, *The True Knowledge of a Man's Own Self* (1602) is specifically physiological knowledge. The book promises to hold the mirror up to nature, to show the reader "the inward parts of the body, from the very hour of conception, to the latest minute of life."[5] "Self" as "a permanent subject of successive and varying states of consciousness" (*OED* C.3) is a much later idea, dating only from the end of the seventeenth century. Woman, sodomy, nation, and race—those later objects of new historicist inquiry—are even more obviously body-based. Early modern misogyny begins with the supposedly defective female body.[6] Sodomy as a legal concept is concerned with certain kinds of physical acts carried out by bodies of a certain sex under certain physical circumstances.[7] "Nation" in early modern usage refers to persons born in the same geographical place; "race," to persons sharing a certain lineage or genealogy.[8] All very physical.

The social constructedness of physiological knowledge has been demonstrated in several landmark books, including Nancy G. Siraisi's *Medieval and Early Renaissance Medicine: An Introduction to Knowledge and Practice* (1990), Gail Kern Paster's *The Body Embarrassed: Drama and the Disciplines of Shame in Early Modern England* (1993), Andrea Carlino's *Books of the Body: Anatomical Ritual and Renaissance Learning* (1994, English translation 1999), and the essays collected by David Hillman and Carla Mazzio in *The Body in Parts: Fantasies of Corporeality in Early Modern Europe* (1997). The *de*constructive possibilities of this constructedness are put to the test in Thomas Laqueur's *Making Sex: Body and Gender from the Greeks to Freud* (1990), a book that has given wide currency to the idea that early modern people saw one sex where we see two. If the sexual organs of females are taken to the inverse of the sexual organs of males, extruded in the latter case only because of males' greater body heat, then the markers of gender become strictly performative—an extreme instance of the arbitrariness of binary meaning-marking.[9] Our postmodern excitement at the prospect needs to be tempered, however, by contemporary witnesses like Helkiah Crooke, who devotes several folio pages to the one-sex model in his encyclopedic *Microcosmographia* (1618)—and rejects it on the basis of recent anatomical studies.[10] In the human body, deconstruction runs up against its greatest challenge. The human body, if nothing else, would seem to *be there,* oblivious to the constructions of language. Judith Butler, in *Bodies That Matter: On the Discursive Limits of "Sex"* (1993), confronts this issue head on and ends up suggesting a *reciprocal* relationship between bodies as physical entities and the construction of those bodies in discourse: "Language and materiality are fully embedded in each other, chiasmic in their interdependency, but never fully collapsed into one another, i.e., reduced to one another, and yet neither fully ever exceeds the other. Always already implicated in each other, always already exceeding one another, language and materiality are never fully identical nor fully different."[11]

As Butler intimates, the body cannot be taken as just another object of new historicist study like child-rearing practices or marriage arrangements or national identity. Inescapably the body presents itself not only as an *object* of study but as a *subject* of study. Language offers one way of knowing the body, but the consciousness that produces that language is already *in* the body, not outside it. Gale Kern Paster's pioneering attempt in *The Body Embarrassed* to reconstruct "the experience *as from within* of bodies that understood themselves and were understood by others in terms of humoral physiology" has recently been extended by Michael C. Schoenfeldt in *Bodies and Selves in Early Modern England* (1999). Schoenfeldt turns to texts by Spenser, Shakespeare, Herbert, and Milton for inside evidence of what it was like to inhabit an early modern body. To do so, Schoenfeldt warns, we must learn to see material reality where our own preconceptions prompt us to see only metaphor: "By urging a particularly organic account of inwardness and individuality, Galenic medical theory gave poets a language of inner emotion whose vehicles were also tenors, whose language of desire was composed of the very stuff of being."[12] In *The Acoustic World of Early Modern England* (1999), I have attempted to use Galenic physiology and the testimony of contemporary writers toward similar ends: to reconstruct the experience of sound in a culture that seems to have been more aurally attuned than ours. By combining a modern scientific understanding of the "hardware" of human hearing with attention to the historical "software" of early modern culture, I have been defining my study as an exercise in "historical phenomenology." Susanne Scholz, in *Body Narratives: Writing the Nation and Fashioning the Subject in Early Modern England* (2000), first sets in place "The Subject's New Body," with its distinctive protocols of self-knowledge and self-government, before turning outward and pursuing the implications of that construction in the formation of national identity and the incorporation of cultural Others into an empire.

What would Michael Foucault think of such projects? In a recent retrospective account of the origins and evolution of new historicism, Stephen Greenblatt has stressed the claims to objectivity in Clifford Geertz's practice of "thick description" as well as in Foucault's notion of *épistémè* as "the mental grid, or code, according to which people process information and live their lives." The title of Greenblatt's chapter on Geertz is "A Touch of the Real."[13] The very possibility of such objectivity is grounded, of course, in Descartes's separation of the thinking mind from the body it inhabits—a move that decisively separates Shakespeare scholars on *this* side of the Cartesian divide from the subjects they study on *that* side. (Note, however, Cynthia Marshall's argument, in her contribution to this forum, that a sense of estrangement between mind and body is frequently exploited in early modern stage scripts.) By insisting on the embodiedness of knowledge—*all* knowledge, even the scholar-critic's knowledge—projects like the ones I've described here may be pointing us toward a new critical methodology, one that combines the phenomenology of perception, as practiced by Greenblatt and his successors.

Not every participant in this forum, as you'll discover, would define her or his work in just this way. Alan Dessen, in the first contribution, is skeptical about the evidence of how bodies were staged for public viewing. In the last two contributions, Jyotsna Singh questions the focus of so much contemporary criticism on the *desiring* body, to the exclusion of the body in its other guises and capacities, while Dympna Callaghan wonders why we have seized on the *material* body as an object of academic inquiry just at this particular moment. Each contributor was asked simply to write out his or her thoughts on the relationship between the body and some other entity. There was no particular agenda. In keeping with forums convened in past volumes of *Shakespeare Studies,* contributors were not asked to provide citations or footnotes, though a few of them have not been able to avoid the impulse. We begin in the most specific, concrete way possible, with the bodies of actors onstage. Drawing on *A Dictionary of Stage Directions in English Drama, 1580–1642* (1999), which he compiled with Leslie Thomson, Alan Dessen provides a detailed catalogue of references to bodies and body parts. Heads, ears, eyes, faces, beards, hair, brains, mouths, tongues, breasts, arms, hands, legs, knees, and feet figure in Dessen's theatrical anatomy lesson. Dessen is cautious, however, about how representative the evidence may be, since often it seems to be unusual effects that call for specific cues. Eyewitness accounts, as he notes, are even trickier to analyze, since the distinction between what was displayed by the actors and what was perceived by viewers is not always clear. The role of language in creating such body effects is Jim Siemon's subject in the next contribution. Time—pace and rhythm in the speaking of lines onstage, historical time in production history—complicate the relationship between body and language. Changes in the interactive dynamics among language, body, and time become especially clear in Siemon's brief look at the production history of *Richard III*.

Antitheatrical polemicists of the sixteenth and early seventeenth centuries are unanimous in stressing the visceral, physiological effects that dramatic performance had on listener-spectators. When Hamlet imagines that an actor, given Hamlet's own "cue for passion," would "amaze indeed / The very faculty of eyes and ears" (3.1.563, 567–68), he is using the word "amaze" in its fundamental physical sense of "stun or stupefy, as by a blow on the head" (*OED*, "amaze," 1). To understand such effects, the next two contributors argue, we need to people the theater's yard and galleries with bodies constituted by Galenic medicine. Just what Hamlet means when he says "cue for *passion*" is Gail Paster's subject. Our own preferred word for such effects, "emotion," belongs to a very different understanding of sensation: where it comes from, what it does to the body, how it presents itself to consciousness. Cynthia Marshall is concerned specifically with the effects of spectacle and sound on bodies in the audience. She takes William Prynne and John Rainolds at their word and investigates the physiological affects represented in scripts, as well as the implied appeal of those affects to listener-spectators.

John Gillies then takes us outside the theater into the world at large as he studies the early modern "scene of cartography." Maps, he proposes, give us clues to the historically changing relationships of human bodies to ambient space. The coordinates of the "new geography" of the sixteenth and seventeenth centuries substituted a thoroughly rationalized space for earlier schemes centered on the individual viewer, on home territory, and on God. Changes in the meaning of the word "room," Gillies argues, serve as an index to these changes in sense of space. Last to take the rostrum are Jyotsna Singh and Dympna Callaghan, both of whom return us to the critical issues that inspired this forum in the first place. Observing the increasing concern of gender criticism with inclusiveness, presence, and representation over the past decade, Singh wonders why the focus of body work has been so insistently placed on the *desiring* body to the exclusion of the working body or the class-marked body or the racialized body. Why, indeed, are we so preoccupied with the body in the first place, Callaghan asks. By insisting on the "brute facticity" of this new object of inquiry, she charges, we may simply be allaying our own postmodern anxieties that we as scholars have nothing *there* as a subject, nothing that we can *see.* In the process, she continues, we are ignoring the concern of much early modern literature precisely with the *unseen.* We are ignoring literature itself. The forum ends, then, not with a unified manifesto on the part of the eight participants, but with very large questions about the relationships between the seen and the unseen, between body and consciousness, between material evidence and subjectivity. The eight of us hope we've given you something to think about—and through.

Notes

1. T. S. Eliot, "The Metaphysical Poets," in *Selected Essays,* 2nd rev. ed. (London: Faber, 1934), 287.
2. On Lacanian theory, see Catherine Belsey, *Critical Practice* (London: Methuen, 1980), and Madan Sarup, *Jacques Lacan* (Toronto: University of Toronto Press, 1992).
3. I refer, of course, to Stephen Greenblatt, *Renaissance Self-Fashioning* (Chicago: University of Chicago Press, 1980).
4. *Antony and Cleopatra* 5.1.21–22 in William Shakespeare, *The Complete Works,* ed. Stanley Wells and Gary Taylor (Oxford: Clarendon Press, 1989), 1031. Further quotations from Shakespeare in the Introduction are taken from this edition and are cited in the main text.
5. Philippe de Mornay, *The True Knowledge of a Man's Own Self,* trans. Anthony Munday (London: William Leake, 1602), sig. A11.
6. Two contributors to this form have written extensively on this connection: Gail Kern Pastern in *The Body Embarrassed: Drama and the Disciplines of Shame*

in Early Modern England (Ithaca: Cornell University Press, 1993), and Dympna C. Callaghan in *Shakespeare Without Women: Representing Women and Race on the Renaissance Stage* (London: Routledge, 2000).

7. On this point I can refer you to chapter 2 in my book *Homosexual Desire in Shakespeare's England: A Cultural Poetics* (Chicago: University of Chicago Press, 1991), 41–54.

8. This distinction between place ("nation") and time ("race") is suggested by Margo Hendricks, "Introduction," in Margo Hendricks and Patricia Parker, eds., *Women, "Race," and Writing in the Early Modern Period* (London: Routledge, 1994), 1–2.

9. Jonathan Culler's *On Deconstruction* (Ithaca: Cornell University Press, 1982) remains the best primer on deconstruction as a methodology for reading texts.

10. Helkiah Crooke, *Microcosmographia: A Description of the Body of Man* (London: Jaggard, 1618), 149–50.

11. Judith Butler, *Bodies That Matter: On the Discursive Limits of "Sex"* (London: Routledge, 1993), 69.

12. Michael C. Schoenfeldt, *Bodies and Selves in Early Modern England: Physiology and Inwardness in Spenser, Shakespeare, Herbert, and Milton* (Cambridge: Cambridge University Press, 1999), 8.

13. Catherine Gallagher and Stephen Greenblatt, *Practicing New Historicism* (Chicago: University of Chicago Press, 2000), 20–31 (on Geertz) and 66–74 (on Foucault). The "grid" as the lowest formation in the three-part structure of an *épistémè* is described on page 72.

The Body of Stage Directions

ALAN C. DESSEN

IDEALLY, DISCUSSION of how the body was presented on the English Renaissance stage should be grounded firmly in evidence from both contemporary records (e.g., eyewitness accounts, Henslowe's records) and playscripts. Indeed, one would expect the plots, dialogue, and stage directions of the five to six hundred extant plays to convey clearly what the original playgoers would have seen. Unfortunately, such is not the case. Rather, most readers do not realize how little evidence has actually survived about the staging of plays in this period—the norm is silence. A few eyewitness accounts from playgoers are available (including several for Shakespeare plays), but these accounts can be singularly unrevealing, often amounting to no more than partial plot summaries. Similarly, scraps of useful information do turn up in Henslowe's inventory of costumes and properties, but again surprisingly little can be gleaned about theatrical practice from these and comparable documents.

Dialogue evidence is far more plentiful, but, whether for the body or other concerns, this material represents shifting sands, not bedrock. Typical is Gertrude's description of Hamlet in the closet scene: "Forth at your eyes your spirits wildly peep, / And as the sleeping soldiers in th' alarm, / Your bedded hair, like life in excrements, / Start up and stand an end" (3.4.119–22). Are we to conclude from this passage (see also *Julius Caesar,* 4.3.279–80) that Richard Burbage had a fright wig or that he had the ability to make his hair stand on end (self-willed horripilation)? Or are such descriptions substitutes for what cannot be bodily displayed to a playgoer? To tease out onstage effects and practice from dialogue is repeatedly to encounter this problem.

To rely primarily on stage directions is, by contrast, to stay within the realm of what was or could have been done in the original productions, particularly when the play in question is linked to a professional company or to an experienced playwright. The exigencies of the playhouse are reflected in so-called "permissive" signals (enter "as many as can be"—Quarto *Titus Andronicus,* A4v, 1.1.72) or other coded or elliptical terms where much is left to the implementation of the players ("Exit Corpse"—Folio *Richard III,* 423, 1.2.226). To build edifices on stage directions, however, is to confront a series of problems. For example, in many instances a reader still cannot distinguish between what was actually displayed onstage and what was left to an auditor's imagination, especially in "fictional" signals where the author of a stage direction slips into a narrative mode so as to tell the story rather than provide instructions for an actor: Jonas "cast out of the Whale's belly upon the Stage" (*Looking Glass for London,* 1460–61).

What follows therefore falls far short of a comprehensive account but rather is a highly condensed summary of specific references to parts of the body provided by a dictionary of stage directions.[1] Omitted are many categories clearly associated with actorly or fictive bodies where body parts are not specified, most notably situations linked to costume, disguise, and various movements. Moreover, even though citations are drawn from a database that includes over 22,000 stage directions from more than five hundred plays that span forty years, the material cited here constitutes a tiny fraction of the extant signals, and those signals, in turn, specify only a fraction of the actual onstage activity.

The obvious point of departure is not fruitful, for actual uses of the term "body" in stage directions are unrevealing. Rather, most of the one hundred examples deal with the introduction and removal of corpses: "Ventidius as it were in triumph, the dead body of Pacorus borne before him" (*Antony and Cleopatra,* 1494–95, 3.1.0); "The dead body is carried away" (*Hamlet,* Q2 H1v, Folio 2000, 3.2.135). Similarly, the term "corpse" is found primarily in funerals and related ceremonies, as when ladies are "winding Marcello's corpse" (*White Devil,* 5.4.65).

The body and the voice may be an actor's basic tools, but, not surprisingly, some bodily features are cited only when a distinctive action is signaled: "exit, biting his thumbs" (*Dick of Devonshire,* 1714–15); "bites out his tongue" (*Spanish Tragedy,* 4.4.191); "cuts their throats" (*Titus Andronicus,* K1v, 5.2.203). In addition to the famous moment in *'Tis Pity* where Giovanni enters with Annabella's "heart upon his dagger" (5.6.9), *Golden Age* provides "a bleeding heart upon a knife's point, and a bowl of blood" (20). Shoulders appear in a variety of locutions, mostly linked to carrying ("the body of the King, lying on four men's shoulders"—*Massacre at Paris*, 1263), taking someone into custody ("claps her on the shoulder"—*2 Edward IV*, 123), or showing favor (Henry VIII enters "leaning on the Cardinal's shoulder"—*Henry VIII*, 317–18, 1.2.0). Signals for the neck are fairly common, usually linked to objects about the neck ("in their Shirts, barefoot, with halters about their necks"—*Edward III*, I3v) or an embrace in which someone hangs about another's neck ("hanging about his neck lasciviously"—*Insatiate Countess*, 3.4.82). The fifteen examples of fingers encompass a wide variety of actions, most commonly "lays his finger on his mouth" to signal silence (*Antonio's Revenge*, 2.2.215) but also to make the sign of the cross (*Perkin Warbeck*, 2.2.83), to threaten ("with his Finger menaces Eulalia"—*Queen and Concubine*, 22), to taste ("takes of the honey, with his finger, and tastes"—*Sejanus*, 5.177), or to torment Falstaff ("They put the Tapers to his fingers, and he starts"—*Merry Wives*, G3r, 5.5.88). Figures lie, sleep, and fall in another's lap or enter with objects in their laps: "They sit: Sneakup's head in the Lady's lap" (*City Wit*, 347); the nurse enters "with the ladder of cords in her lap" (Q1 *Romeo and Juliet*, F3r, 3.2.31). Most of the roughly twenty examples of heels are found in the locution "trip up" or "strike up his heels" ("to cause to fall"—*Roaring Girl*, 2.1.331), but figures are also pulled onto or off the stage by the heels ("draweth in Rotsi by the heels groaning"—*Devil's Charter*, K4v)—and to stage a famous moment Achilles enters "with an arrow through his heel" (*1 Iron Age*, 332).

Widely cited are beards and hair, with both terms regularly linked to disguise, as when a previously disguised figure enters "without hair or beard" (*Wit of a Woman*, 1662). Most common is the pulling or taking off of such items: "Pulls his Beard and hair off" (*Island Princess*, 169); "casts off his Peruke, and Beard" (*Novella*, 177). When not linked to disguise, beards are associated with age or signal a disheveled state: "a long white hair and beard" (*Picture*, 2.1.85); "all ragged in an overgrown red Beard" (*Caesar and Pompey*, 2.1.0). Occasionally the focus is upon grooming, as in "looking in a glass, trimming his Beard; Giacopo brushing him" (*Love's Sacrifice*, 676–77), while in the distinctive humiliation of Edward II his tormentors "wash him with puddle water, and shave his beard away" (*Edward II*, 2301).

Hair is cited often, most notably when a female figure enters with her hair loose, disheveled, or about her ears to convey that she is distraught with madness, shame, rage, extreme grief, or the effects of recent violence: enter Franceschina "with her hair loose, chafing" (*Dutch Courtesan*, 2.2.0); enter Ophelia "playing on a Lute, and her hair down singing" (Q1 *Hamlet*, G4v, 4.5.20). In addition, disheveled hair is one way of signaling "enter ravished": "The Soldiers thrust forth Theocrine, her garments loose, her hair disheveled" (*Unnatural Combat*, 5.2.185). Loosened hair is also linked to women undergoing public penance or condemned to death: "Mistress Shore in a white sheet barefooted with her hair about her ears, and in her hand a wax taper" (*2 Edward IV*, 165). A few male figures appear with disheveled hair, including the fugitive Humber with "his hair hanging over his shoulders" (*Locrine*, 1573–74). As to actions, most common are female figures who are drawn, pulled, dragged, led, or trailed by their hair: "she draws one of the ladies by the hair of the head along the stage" (*Tom a Lincoln*, 2620–21). As a sign of vexation a figure "Tears his hair" (*Yorkshire Tragedy*, 487), whereas grooming can be performed by both men and women: Bellafront "with her bodkin curls her hair, colors her lips" (1 *Honest Whore*, 2.1.12); "Novall sits in a chair, Barber orders his hair" (*Fatal Dowry*, 4.1.0). A previously disheveled figure enters "his hair and beard trimmed, habit and gown changed" (*Lover's Melancholy*, 5.2.0); a woman who has been disguised as a man reveals her identity when she "discovers her hair" (*Philaster*, 144/416).

Since boy actors played female roles, references to bosom and breast would seem to be of particular interest, but the actual citations often are not helpful. Bosom can refer to a man or woman's chest ("flies to his bosom"—*Match Me in London*, 5.3.0) or the garment that covers that part of the body ("He plucks it out of his bosom and reads it"—*Richard II*, H4v, 5.2.71; "Opens his bosom, and puts them [severed hands] in"—*Selimus*, 1436). The two senses are sometimes hard to distinguish, as when a figure appears with "a white Rose in her bosom" (*Warning for Fair Women*, I1r). The roughly thirty references to the breast mostly denote a man's or woman's bosom or chest. The few other likely references to a woman's breasts are a Caroline dumb show where "they return her child, she points to her breasts, as meaning she should nurse it" (*Bloody Banquet*, 855–56) and possibly "they bind her to the Chair, the Eunuch much fears her breast" (*Fatal Contract*, I3r). More typical are "Sets the Garland on her breast" (*King John and Matilda*, 87) and "with Jewels and a great crucifix on her breast" (*Second Maiden's Tragedy*, 1930–31). Most of the signals are for a variety of actions involving men: "walks sadly, beats his breast" (*Jovial Crew*, 445); "He lays his breast open, she offers at with his sword" (Folio *Richard III*, 371, 1.2.178).

The many references to the head (roughly 220) consist of severed heads (mostly human but also of animals killed in a hunt); locutions in which objects are placed on the head (most commonly crowns and garlands); bloody, broken, and bare heads; and a wide variety of actions. Severed heads are specified in over twenty-five plays ("Dead men's heads in dishes"—*Battle of Alcazar* plot, 98); related actions include "Her head struck off" (*Virgin Martyr*, 4.3.179) and "takes a dead man's head upon his sword's point holding it up to Edmond's soldiers they fly" (*Edmond Ironside*, 989–91). Heads are described as black, white, bloody-bleeding, and most commonly broken (*Arden of Faversham*, 840, 1682). The most often signaled action is the shaking of heads (*1 Henry VI*, 2448, 5.3.19), but figures are also directed to scratch, hang, raise, and nod their heads. Blows to the head are common: "striketh six blows on his head and with the seventh leaves the hammer sticking in his head" (*Two Lamentable Tragedies*, C4r). Other actions include "*declines his head upon her neck*" (*Hamlet*, Q2 H1v, Folio 1993, 3.2.135); "holds his head down as fast asleep" (*If This Be Not a Good Play*, 4.4.16); "Lays his Hand on his Head" (Folio *3 Henry VI*, 2453, 4.6.68). Unusual are "his head shaved in the habit of a slave" (*Believe as You List*, 2322–23) and Rafe "with a forked arrow through his head" (*Knight of the Burning Pestle*, 229).

Parts of the head are also cited regularly, often in familiar locutions. Somewhat surprising are the five references to brains both as verb and noun linked to violent death, as when Bajazeth "brains himself against the cage" (*1 Tamburlaine*, 2085) or D'Amville inadvertently "raises up the ax, strikes out his own brains" (*Atheist's Tragedy*, 5.2.241). The few references to the cheek are linked to the application of cosmetics (*1 Honest Whore*, 2.1.0) or to a kiss (*Devil's Charter*, E1r). The mouth is found in a variety of locutions and actions, most commonly stopping or laying a finger on one's mouth to gain silence ("The Guard lead off Lamia stopping his mouth"—*Roman Actor*, 2.1.239) but also objects placed in the mouth, as when the captive kings draw in Tamburlaine's chariot "with bits in their mouths" (*2 Tamburlaine*, 3979). The ear appears regularly in the locution "hair about the ears," in making sounds (usually whispering) in the ear (*Antony and Cleopatra*, 1378, 2.7.38), and in acts of violence, most commonly a box on the ear (*Doctor Faustus*, A-905) but also "cuts off the Cutpurse's ear, for cutting of the gold buttons off his cloak" (*Massacre at Paris*, 622). The few references to the nose are mostly linked to violent actions: "wrings him by the nose" (*Woman's Prize*, 23); "Cuts off his Nose" (*Edmond Ironside*,

708). Eyes are cited when covered, usually by a patch (*Roaring Girl,* 5.1.55) but twice by glass (*White Devil,* 2.2.23; *New Trick,* 252), and in a variety of related locutions, as when figures fix their eyes upon someone or something ("fixeth his eye on Buckingham, and Buckingham on him, both full of disdain"—*Henry VIII,* 177–79, 1.1.114) and in actions involving tears ("wipes his eyes"—*Wise Woman of Hogsdon,* 316). The roughly seventy-five examples of "face" consist of veils and other items on, over, covering, or hiding the face (e.g., *Titus Andronicus,* K2r, 5.3.25); colors on the face ("her face colored like a Moor"—*Devil's Law Case,* 5.6.29); bloody and wounded faces ("their heads and faces bloody, and besmeared with mud and dirt"—*Doctor Faustus,* B-1490–91), and a wide variety of actions, most commonly when figures fall on their faces (*Two Noble Kinsmen,* C4r, 1.4.0) or throw something in another's face (*Renegado,* 5.3.115).

As to "limbs," the term itself is found only twice in stage directions, both times as part of a banquet course composed of human parts: "A banquet brought in, with limbs of a Man in the service" (*Golden Age,* 21); a servant "bringing in Tymethes's limbs" (*Bloody Banquet,* 1715–16). References to the leg are usually to "make a leg," a male version of the curtsy ("Snatches off his hat and makes legs to him"—*Revenger's Tragedy,* G3r); stage properties ("He pulls off his leg"—*Doctor Faustus,* B-1561); and a scattering of other actions and usages ("As they open the stocks, Wasp puts his shoe on his hand, and slips it in for his leg"—*Bartholomew Fair,* 4.6.77). Although over three hundred figures are directed to kneel or kneel down (a small percentage of the actual onstage kneelings), references to knees are less common (roughly twenty-five). Locutions include bending or falling on one's knees ("They all bend their knees to Caesar, except Caradoc"—*Valiant Welshman,* I3v) or more simply being on one's knees, as with a servant or messenger ("brings a bowl of wine, and humbly on his knees offers it to the King"—*1 Edward IV,* 61). Abject figures "go off on their hands, and knees" (*New Way,* 1.1.98); children can be placed on one's knee (*Dido,* 0); *Fawn* provides "Zuccone, pursued by Zoya on her knees" (4.280); a woman teasing a misogynist "sits on his knee" and "rises from his knee" (*Woman Hater,* 141).

The foot is found regularly in such locutions and actions as "stamps with his foot" ("He stamps with his foot, and the Soldiers show themselves"—Folio *3 Henry VI,* 189–90, 1.1.169), being barefoot (usually associated with mourning or penance, as in "barefoot, with some loose covering over his head"—*David and Bethsabe,*

972), and the kissing of a foot as a sign of homage or abasement ("being presented unto the Pope, kisseth his foot, and then advancing two degrees higher, kisseth his cheek"—*Devil's Charter,* E1r). Other distinctive actions include "His foot on the Doctor's breast" (*Bashful Lover,* 5.1.135) and "sets his foot afore him, and he falls with his basket" (*Bartholomew Fair,* 4.2.32). The plural "feet" is found primarily in variations of "at his/her feet": "lay down their properties at the Queen's feet" (*Arraignment of Paris,* 1213); "The maids sit down at her feet mourning" (*Broken Heart,* 4.4.0).

References to the arm and hand are plentiful. Bloody arms are common ("unbraced, his arms bare, smeared in blood"—*Antonio's Revenge,* 1.1.0); figures are stabbed or hurt in the arm (*Edward I,* 894); a wounded figure may enter "with his Arm in a scarf" (*Coriolanus,* 746–47, 1.9.0). The wide range of actions also includes holding, pulling, or binding arms; taking, holding, supporting, or catching another in one's arms/by the arm; sinking or falling in someone's arms; pulling, taking, or leading by the arm; and wreathing, folding, or spreading arms. Of the nearly five hundred examples of "hand," the most common locution is to enter with an object in one's hand but also signaled are kissing a hand (over forty examples); wringing hands; entrances hand in hand; a variety of actions such as holding, taking, joining, and offering hands; and severed hands. Examples include "Holds her by the hand silent" (*Coriolanus,* 3539, 5.3.182); "he offers to stab himself, and she holds his hand" (*Tom a Lincoln,* 38–41); "kneels down and holds up his hands to heaven" (*Arden of Faversham,* 1475–76); "beckoning with her hand" (*Sir Thomas More,* 1080); "fight hand to hand" (*1 Henry VI,* 2460–61, 5.3.29). Signals for severed hands include "a dead man's hand" (*Duchess of Malfi,* 4.1.43); "He cuts off one hand" and "Cuts off the other hand" (*Edmond Ironside,* 700, 702); "He cuts off Titus's hand" (*Titus Andronicus,* F2r, 3.1.191); and a torment in hell includes "Hand burnt off" (*If This Be Not a Good Play,* 5.4.41). Also distinctive are several supernatural hands: "A hand with a Bolt appears above" and "The hand taken in" (*Prophetess,* 388).

As indicated by signals already cited (severing of a hand, biting out of a tongue, cutting off of a nose or ear), plays display onstage violations of the body despite the obvious practical difficulties. Most famous is the blinding of Gloucester in *King Lear* (where typically neither Quarto nor Folio offers a stage direction for that action—again, the norm is silence), but *Selimus* provides "Pulls out his eyes" (1415), and at the climax of a bloody revenge tragedy

"The conspirators bind Piero, pluck out his tongue, and triumph over him" (*Antonio's Revenge,* 5.3.62). The rare uses of "deformed" appear to denote "ugly" rather than "misshapen" (*Women Pleased,* 286), but occasionally a soldier home from the wars is introduced without a limb or otherwise disfigured: "three soldiers: one without an arm" (*Maidenhead Well Lost,* 114); "Wallace, like a halting Soldier on wooden stumps, with Mountford dumb, and Glascot blind" and "Beaumont with a wooden stump" (*Valiant Scot,* E1v, F1r). Lavinia is brought in "her hands cut off, and her tongue cut out, and ravished" (*Titus Andronicus,* E2r, 2.4.0) and later "takes the staff in her mouth, and guides it with her stumps and writes" (G1r, 4.1.76). If one factors in as well the various properties (numerous severed heads, a dead man's hand, detachable legs, limbs as a dinner course), the violated body can be a vivid presence onstage.

To end with such examples, however, is perhaps to misrepresent the evidence. For a variety of reasons, many aspects of the actorly or fictive body obvious to the first playgoers are not cited in the early manuscripts and printed texts and consequently must be fleshed out by readers today. The paucity of references to the throat, tongue, thumb, fingers, cheek, nose, and eyes may therefore be misleading and may blur effects that can be provided by a skilled actor. Even the more plentiful citations of arm, hand, head, and foot provide only a fraction of the possibilities for conveying states of mind or distinctive actions. Rather, experienced playwrights, particularly those attached to theatrical companies (e.g., Shakespeare, Fletcher, Heywood, Massinger, Brome), could take for granted and therefore build on the professionalism and expertise of their actor-colleagues so as to take a "leave it up to the players" approach rather than the "spell it all out" attitude associated with amateur playwrights.

What did need spelling out, however, were distinctive actions and items that were not part of standard procedures and required some special attention: violations of the body, supernatural events, other special effects, dumb shows, masques-within-plays. Indeed, from the stage directions in a small set of plays (e.g., *2 Henry VI; Antonio's Revenge; Whore of Babylon; Devil's Charter; Tempest; Prophetess; Hengist*) a clever reader could extract a truly bizarre picture of what regularly "happened" on Elizabethan, Jacobean, and Caroline stages. Still, whether presented naturalistically or imaginatively, the violated body did play a significant role in some tragedies and histories, just as beards and hair clearly were basic to actorly representations. Evidence from stage directions does not answer many questions about the body but can extend our sense today of the relevant theatrical vocabulary shared then by playwrights, players, and playgoers.

Notes

1. Alan C. Dessen and Leslie Thomson, *A Dictionary of Stage Directions in English Drama, 1580–1642* (Cambridge: Cambridge University Press, 1999). For full documentation and an explanation of procedures, short titles, and working assumptions readers should consult the dictionary itself.

Between the Lines:
Bodies/Languages/Times

JAMES R. SIEMON

"The relation to the body is a fundamental dimension of the habitus that is inseparable from a relation to language and to time."
—Pierre Bourdieu, *Logic of Practice*

KEIR ELAM HAS RECENTLY noted the (re)turn of critical attention from fascination with language to concern with the body, and especially with the actor's body, as a site where "social history, dramatic history and stage history interrogate each other."[1] Evidently agreeing with Elam that "perhaps the most serious limit of recent body criticism is its lack of reference to performance," Barbara Hodgdon (following Joseph Roach) has rightly emphasized historical and material reasons for considering "the" performing body as bodies, while W. B. Worthen's critique of the lack of attention paid to earlier stage practice in recent constructions of text/performance relations has further offered reasons to consider language as languages.[2] What follows will pursue these leads, drawing on M. M. Bakhtin and Pierre Bourdieu—two theorists of the interrelation of (multiple) languages and bodies—and attempt to suggest how stage history might enrich current discussions by attending to the element of time.

In a general way, Shakespeare studies has grown accustomed to conceptualizing bodies in plural senses—as carnivalesque, gendered, alimentary, scattered, enclosed, tremulous, leaky, anatomized, queer, and pained, among others. Similarly, the field has recognized multiplicity among early modern discourses, including those invoking poverty, race, gender, economy, and religion. But languages and bodies may be considered as plural in a related but different sense derived from key concepts of the Bakhtin circle and Pierre Bourdieu. For Bakhtin as for Bourdieu, historical bodies and languages are always plural and yet interactive, distinguishable yet tied to class, group, generational, and professional struggles for position and advantage that implicate them within one another. Idiolects, jargons of groups, sects, trades, regions, and eras do not take shape without traces of their co-formation by antagonistic intersections with one another. Similarly, postures, deportments, intonations, even bodily dimensions implicate embodied differential categories of social definition, distinction, and tastes. Furthermore, bodies and languages are integral to one another. Even such apparently "bodily" states as hunger are not felt independently of sociolinguistic implications (such as the resentment of the politicized peasant or the joyful fulfillment of the fasting dieter). Conversely, bodies bear socially determined schemata of perception, action, and configuration that contribute even to such high-level "verbal" products as philosophical or aesthetic discourses (see Bourdieu on Flaubert's sexuality or Heidegger's nature hikes). Resisting mutually producing binarisms of language and body, concepts like Bakhtin's utterance and Bourdieu's habitus take human reality as shot through with accent marks left by social groups and their struggles in and on bodies and words. Such ideas are not foreign to students of Elizabethan England, where one often encounters a "reciprocity of social and somatic formation."[3] Thus one finds terms with strong social implications that carry ambiguous verbal/bodily sense. Puck scorns the Mechanicals for "swaggering" (Riverside *Midsummer Night's Dream* 3.1.77)—a term that may denote boasting or strutting—when, in fact, they neither brag nor even stand: as "rude" commoners their proximity offends the Fairy Queen's dignity; they "swagger" merely by being the wrong sort in the wrong place at the wrong time.

As this example suggests, a consideration of the plural bodies and languages constituted by feminisms, materialisms, and historicisms also demands that one consider times, not just in the familiar sense of historical periods but in the more intimate, physical yet deeply sociohistorical, senses of pacing, articulation, and deportment. Hamlet's pronouncements on language and body, on "word and action," pit modes of timing against one another. Either actors "speak the speech . . . trippingly" while "us[ing] all gently . . . with temperance" and "smoothness," or they "mouth it" like a "robustious fellow" while "saw[ing] the air," "strutt[ing] and bellow[ing]" (*Hamlet* 3.2.1–33). In his account, timing joins such theatrical elements as intonation ("accent"), bodily configuration ("robustious"), and behavior ("gait") in being correlated with an offstage social polarity that opposes the "barren and incapable" to the "judicious." Through the alchemy of Hamlet's habitus, these socially particular value judgments appear to him as "nature"—"the very age and body of the time"—simply and already "there" to be reproduced on stage without being "overdone, or come tardy off." Hamlet's three sources of authority—behavior "natural" to contemporaries, the text as "set down," and theatrical techniques recognized by the "judicious" (but not by the "unskillful")—offer a provisional starting place for further consideration of timing in a specific stage history.

Richard of Gloucester has struck many, from G. B. Shaw to Jan Kott, as puppet-like or mechanical. One can see where such a notion comes from. Shakespeare's Richard is constituted as an intersection of a grotesque physical body (a "lump of foul deformity"), a ragtag verbal inheritance (from "odd old ends stol'n forth of holy writ" and elsewhere), archaic theatrical device ("moraliz[ing]" "like the formal Vice, Iniquity"), and a mechanical struggle against space and time (laying claim to "all the world to bustle in" while he limps "halting by"). In light of these pronounced physical determinations, it is worthwhile remembering Richard's specifically textual determinations. Not only is his narrative taken, often verbatim, from a line of providentialized history, he is a cliché for tyranny and deformity (as in anti-Cecil libels). The play emphasizes the character's limits by making him, alone among Shakespearean protagonists, not only (re)introduce himself as like himself before the action begins but also perform under a title—the Tragedy of "Richard the Third" (F1) or of "King Richard the third" (Q1)—that predefines his royal trajectory. Finally, the play is highly formulaic, "relentlessly iambic," and frequently "elephantine in its ironies."[4]

Yet despite obvious determinants—theatrical (the Vice), textual (the More-Holinshed line), and behavioral (the deformed Cecil)—some have found in Richard the first Shakespearean "voice of a fully developed subjectivity,"[5] or the dramatized voice of a writerly male subjectivity.[6] Richard's own wonderful pun announces him "determined to prove a villain," thereby constituting himself at an uncertain intersection between predetermination and self-determination: like a modern subject, perhaps, or an early modern subject caught up, like Faustus, in debates about predestination.

The tensions suggested by the Shakespearean pun are clearly registered by the theatrical abbreviation that dominated two hundred years of the play's production history. (A. C. Sprague witnessed a performance of Cibber in Boston as late as 1930.) Although Cibber's 1700 adaptation cut the Shakespearean text (eliminating Margaret, Clarence, the murderers, Hastings, Edward IV, and more) to focus on Richard, it added hundreds of lines supplying linkages, transitions, and motivations for him. Upon this reduced text, performers labored further. David Garrick, in particular, shocked Cibber himself by inscribing his text with a new mode of stage behavior. Aiming "to shake off the Fetters of Numbers" on behalf of "nature," Garrick added pauses, and gave the eighteenth century something it wanted and could recognize, as it were, between the lines: a new density of recognizable feelings.[7] John Genest claimed Garrick's emotions "were legible in every feature of that various face—his look, his voice, his attitude changed with every sentiment."[8] None took up "natural" timing more influentially than Edmund Kean, whose legacy survived long after performers had renounced Cibber's text, and long after offstage behavior had forgotten the eighteenth-century man of sentiment.

Kean's micro-interventions in timing were everywhere, from line to line, word to word, even syllable to syllable. While some thought he could project "a beautiful style of deliberate triumph" through a strategic pause, others complained about "long pauses ... not only between words, but between syllables of the same word." William Hazlitt objected to his "making every sentence an alternation of dead pauses and rapid transitions."[9] Kean's labor of temporal appropriation also manifested itself in larger effects.

In keeping with eighteenth-century interests in character, Cibber's text had elaborated on Richard's death, which Qq and F give only as "They fight. Richard is slain." Cibber added a speech for Richard and a farewell to his "aspiring soul." From this Kean constructed a signature piece of physical theater that turned Richard into a thing that would not die: "*[Kean] fights furiously back & forth—in turning looses* [sic] *balance, falls on his knee, & fights up—in turning receives Richmond's thrust—lunges at him feebly after it—clenchy* [sic] *is shoved from him—staggers—drops the sword—grasps blindly at him—staggers backward & falls—head to R H—turns upon right side—writhes, rests on his hands—gnashes his teeth at him (LH)—as he utters his last words—blinks—& expires rolling on his back.*"[10]

Beyond Cibber's wildest inventions, Kean, as Byron recognized, rendered Richard a Romantic hero, especially through his physical rendition of the death. Leigh Hunt wrote: "He stood looking the other in the face, as if he was already a disembodied spirit, searching him with the eyes of another world; or as if he silently cursed him with some new scorn, to which death and its dreadful knowledge had given him a right." Most famously, Hazlitt wrote: "He fought like one drunk with wounds; and the attitude in which he stands with his hands stretched out, after his sword is taken from him, had a preternatural and terrific grandeur, as if his will could not be disarmed, and the very phantoms of his despair had a withering power." But over time Kean's bodily action evolved in a way that troubled Hazlitt: "He at first held out his hands in a way which can only be conceived by those who saw him—in motionless despair—or as if there were some preternatural power in the mere manifestation of his will: he now actually fights with his doubled fists, after his sword is taken from him, like some helpless infant."[11]

In performance, Kean's body became grotesque and disconcerting rather than heroically Romantic, but given the operatic improbabilities of Kean's earlier staging, what truly bothered Hazlitt may lie elsewhere than in a violation of "nature." Clearly, the problem was not that Kean had departed from any written "text." Rather, Hazlitt is disgusted by an enactment of physical impotence instead of supernatural "will," and this metaphysical queasiness is linked to his suspicion that Kean had gotten his physical model in the wrong place, from the wrong sort of people: "from seeing the last efforts of Painter in his fight with Oliver."[12] If Kean's legend had been heightened in some circles by his watching public executions to learn how to die on stage, watching prizefighters was not the same sort of thing.

In any case, while Kean himself claimed to take authority from nontheatrical bodies and behavior, his innovations survived theatrically in specific acting "points" and in a vocal pace that helped authorize the speech and behavior of later actors, even when they had rejected Cibber's text and Kean's style. Macready's elaborately formal style still incorporated pauses to signal emotional transitions, and while he dropped Cibber's death speech, he retained Kean's stare: "the fiendish glare with which he regarded his victorious foe, gave to his eyes a resemblance to coals of fire fading into white cold cinders; the gaze became dull and unmeaning; the eyelid quivered and dropped—and the tyrant was no more."[13]

When in the 1870s Henry Irving finally rejected Cibber's text entirely, he nevertheless continued to speak and act like Kean performing Cibber, even though the words had largely changed. Irving trimmed about 1,600 of the 3,600 lines of the Shakespearean text but injected "innumerable pauses," as Henry James complained. To register a "heroical temper" in the last act, Joseph Knight wrote, "he lengthened out the syllables of words until they seemed interminable, and his utterance grew inarticulate—he marred the presentation by grimace and by extravagance of gesture." Directly modeling his actions on Kean (as G. B. Shaw lamented), Irving attempted to better Kean's physical point: topping the "glare of baffled hate and malignity which he fixes on Richmond . . . [Irving] gnaws his adversary's sword."[14]

Irving, with his "heroical" pauses and sword-biting, was one of the vocal prototypes for Olivier, but rather than seek the precise interaction of Irving, Donald Wolfitt, Hitler, Jed Haris, and the Big Bad Wolf struggling within that complex voice,[15] let us consider pauses and timing in the remarkable 1992 Sam Mendes/Simon Russell Beale RSC production. This production paradoxically takes the play back to someplace that Shakespeare's words arguably had never gone but that had been present in the sources all along. Building on the bodily legacy that we have traced back through Irving to Kean and probably to Garrick—a legacy that has developed in a dialogical relationship with the words of Cibber or Shakespeare—the Mendes/Beale production uses pauses and hesitations in a powerfully political way that is truer to Shakespeare's textual sources than is Shakespeare. One episode that is strikingly omitted from Shakespeare's *Richard III* is the tense, highly political game of pauses and silence played between More's own mentor, Morton, and Buckingham as Morton attempts to win him for the anti-Richardian resistance: "The duke [of Buckingham] somewhat maruelling at his [Morton's] sudden pauses, as though they were but parentheses, with a high countenance said: 'My lord, I euidentlie perceiue, and no lesse note your often breathing, and sudden stopping in your communication; so that to my intelligence, your words neither come to anie direct or perfect sentence in conclusion, whereby either I might perceiue and haue knowledge, what your inward intent is now toward the king, or what affection you beare toward me" (Holinshed, *Chronicles* [1587] 3:737). Given that this episode represents arguments for violently deposing an hereditary monarch, and shows an honored cleric dramatically employing them, it is probably no accident that Shakespeare did not dramatize it, nor that More himself leaves it incomplete, nor that Hall's "pauses" and "parentheses" are so prominent, nor that Holinshed's marginal note carefully attributes it to Hall: "Here endeth Sir Thomas More, & this that followeth is taken out of master Hall."

The Shakespeare Centre film of the Mendes/Beale production records what some reviewers noticed: despite its broad conception (Beale repeatedly enters to barking dogs and physically resembles, as reviewers put it, Uncle Fester), the performance is riddled with pauses that suggest neither nineteenth-century Romantic heroism nor eighteenth-century sentiment but a late-twentieth-century sense of the micro-pragmatics of political power. This is not something "there" in Shakespeare's words (except possibly when Shakespeare's Richard, uncharacteristically, fails to respond to little York's taunts or when Queen Elizabeth temporizes) but represents instead the performers' own work, physically building on the historical labors of previous generations of actors. In this aspect of the production, the actors are not so much verbalizing a text; they are not exactly speaking or even acting "Shakespeare," but rather, as James Norris Loehlin puts it, they are "playing politics," using strategic silences that "themselves vividly convey the power relations" that embrace the characters and implicate the play's audiences.[16] When Richard and Richmond finally descend to grapple in a pit of dirt, the metaphor is as clear as the filth that clings to them both, but it is in the moments between the words that fear, self-interest, revulsion, and domination speak far louder of the insidious struggles that contaminate everyone on the stage.

Although this final scene could be moralized into meaning that all politics is dirty, such language could not do justice to the implications raised by the production's pauses and hesitations. In some visions, all politics might end in the pit, but on the stage what might be sensed—between the lines—is a nightmare version of the infinite negotiations that are taken, endured, and resisted in everyday life. It is not a matter of heroic will, or lively sentiment, or providential agency, but struggle—the kind of thing that may be heard often enough in silences. To an early modern theatrical habitus, pauses might be a site of primary anxiety, of bodily failure to live up to one's verbal role (think how powerfully Shakespeare represents pauses as failures, as being "out" of one's part—Francis the Drawer, the Mechanicals). In a world that has seemed to deprive many of any single big narrative, pauses might be instead, as they appear in the RSC production, a site for defining something resembling agency.

Notes

1. Keir Elam, " 'In what chapter of his bosom?': Reading Shakespeare's Bodies," *Alternative Shakespeares*, vol. 2, ed. Terence Hawkes (London: Routledge, 1996), 142.

2. Barbara Hodgdon, "Replicating Richard: Body Doubles, Body Politics," *TJ* 50 (1998): 207–25; W. B. Worthen, "Drama, Performativity, and Performance," *PMLA* 113 (1998): 1093–1105.

3. Susanne Scholz, *Body Narratives* (New York: St. Martin's, 2000), 10.
4. Julie Hankey, *Richard III* (London: Junction, 1981), 1.
5. Janet Adelman, *Suffocating Mothers: Fantasies of Maternal Origin in Shakespeare's Plays* (New York: Routledge, 1992), 1.
6. Eve Rachel Sanders, *Gender and Literacy on Stage in Early Modern England* (Cambridge: Cambridge University Press, 1998), 146.
7. Scott Colley, *Richard's Himself Again: A Stage History of* Richard III (New York: Greenwood, 1992), 41.
8. Colley, *Richard's Himself Again*, 39.
9. Colley, *Richard's Himself Again*, 67, 64, 64–65.
10. Alan S. Downer, ed., *King Richard III: Edmund Kean's Performance as Recorded by James H. Hackett* (London: STR, 1959), 98.
11. Colley, *Richard's Himself Again*, 76, 75, 76.
12. Downer, ed., *King Richard III*, xxxii.
13. Colley, *Richard's Himself Again*, 80, 86.
14. Colley, *Richard's Himself Again*, 130, 138, 139.
15. Colley, *Richard's Himself Again*, xi.
16. James Norris Loehlin, "Playing Politics: *Richard III* in Recent Performance," *Performing Arts Journal* 15 (1993): 80–94.

The Body and Its Passions

Gail Kern Paster

"The history of the body," Shigehisa Kuriyama has recently written, "is ultimately a history of ways of inhabiting the world."[1] I would add to this wise sentence the chiastic corollary that this history is also about how the world inhabits the body. As the recent intellectual history of prodigies, wonders, and monstrous births has reminded us, the natural world of early modern Europe in practice and conceptualization resembles ours only in part. Its organization was analogical: a network of analogy and mutual functionality enlivened all animate life in a hierarchical continuum of ensoulment (*empsychos*) ascending from vegetables, to imperfect animals such as sponges, to perfect animals such as birds and mammals, and finally to the human being, uniquely endowed with an intellective soul. The human body, though set apart from animals, vegetables, and minerals by the existence of the rational soul, was nevertheless joined indissolubly to the rest of ensouled nature on the universal scale. Perhaps most important, it shared all of its passions with the animals stationed just below. Descartes succeeded in disturbing this continuum and beginning its slow demise when he rejected the existence of the vegetable and sensitive souls, reduced the body's three kinds of spirits (natural, vital, and animal) to only the last of these, and altogether denied thought and passion in animals. The body did remain central for Descartes's thinking about how the soul received, organized, remembered and felt about information from the outside world. Nevertheless, it remains true that Descartes set in motion the gradual process towards abstraction and dematerialization that, in the eighteenth century, overtook early modern discourses of body and mind.

Because body-mind interactions still tend to be conceptualized in post-Enlightenment terms, it is helpful to be reminded of the organic unity of body, mind, and soul when we read early modern discourses of the passions—or what, since the late seventeenth century, have been called the emotions. We now understand the emotions generally as psychological events that arise from some internal or external stimulus and produce bodily effects (an elevated heart rate, pallor or flush, goose bumps, and other fight-or-flight mechanisms). But, for the early moderns, the passions or perturbations of mind were fully embedded in the order of nature and were part of material being itself—one of the six "non-natural" factors along with diet, sleep, rest or exercise, air, fullness or emptiness that constituted any body's given state of health at any moment in time. The passions operated upon the body very much as strong movements of wind or water operate upon the natural world: they were the body's internal climate of mood and temper, inward motions carried to the sentient flesh by the animal spirits. It is to such stirrings of the passions that Iago refers in reminding his gull Roderigo that human beings have "reason to cool our raging motions, our carnal stings, [our] unbitted lusts" (Riverside *Othello,* 1.3.330–31). His term, "raging motions," carries a strong sense of the animal spirits as liquid currents moving within the body to alter what it knows and how it feels.

This materialism in early modern thought means, among other things, that affective discourses in the period always presuppose embodiment just as bodily references always assume an affective context or consequence. In the brief space allotted to me for the rest of this essay, I would like to suggest how keeping the materiality of the passions in our minds may make a difference in reading even the most familiar of texts. By doing so, we may begin to rethink not only how the body inhabited the early modern world but how that world inhabited the body.

Take, for example, the wordplay between Hamlet and Guildenstern after Claudius has abruptly halted Hamlet's production of *The Murder of Gonzago* at the instant the poison is poured into the sleeping Player King's ear. "The King, sir," Guildenstern reports to the momentarily jubilant prince, "is in his retirement marvellous distemp'red" (Riverside *Hamlet,* 3.2.299, 301). Since the received meanings of "distemper" included intoxication, Hamlet's reply—"With drink, sir?"—may be disingenuous, but it is lexically apropos. He facetiously ignores the part he himself has played as cause of the king's distress and substitutes Claudius as the culprit. The self-defensive jibe is both personal and political, given the disapproval Hamlet has already expressed in 1.4 about Claudius's indulgence in public drinking games and the national shame attendant thereon. Guildenstern's perhaps surprised, perhaps exasperated correction of the prince's willful misunderstanding—"No, my lord, with choler"—is thus probably intended to clarify and narrow distemper's range of reference. The king is not drunk nor (as Guildenstern might imagine Hamlet to be hoping) is he fearful. The passion that distempers him is anger.

It is helpful to recognize that, with no loss of meaning or efficacy here, Guildenstern might easily have used "anger" to describe Claudius's passion in the first place. The humoral term "choler" keeps Claudius's emotions strongly within the flesh, choler being at one and the same time body fluid and raging motion, yellow bile and anger. The passions and humors were known to be closely allied, as the English Jesuit Thomas Wright explains in *The Passions of the Mind in General*: the "Passions ingender Humours, and humours breed passions."[2] Guildenstern's locution thus returns us to a moment in the history of bodies, minds, and souls when bodily fluids could still carry the full weight of a character's destiny, a moment when dense causal networks linked body, mind, culture, and the physical world. Indeed, it is because he uses the word "choler" that Hamlet can continue, with rude semantic pertinence, to taunt Guildenstern about the king's distemper and his own therapeutic recommendations for curing it: "Your wisdom should show itself more richer to signify this to the doctor, for me to put him to his purgation would perhaps plunge him into more choler" (305–7). As G. R. Hibbard notes in the Oxford *Hamlet*, Hamlet's sardonic reply brings together three forms of purging—medical, legal, and spiritual—though his reference to Claudius's physician ensures that medical purgation is the primary sense operative here.

Purgation was, in fact, prescribed for choler. The Puritan diarist Ralph Josselin records taking syrup of roses for an attack of ague: "wrought very kindly with me, gave me 9 stools brought away much choler." Here, the idea of purgation allows Hamlet both to flaunt his mock-concern for Claudius and to threaten the king indirectly with a bloodletting. The more humiliating option—Hamlet's sly implication that Guildenstern would be stupid enough to ask him, not the doctor, to administer a cathartic dose to Claudius either rectally or orally—brings us close to a cluster of early modern health practices and habits of thought. If bodily fluids *were* the stuff of emotions, then to alter the character and quantity of a body's fluids was to alter that body's passions and thus that body's state of mind and soul. Hamlet, putting himself scandalously in the position of Claudius's physician, imagining himself administering a purge to the royal body, allows the king's body to become the stuff of a humiliating practical joke, an anally sadistic jest-book prank of the sort that a Scogin might deliver to one of his opponents. In that sense, the aborted production of that other practical joke, *The Murder of Gonzaga,* can be regarded as a failed purging for Claudius, an uncathartic catharsis—an aggravation of his choler rather than the agent of its release, though it has had the psychophysiological effect on Claudius that Hamlet had desired. The sight startles the King into publicly betraying a passion—though how to interpret that passion as fear or anger or guilt is precisely the unspoken issue in this dialogue.

As Hamlet's puns and wilful misunderstandings in this exchange suggest, the force of his remarks to Guildenstern depends upon a commonplace semantic overlap between physiological and political discourses. In 1600, the imbalances or disturbances to which the word "distemper" could refer involved disorder in the body politic, disturbance of climate and air, or general imbalances and a disproportionate mixture of parts. The spectacle of a player king being murdered by his player nephew would thus cause distemper not only in the "real" king but—for different reasons and with a different set of emotions—in the guests invited to the court performance as well, themselves representative of the national culture and the larger body politic. As with so many other events in the play, the disturbance brought about locally by the scandal of *The Mousetrap*—a commotion simultaneously physical, psychological, and political in nature—affects the onlookers' bodies, minds, and sense of political well-being. The court's distemper will require the physical, spiritual, and political purgations finally achieved by the spectacle of poisonings and bloodlettings at play's end.

But I want to suggest an even wider context for Hamlet and Guildenstern's exchange here in 3.2, one which involves the causal networks of body, mind, and world invoked by the words of player nephew Lucianus as he pours poison into the sleeping Player King's ear:

> Thoughts black, hands apt, drugs fit, and time agreeing,
> [Confederate] season, else no creature seeing.
> Thou mixture rank, of midnight weeds collected,
> With Hecat's ban thrice blasted, thrice [infected],
> Thy natural magic and dire property
> On wholesome life usurps immediately.
>
> (3.2.256–60)

The incantatory quality of these lines results, I think, as much from the succession of feminine couplets as from the demonic imagery. But I am more interested in the cosmology implied and rhetorically constructed by Lucianus's melodramatic set of fatal convergences—first, a correspondence in his body between murderous mind and its physical agents, the "apt" hands; then a correspondence between this body and the natural world that it finds so convenient for its intents. The picture is not one of a disembodied mind instrumentalizing a set of neutral objects—hands, weeds, drugs, time, and the natural world—but rather of a co-conspiracy of like material agencies. Political terms of confederacy and usurpation undergird these analogies even as they emphasize the political meaning of the event. Putting Lucianus's mind fully into his body is to see a mind (like Claudius's) blackened symbolically with evil intention, physically with choler or rage; it is to understand hands "apt" in two senses, as both physically capable and in effect morally willing. This human agency is itself met and extended responsively by properties inherent to nature, time, and the "confederate" season. Time "agrees" with the murder not only by providing Lucianus with his opportunity but, in league with the season, by providing times of day when the different properties in life forms change in response to the natural and cosmological environment. Thus a poisoner would collect weeds at midnight for maximum toxicity, weeds that work metonymically here to become the natural symbols of as well as agents for black thoughts. Though the mixture's rankness has presumably been augmented by witchly words, the weeds' toxic cycles belong to them alone, as their "dire property." In Lucianus's words, then, we should recognize the cosmological assumptions common to the multiple puns on distemper, choler, and purgation in the conversation between Hamlet and Guildenstern that takes place so soon thereafter. In both speeches, human passions—here the passion of anger—occur fully within the natural order, take on an elemental force and character contingent upon a fully realized, if only partially articulated set of correspondences between inner and outer worlds, between the human body and the world in which it feels and acts in continuous, dynamic reciprocity.

These same correspondences inform the scene's rhetorical and emotional climax when Hamlet, picking up the demonic accents and mood of the murderous Lucianus, melodramatically proclaims his own state of mind:

The Body and Its Passions 49

> 'Tis now the very witching time of night,
> When churchyards yawn and hell itself [breathes] out
> Contagion to this world. Now could I drink hot blood,
> And do such [bitter business as the] day
> Would quake to look on.
>
> (3.2.388–92)

Midnight as represented here is both frightening to the imagination and physically unhealthy, with churchyards yawning up not only ghostly visitors to trouble the conscience but also noxious exhalations to trouble the porous flesh of the humoral body. But even more important for the psychological and physiological correspondences I have been tracing is the literalizing trope of Hamlet's bloodthirstiness. I read this declaration as the physiological expression of a new mood and interest, a change in materialized consciousness brought about by the provocative images of the play, Claudius's reaction to it, the sharp exchange with Guildenstern, and Gertrude's invitation to her closet. As Hamlet's impulse to drink blood becomes indistinguishable from a desire to shed it, killing becomes a drinking that expresses the moment. The heat of the new blood contains courage and capacity to act as *its* properties, properties it would transmit to the drinker when ingested. At this moment, the word of the father—the imposition to revenge—overlaps fully with therapeutic protocols, as Hamlet imagines himself suddenly (if momentarily) ready to kill.

Human blood was one of the bodily fluids—along with breast milk, urine, and mummia—to be ingested for therapeutic purposes. In *Three Books on Life* (II.xii), Ficino recommends it as an antidote to the cooling and drying processes of melancholy old age, to be taken with an equal amount of sugar and wine under a waxing moon. Blood would also serve as an antidote to the drying and cooling effects of mourning. Thus Hamlet's thirst here bespeaks his natural embeddedness in the world and an openness to the cues of time and season. He proclaims his readiness "now" for the heart-stimulating, anger-inducing drink of "hot blood," proverbially recommended (according to Hibbard) as an incitement to homicide. Even as he promises himself not to let "the soul of Nero enter this firm bosom," to "speak [daggers]" to his mother "but use none" [3.2.394, 396], we should note echoes of the earlier discourse of purgation, with words uttered in choler functioning as purgative agent for Gertrude's imagined spiritual opening and substituting for the physical daggers that he vows not to employ.

That Hamlet expresses the need for an external stimulant seems less important to me than his desire to incorporate the behavioral properties belonging to another's differently tempered blood. We ought, I think, to interpret this new appetite as a sign of release from melancholic depression, the burgeoning of a desire to be ready physiologically and psychologically for sudden physical action (like stabbing through an arras). The fragility of such a transformation goes without saying, on at least two counts. One comes from Hamlet's own sense of how hard won and soon lost any change in temper must be. In the very next scene, he begs the Ghost not to look upon him with pity,

> Lest with this piteous action you convert
> My stern effects, then what I have to do
> Will want true color—tears perchance for blood.
>
> (3.4.128–30)

Tears for blood, weeping for drinking—such are the swift metamorphoses of humoral corporeality. Thus the second count comes from humoralism generally, a way of thinking about bodily behavior that finds it much easier to account for a subject's moment-to-moment transformations in mood and actions than to account for emotional steadiness and a high degree of psychological self-sameness. For self-sameness presupposes disembodied consciousness, not the humoral subject's full immersion in and continuous interaction with a constantly changing natural and cultural environment.

For these inhabitants of Elsinore, I have been arguing, as for the onlookers at the Globe, the passions occurred within the natural order and belonged to it. In the early modern version of inwardness the psychological and the physiological were conceptually fused. Only with great difficulty can we read the early modern passions *as from within* an early modern body-consciousness. But we can move closer to such a reading if we can begin to imagine what it feels like to want to drink hot blood.

Notes

1. Shigehisa Kuriyama, *The Expressiveness of the Body and the Divergence of Greek and Chinese Medicine* (New York: Zone, 1999), 237.

2. Thomas Wright, *The Passions of the Mind in General,* ed. William Webster Newbold (New York and London: Garland), 64.

Bodies in the Audience

Cynthia Marshall

"A POX OF THIS GOUT!—or a gout of this pox!" mutters Falstaff (Norton *2 Henry 4*, 1.2.223), neatly demonstrating how the insistent body disrupts metaphorical abstraction. Yet by a curious circularity, that body in all its fleshy reality occasions proliferating metaphors, both from Falstaff himself as here and from those who would describe or indict him. A "huge hill of flesh," Falstaff is at once an actor on a stage and a "roasted Manningtree ox with the pudding in his belly" (Norton *1 Henry 4*, 2.5.224–5, 412–13), his body simultaneously the stable physical ground of Prince Hal's—and the Henriad's—existence, and a tissue of imaginative linguistic phrases from Shakespeare's pen.

Falstaff offers a salutary example of how language and the body interanimate one another. His example is relevant not only to the question of bodies on stage in early modern theaters but to that of bodies in the audience, given that surviving accounts of audience response can seem to modern readers impossibly metaphorical. What, for instance, is William Prynne describing, or imagining, when he writes (in *Histriomastix* [1633], 340–41) that events on stage "devirginate" maidens in the audience? We err in the direction of literalism if we suppose Prynne to see Cupid's dart physically piercing the bodies of innocent viewers, and yet Prynne is not exactly speaking metaphorically either: he believes that playgoing presents physical danger. Prynne tends to a hysterical compounding of physical symptoms with higher-order offenses, although by the standards of the day he is not neurotic. His notion of theater audiences as receptive and vulnerable is fueled by moral outrage and entirely in keeping with the antitheatricalists' habitual discounting of viewers' ability to withstand the insidiously overwhelming powers of theatrical spectacle. John Rainolds writes similarly of theatergoers catching an "ague" that ambiguously mutates into, or carries with it as symptom, the "phrensie" of speaking tragic verse, "so that the whole citie was full of pale and thinne folke, pronouncing like stage-players, and braying with a loude voice" (*Th'overthrow of Stage-Playes* [1599], 118). In Rainolds's anecdote, as regularly in antitheatrical rhetoric, theatrical influence is deemed infectious.

Efforts to assess the playgoing experience in early modern England need to take better account of the role of emotion or affectivity, because of the way it inflects the body that comes sporadically into view in these accounts. While one hesitates to endorse the antitheatricalists' view of the audience as feminized and disempowered or to countenance their hostility toward theater in general, it is also true that our modern disciplinary organization encourages an emphasis on drama's intellectual and aesthetic effects, at the risk of overlooking the terms within which the plays' original audiences would have received them. In the early modern era, when intellect and will were seen as subject to the dangerously unravelling effects of emotion (or, as they were called, the passions), and when humoral psychology defined the passions themselves as physical, the excitements of theatergoing were not limited to the cognitive level. With psychology and physiology compounded within the humoral regime, theater's emotional effects were felt by bodies in the audience—metonymically, not metaphorically. When Prynne imagines maidens so strongly wrought upon by the events on stage, as when he imagines cross-dressed actors "degenerat[ing]" into women (197–98), his outraged rhetoric accords with the more sober writings of humoral theorists, for whom the passions in fact provided linkage between body and soul. Nicolas Coeffeteau's *Table of Humane Passions,* translated into English in 1621, follows Aquinas in explaining how the sensitive soul mediates between its rational and appetitive counterparts, with the passions fostering the link between the higher, rational portion of the self and the lower, appetitive part. By arousing the emotions, theater exercised this link, bringing viewers' rigidly upright selves into contact or conjunction with their physical or appetitive natures. Or in the more vividly conceived terms of Stephen Gosson, theatrical sensations by "the privie entries of the eare slip downe into the hart, and with gunshotte of affection gaule the minde, where reason and vertue shoulde rule the roste" (*Schoole of Abuse,* 1579 [sig. B7]).

Within the plays themselves I find warrant to take such aspects of antitheatrical rhetoric seriously. In *As You Like It,* Phoebe's reasonable argument that "there is no force in eyes / That can do hurt" might momentarily loosen the shaft of Cupid's devirginating arrow, but Silvius understands with the wisdom of experience how the emotions of viewer and viewed, not the physics of light, are determinative in these interactions:

> If ever—as that ever may be near—
> You meet in some fresh check the power of fancy,
> Then shall you know the wounds invisible
> That love's keen arrows make.
> (Norton *As You Like It,* 3.5.26–27, 29–32)

Phoebe, of course, herself promptly feels the "wounds invisible" of Ganymede's scornful glance. The episode's animation of Petrarchan cliché grounds erotic emotion in the suffering body, and it suggests the contagious quality of such experiences, in keeping with the antitheatricalists' fears. A central point of theatrical performance was to put viewers into a case rather like Phoebe's—if not necessarily to cause them to fall in love, then to enable them to experience an upheaval of psychic organization through the working of extreme emotion.

As we have become more aware of the details of the construction of early modern theaters and of the social interactions within them, the relevance of material aspects of playgoing has come strongly to the fore. Yet "playgoing" names the activity of a motivated, empowered subject, whereas it seems to have been the goal of many plays to shatter and undo that organized subjectivity or selfhood, as the antitheatricalists feared, and the goal of playgoers themselves to experience radical emotional excitement. One way theater provided this cathartic release was by promoting emotional excess, which would have been experienced physically as well as psychologically. With emotion understood and experienced as an affair of both the humoral body and the perceptive intellect, the body served as what Maurice Merleau-Ponty calls "expressive space."[1] The other way plays sought to shatter viewers was by highlighting discontinuities between the body and the soul or self. Much of our own era's theoretical work on "the body" depends on a phenomenological awareness of how we live in and through our bodies but do not quite coincide with them. A similarly riddling sense of the body as an ambiguous site of subjectivity is at work in the drama of Shakespeare's day. Many plays of the period seem to have been intent on exposing the phenomenology of the body, bringing to viewers' awareness the seam between physical and thinking components of the self, and foregrounding the alien and unwieldy nature of the former. Certainly a metaphysical split between mind and body was known in the early seventeenth century, although the division we call Cartesian was not as sudden or as definitive as some modern commentators suppose. Early modern drama was deeply and precociously engaged in working out what it means to live as a conscious self within a mortal body.

While the antitheatricalists tend to write of early modern drama as an affair of relentless erotic titillation, we are likely to be struck by how prominently bodily violation and physical violence figure in the plays. Rather than simply reflecting a violent culture, this aesthetic of violence served a phenomenological purpose. In the theater, the representation of physical pain calls attention to bodiliness in a complex way—Herbert Blau calls the source of staged pain "the most serious question in acting."[2] The actor's peculiar goal is to extend the sense or sensation of suffering to viewers, whose sympathetic bodies might accordingly feel imagined pain. Often plays pressure sympathetic identification toward some sort of physical participation. When Gloucester's eyes are put out in *King Lear,* viewers are famously called into involvement. The viewer who covers his eyes in horror at the crime enacts the blindness Cornwall creates. Late in the play, Kent's line "Break, heart, I prithee break" simultaneously calls for the king's release from suffering and registers sympathetic grief as a physiological response, one that Kent himself accomplishes in the "journey" (Norton *Tragedy of King Lear,* 5.3.287, 296) on which he embarks at the conclusion. *King Lear* thus models for its audiences an emotional response so radical that the body is undone, broken. Staged violence is sometimes matched by words precisely geared to make viewers cringe, as when Leontes assaults Antigonus:

> You smell this business with a sense as cold
> As is a dead man's nose. But I do see 't and feel 't
> As you feel doing thus; and see withal
> The instruments that feel.
> (Norton *Winter's Tale,* 2.1.153–56)

The "business" Leontes refers to (his wife's affair with his friend) is purely imaginary, yet he claims to "see 't and feel 't" palpably, and employs violence against Antigonus to demonstrate the validity of his claim. Elaine Scarry has written compellingly of the way violence serves to ground epistemic doubt and resolve moral ambiguity, as it does for Leontes here. Viewers implicated by Leontes' deictic statement—"as you feel doing thus"—would experience the body as "expressive space," in Merleau-Ponty's term.

Because subjective dependence on the body encourages the assumption that it is real and trustworthy, the most powerful moments of theatrical phenomenology are those that combine the uncanny effects of a body whose status is uncertain with an ambiguous or oscillating demand for emotional response. The maimed Lavinia is a striking instance: although hardly unique in a play in which many limbs are "lopped," Lavinia inspires particularly troubled responses. Her uncle's agonizingly prolonged description of her "body bare / Of her two branches" (Norton *Titus Andronicus*, 2.4.17–18) focuses viewers' attention on her blasted shape, challenging norms of bodily integrity through the specter of an incomplete body. The many maimed (headless, handless, tongueless) bodies represented in *Titus Andronicus* offer a mirror stage gone tragically amuck: in place of the "statue" or "orthopaedic" image of bodily totality that Lacan's paradigmatic infant admired, viewers of this play confront the fragmented body of the disintegrating individual. In its final scene the play even reduces human flesh to food. Yet Lavinia's continued presence onstage as she struggles to communicate and to achieve revenge challenges a temptation to objectify her as victim; a mutely provocative stage presence, she functions as both subject and object. Perhaps Lavinia most discomfits viewers because of the way Marcus's address eroticizes her maimed appearance. His references to her arms as "circling shadows kings have sought to sleep in," her "rosèd lips," her "honey breath" (2.4.19, 24, 25), offer her, pornographically, as an object of desire. Presumably few in the audience would ever respond lustfully to this harsh spectacle, although similar conjunctions of violence and sensuality appear in the imagery of martyrdom. There too the goal was to provoke a visceral response.

In any theater, audience members can be expected to feel their own physical vulnerability when violent outrages against human bodies are represented onstage. But while a valuation of anatomical integrity seems to be transhistorical, early modern bodily understanding was inflected by a set of norms and codes rather different from our own, and plays accordingly engage bodies in ways that are distant from our experience. For instance, in John Ford's *The Broken Heart,* the despairing, lovesick Orgilus accomplishes suicide by phlebotomy, following to mortal extreme the standard therapeutic treatment for erotomania: bleeding the patient until he or she lost consciousness. For those members of the seventeenth-century audience who had experienced phlebotomy (most likely a significant number, since it was widely practiced for an astonishing variety of ailments), Orgilus's grisly suicide would evoke a horrified sympathy that might literally be felt on the pulse. Orgilus describes his death in anatomical terms, but despite the scientific discourse his evocation of the physical effects and sensations of bleeding to death would be comprehensible to viewers:

> So falls the standards
> Of my prerogative in being a creature.
> A mist hangs o'er mine eyes; the sun's bright splendour
> Is clouded in an everlasting shadow.
> Welcome, thou ice that sitt'st about my heart;
> No heat can ever thaw thee.
> (Oxford *Broken Heart*, 5.2.150–55)

Because early modern physiology understood the heart to be the hottest organ, Orgilus's description gives extra point to the physiological fact that severe blood loss causes body temperature to drop.

That viewers sought out and paid for theatrical experiences of this sort suggests that extreme emotion—the sort that devirginated the body or forced it into disorienting awareness—was felt as pleasurably cathartic, despite moralists' counsel against it. However Aristotle might have defined catharsis (moral purification and social purging have usually been suggested) the term's conflation of the emotive and the physical makes good sense in relation to the early modern era. When the playgoing populace submitted themselves to the harrowing effects of represented violence and emotional laceration, orderly subjectivity was dispatched in the face of overwhelming feeling. Through these sorts of theatrical encounters, timely questions of subjectivity, power, and embodiment were engaged emotionally and physically, as well as politically and intellectually.

Notes

1. Maurice Merleau-Ponty, *Phenomenology of Perception*, trans. Colin Smith (London: Routledge & Kegan Paul, 1962), 146.
2. Herbert Blau, *The Audience* (Baltimore: Johns Hopkins University Press, 1990), 163.

The Body and Geography

JOHN GILLIES

"TRADITIONALLY," which is to say in most times and places prior to the "New Geography" of early modern Europe, the tie between the body and geography ("description of the earth") has been primordial, intimate, and manifold. According to modern phenomenology, the body is made for earthly space, as—in an immediate sense—earthly space becomes manifest through the perceiving and feeling body. Bodies not only perceive space or things-in-space through any combination of their five senses, but their very design—their "handedness," their slightly uneven bifurcatedness—orientates or situates them qualitatively within space and fits them to manipulate things-in-space. Bipedalism not only equips the body to move through space but propels it as well.

Little wonder, then, if traditional geographies or pictures of the earth are deeply imprinted by the body. One primordial entail of the body is "the practice of dividing the circle of the horizon into four cardinal directions," which (as a historian of religion writes) "is almost universal." Only with the development of a concept of *azimuth* (whereby one point was fixed on the horizon) did this directional scheme become "more abstract and useful." Azimuth itself, however, is also keyed to the body; to the felt value of one direction over (and indeed against) another. East is sacralized in Jewish and Christian tradition ("and, behold, the glory of the God of Israel came by the way of the East," Numbers 2.2.3). West and north are ominous. However, as east is (roughly) the direction of the rising sun, it tended to be sacralized by other religions as well. For this reason, and because of the growing importance of Jerusalem, the Jewish (and the traditional Christian) geographies tended to be keyed to Jerusalem as to a sacred center rather than to the sacred direction. As such, they resembled other *omphalos-* (or navel) centered cosmographies, such as ancient Greek and Chinese. In such cosmographies, geographic boundaries are equally valorized if somewhat paradoxical. Conceding that there is indeed earth beyond the boundaries of the earth, such boundaries assert the limits of the properly human or habitable. Beyond the limits of the Greek *oikumene* (or "house-world") are wild beasts, monstrous bodies, impassible deserts, mountains, ocean, insufferable heat or cold. Even within the *oikumene,* the rooms (continents) were of variable quality. Following Herodotus, the Hippocratic treatise *Airs Waters Places* pronounces that Europeans "will be well nourished, of very fine physique and very tall," because Europe is "situated midway between the heat and the cold [and] is very fruitful . . . very mild." Asiatics, on the other hand, are "less homogeneous . . . because of the changes of the seasons and the character of the region." If human races tend to be geographically imprinted in traditional geographies, so too the geographic image—the *imago mundi*—fairly glows with affect. (To the Beowulf poet, the earth is "wlite-beorhtne wang, swa waeter bebugeth" or "a gleaming plain girdled with waters.") From late Roman thought (primarily Macrobius) into the Renaissance, it was commonplace to think of the world as a macrocosm in which the human body was recapitulated as microcosm. Again, the "world of earth" (*Orbis Terrarum*) was astrologically predicated by the environing spheres.

In all these contexts, the primary fact about early modern geography is the emptying of the body from the world picture. The so-called "New Geography" can be thought of as an amalgam of the new geographic discoveries (vast new lands and oceans) with the dramatic developments in cartographic science that had made these discoveries possible. In none of the three standard narratives of the New Geography is the body a real player. For the post-Baconian, scientistic narrative, the key development is an "objective" spatial awareness predicated on a mathematical "graticule" (keyed to itself alone) from which precisely the bodily "geography of myth and dogma" is absent. For the deconstructive and materialist critique of this narrative stemming from Henri Lefebvre's *Production of Space,* the new cartography is seen as a Faustian demiurge, actively producing the regimented spaces of an emergent capitalist order in the service of which traditional spaces are consigned to the trash-heaps of history, myth, and legend. (For Lefebvre, it is axiomatic that the "space of the inhabitant" and of tradition alike is as helpless as Goethe's Philemon and Baucis before Faust's stupendous conversion of their pastoral retreat into a heavy-industry park.) In a third and phenomenologically keyed narrative, the new cartography decisively entrenches the relatively plastic and neutral concept of "space" at the expense of the innately human, value-laden (and body-bound) category of "place."

These differing narratives of the New Geography all concur in one thing: the relegation of the body from the new world picture. This does not mean that archaic, body-related habits of thought do not persist. (The ancient Hebrew formulation of "the ends of the earth" remains current, as does the idea of monstrous races.) But it does mean that body and map stand in a new relation to each other. Maps are still handled by bodies and thus retain their tops and bottoms and sides, but the top of the map is now "north" and no longer coincident with a sacred direction. There are no sacred directions in the post-Ortelian world map (even though a certain directional bias and meaning is unconsciously asserted). The body is no longer overtly figured in the map. There is no *omphalos,* no point of geographic convergence, no navel linking earth to heaven. Even though bodies abound in the margins of the ornate *Carte à Figures,* they are just that: marginal. Nor is there any technical provision for "privileging" simply remarkable places. (The "Red Sea" is no longer necessarily red, as on medieval maps.) Color itself is no longer a core aspect of geographic signification, but optional, decorative, parergonal. (Coloring was done after the stage of engraving, which itself followed a long way after the cartography proper.) The map no longer glows with affect.

In one account, the loss of bodily authority had frightening consequences. Unmirrored in the map, the body was lost, disoriented, fragmented. Donne's *Anniversaries* testify to the panic of a body unable to recognise an *oikos* (an answerable architecture) in the heavens. In the geographic counterpart to these poems, "Hymn to God my God in my Sickness," Donne attempts to anthropomorphize an Ortelian world map in the image of his own dying body—searching it for a navel, a sacred cord between this world and the next, but finding only disintegration or at best a sonorous nostalgia for the placial hospitality of the old geography. There is of course a more upbeat account (one indulged by Donne himself as erotic cartographer) in which the map promises the body more and better room than it has ever known. While the body may not be in the map, it enlarges itself thereby—treating the map as a plastic space for the projection or extension of desire. Like Tamburlaine's sword, the map is now a kind of mental hand-prop, an organ of imaginative prehension.

The new partnership of body and map is staged in an early modern topos, most familiar today in the Marlovian and Shakespearean phrase "great riches in a little room" or Donne's "one little room" that is "an everywhere," but in fact the invention of geographers—such as William Cunningham, who praises maps for their convenience in contracting the wide world within "a warme & pleasant house, without the perill of the raging Seas: danger of enemies: losse of time: spending of substaunce: werines of body or anguishe of minde." It is as if the interior is that much cozier for the presence of a map: the beguiling image rather than the overwhelming substance of lands and seas, the goal of travel without the pains of travel. Far from disturbing the body, the contemplation of cartographized exteriority actually intensifies the body's sense of housedness, of cocoonment. The burning and frigid zones collapse into the comfort zone as into a overstuffed armchair.

In view of Gail Kern Paster's argument that early modern ideas of "the passions" presupposed a body directly impacted upon and interpenetrated by the natural world, what might have been the consequences of such cocoonment for the body's powers of affect? Sheltered from the perils of travel, Cunningham's cartographer is alike preserved from the vicissitudes of passion ("anguishe of minde"). The scene of cartography has but one actor, one character. With no love interest (outside of the protagonist himself) and no antagonist, there is no *agon,* no storm of passion such as imagined in strikingly geographic imagery by Thomas Wright: "wee may compare the soule without passions, to a calme sea . . . but the passionate to a raging gulfe swelling with waues, surging by tempests, minacing the stony rockes, and endeuoring to ouerthrow mountaines" (*The Passions of the Minde* [1601], 100). Somewhat like Cunningham, who opposes the terrors of voyaging to the pleasures of map-reading, Wright opposes a Thalassically liquid passion to the calibrated certainties of intellect. The wise man maps his passions, determining their whereabouts by reference to the stars: "An angry man raiseth brawles . . . men had neede of an Astrolabe alwayes, to see in what height or eleuation his affections are" (10). Just as he never gets his feet wet or his hands dirty, so cartographic man avoids getting hot under the collar.

Visual forms of the scene of cartography can be found in Vermeer's bourgeois interiors, where maps constantly feature as backdrops to the mundane domesticities enacted before them. Two almost academic variants of the topos are found in "The Geographer" and "The Astronomer"—each posed by the same stylishly begowned model, each figure poring over maps or globes within the privacy of his study. A phenomenological reading these paintings might suggest that the "far sphere" (the space of the eye) is brought within the ambit of the "near sphere" (the *Kernwelt* or space of touch). One notes the "distant" gaze of "The Geographer" in particular. Focusing neither on the map on the table below him nor on the window behind, he gazes into an indeterminate mental distance between both. (There is evidence that at an earlier stage of this composition the head had been down and the gaze fixed upon the map.)

How different is this cartographic mise en scène from that figured by the medieval TO map. Such a map was either hung in a church (itself "oriented" towards the sacred direction) to inspire recognition of the redemptive plan inscribed within its geographic content, or routinely figured in the plataea of the Mystery plays as the literal mise en scène of earthly existence. The pull of the TO map was centrifugal rather than centripetal, invoking the pilgrim rather than the voyager (return to origin rather than far horizon), and perambulation rather than sedentary scheming. Redemption rather than romance was the narrative key; the journey was not to "California" but the foot of the cross.

The difference between the respective "scenes" of the old and new geographies is epitomised in the shift (over a corresponding period) in the meaning of the word "room." The "little room" that Marlowe and Shakespeare imagine as the site of "great riches" represents a substantial narrowing of an earlier spectrum of meanings associated with this word. Old and Middle English "rum" is not necessarily or even primarily an "interior portion of a building." In Old English, "rum" is more often an adjective or adverb than a noun (and when a noun, as in *Judith,* signifies "opportunity"). In *Beowulf,* a grieving father finds his fields and dwelling ("wongas and wic-stede") all too large ("eall to rum") now that his son is dead. "Rum" here evidently means something like "spacious"—a roominess rather than a "littleness"—intimately tied to bodily percept and affectivity. A rift opens up between "rum" and the body in the Middle English usage of "a particular portion of space." Finally, from 1457, the word takes on the sense of "an interior portion of a building."

Considered within the scene of cartography, "room" can be said to have withdrawn from "rum"'s archaically vague and yet bodybound claim to "spaciousness." In addition to being "little," "room" is now an interior and a noun. It is an object rather than a precept, a static shell rather than a supple and body-following adjective or adverb. For its part, "space" now seems immensely large once contrasted with "room" (rather than coextensive with "rum"). "Space" had been held back by "rum." Even in its extensive form, "rum" was never the equal of "space." Where space was and is, "continuous, unbounded or unlimited extension in every direction," "rum"—because of its necessary tie to the body—could never be bigger than "enough." With no anchorage in the body, "space" could be infinite ("I could be bounded in a nutshell and count myself the king of infinite space, were it not that I have bad dreams"). Equally, space was untextured, unfelt, colorless, and potentially monstrous ("O indistinguished space of womens' will"). There was no space for "rum" in the maps of the New Geography. (By contrast, "rum" was the only kind of space on the TO map.) So unqualitied, indeed, was the space of the New Cartography, that it was not necessarily or even primarily geographic. In early modern anatomy textbooks, the body itself becomes the object of the cartographic gaze (the body as *Korpor* studied by the body as *Lieb*, the dead mapped by the living).

In terms of the body, the early modern "scene of cartography" is a paradox. Having withdrawn from the "space" of the map—as from its own primordially vague claims pon spaciousness—the "room" was nevertheless fundamental to the cultural image of the map, particularly that of the world map. It is as if the cartographer's room had become the unconscious equivalent of the ancient *omphalos,* the link between the map and the human world, the human body. In the "scene of cartography," "room" complements "space" precisely because represented as its opposite. The exterior contracts into the map, and the body within the room. Neither is the other. But together, they are going places.

Whose Body?

Jyotsna G. Singh

INCLUSION, PRESENCE, AND REPRESENTATION have provided the impetus for much work in gender studies in the past decade. Carol Neely took the occasion of an essay in 1995 to reflect on the difference between feminist work in the 1990s from feminist work in the 1970s: "Since writing my essay 'Women and Men in *Othello*' in 1973, I have had much time and many incentives to rethink *Othello*. I have been brought face to face with issues I overlooked earlier by teaching the play in many contexts and teaching women's studies and . . . including work by contemporary women writers of color. Simultaneously I have been influenced by the turn towards history in Renaissance studies and by the critique of essentialism and emphasis on difference in feminist theory."[1] In their introduction to the volume in which Neely's essay appears, Deborah E. Barker and Ivo Kamps remark on the same changes:

> Although it is certainly not free from the still powerful forces of conservatism and patriarchy within both the academy and culture, [Shakespearean] gender studies has left the critical margins and justly taken a position at the very centre of academic discourse. Occupying the centre often brings with it the inevitable danger of institutional co-optation, but even the most cursory glance at the actual work done in gender studies confronts us with its radical *difference* from the scholarship produced in any other moment of our history.[2]

Kamps' and Barker's claims undoubtedly reflect a critical consensus about gender studies (along with its earlier incarnation, feminist criticism), namely, that it has emerged as a distinct and dominant field within Shakespeare scholarship. In considering how we arrived at this moment of dominance, so to speak, critics generally consider this development as a progression toward new historical knowledge and innovative critical strategies for reading and rewriting gender. Thus, Shakespearean gender critics today have moved far beyond literary analysis and toward a broader ideological critique of discursive modes and social practices by which any culture perceives and represents itself. Specifically, in the year 2000, the idea of "progress" among Shakespearean gender theorists is based on an awareness of past omissions and accompanying claims of inclusion via representation on many fronts. Among these claims are that feminists have retrieved the silent voices of Renaissance women and other marginalized groups from the historical archive;[3] they have recognized early modern Europe's racialized others such as Othello and Caliban in terms of their struggles within European, colonial patriarchy;[4] and finally, psychoanalytical, Foucauldian, and queer theory interrogations of sexuality have illuminated the complex formation of early modern selves, especially in terms of the "erotic body"—heterosexual, homosexual, lesbian—as a site for "inscriptions of ideology and power."[5]

Yet, as Dympna Callaghan has recently suggested, it is important to assert a distinction between mere "visibility" and "representation in its political sense (namely representing the interests of a particular constituency)." Using Shakespeare's works as a site from which to "address the stakes of representation," Callaghan provocatively questions "what it means to secure cultural and political representation in [European] patriarchy for women and other oppressed groups."[6] While she focuses on the representation and impersonation of persons not present on Shakespeare's stage—women, Africans, and the Irish—I want to examine the dynamics of inclusion and representation within Shakespearean feminist/gender studies. And I do so by looking backward in order to map the terrain of both our past and future interventions in the dominant, patriarchal cultural formations.

Under the rubric of "gender," for instance, what categories of identity and experience have Shakespearean feminists privileged, perhaps to the omission of others, in the past decade? Given that institutions and practices such as courtship, marriage, and the family are so central to Shakespeare's plays, it is understandable that feminist critics have been drawn to these topics. Thus, feminist critics in the 1970s and 1980s performed pioneering work in revealing the patriarchal bias of earlier critical work on these "timeless" institutions. They did so by demonstrating how notions of femininity and masculinity underpinning these social structures are produced and managed through cultural discourses—an ideological process that we now take as a given in any work on gender.[7]

Whose Body? 65

With Foucauldian conceptualizations of sexuality and power as its basis, the formation of gendered identities has continued to be of interest to Shakespearean gender scholars. In fact, the notion of sexuality as a site of anxiety, contestation, and subversion has provided the impetus for much recent work, producing emancipatory and more inclusive discourses on sexuality and sexual difference. As a result, the inclusion of the body—often the *desiring* body—characterizes many studies on gender in the past decade; these range from the relation between erotic desire and the construction of male and female subjects in Shakespeare[8] to the work of Gregory Bredbeck (*Sodomy and Interpretation: Marlowe to Milton*) and Jonathan Goldberg (*Sodometries: Renaissance Texts, Modern Sexualities*),[9] among others, which counters the patriarchal construction of sexual identities via "dividing practices that set homosexual off from heterosexual";[10] instead, they intervene in such binary formulations by emphasizing the instability of all sexual categories, especially as generated by the term "sodomy"—both in the early modern society and in our own time."[11] Other, more recent examples of similar approaches are Stephen Orgel's *Impersonations: The Performance of Gender in Shakespeare's England*, which historically accounts for sexual values and practices represented in the drama and society of the period, and Traub's essay on the clitoris, which relates anatomies and travel narratives in the Renaissance to show varying representations of and responses to same-gender female eroticism.[12]

The political implications of such approaches in the past decade are important: they have illuminated the formation of minority sexual identities and politics; they have offered a historical reappraisal of the ideological underpinnings of these identities; and finally, and perhaps most significantly, they have challenged the sometimes homogenizing effects of popular identity politics whereby particular groups set up exclusionary norms for what it means to be a black man, a lesbian, a homosexual, and so on. Overall, however, while work on sexual difference has successfully included sexual minority voices and experiences, the question still remains as to how it has shaped the direction of future work on gender. Has "desire" as a category of analysis in early modern studies (as in other periods) by now become an over-used term? It seems to have become a catch-all label that defines early modern (or contemporary?) identities above all as desiring, erotic selves. The pervasiveness of this term is not incidental given that desiring (and consuming) bodies are central to our culture of late capitalism, vividly illustrated in the unabashed (and generally parodic) display of erotic desire on television in endlessly proliferating forms. Having said that, I do not propose that we should abandon the term "desire," only that we may we may rethink and reformulate its role and significance in subject-formation in the future.

A different and compelling perspective on desire in Renaissance gender studies has very recently been articulated in *Bodies and Selves in Early Modern England,* in which Michael Schoenfeldt moves beyond purely social constructions of desire as well as psychoanalytic explanations of it; instead, he draws on the influence of Galenic humoral physiology to emphasize a "particularly physiological mode of self-fashioning" in the Renaissance—and to show that "this self is far more than just an effect of discourses, or the product of socio-cultural discourses, institutions, and practices."[13] Drawing on Foucault's later work on self-regulation, he diverges from the new historicist and psychoanalytic focus on desiring subjects. Instead, he states that the "Renaissance seems to have imagined selves as differentiated not by their desires, which all more or less share, but by their capacity to control these desires." Thus, where "we are prone to situate identity on the axis of sexual desire, the Renaissance tended to locate identity amid the control of a variety of appetites, including the sexual." Furthermore, Galenic medicine, according to the critic, was more "relational" than explicitly gendered, thus often undoing "the masculinist framework it was so frequently used to buttress."[14]

How does this historical phenomenology with its more gender-neutral or cross-gender readings of the regulation of desire contribute to the project of gender studies? Is this an inclusive move toward the formation of corporeal rather than simply gendered selves? While such questions are debatable, this study nonetheless signals the future of gender studies in moving beyond the earlier focus on the social construction of the erotic body and toward rethinking the function of desire within new and different modes of identity formation. Such a move can also lead to displacing the desiring body with other images such as that of the laboring body—both gendered and ungendered. Shakespeare's plays offer us many images of class-marked bodies—laboring, diseased, desexualized—and a revaluation of their dramatic and ideological function would be productive. Thus, while inclusion remains a worthwhile goal, we should also continue to attend to the dynamics and effects of this process.

Notes

1. Carol Neely, "Circumscriptions and Unhousedness: *Othello* in the Borderlands," in *Shakespeare and Gender: A History*, ed. Deborah E. Barker and Ivo Kamps (New York: Verso, 1995), 302.
2. Deborah E. Barker and Ivo Kamps, introduction to their *Shakespeare and Gender: A History*, 17.
3. Margaret Ferguson, Maureen Quilligan, and Nancy J. Vickers, eds., *Rewriting the Renaissance: The Discourses of Sexual Difference in Early Modern Europe* (Chicago: University of Chicago Press, 1986), 1–50.
4. Karen Newman, "'And wash the Ethiop white': femininity and the monstrous in *Othello*," in *Shakespeare Reproduced: The text in history and ideology*, ed. Jean Howard and Marion F. O'Connor (London: Methuen, 1987); Jyotsna Singh, "Othello's Identity, Postcolonial Theory, and Contemporary African Rewritings of *Othello*," in *"Race," Writing, and Difference in Early Modern Europe*, ed. Margo Hendricks and Patricia Parker (London: Routledge, 1994): 287–99.
5. Valerie Traub, *Desire and Anxiety: Circulations of sexuality in Shakespearean drama* (London: Routledge, 1992), 9.
6. Dympna Callaghan, *Shakespeare Without Women: Representing gender and race on the Renaissance Stage* (London: Routledge, 2000), 5, 7–9.
7. Lisa Jardine, *Still Harping on Daughters: Women and Drama in the Age of Shakespeare* (Brighton: Harvester, 1983), 1–50; Catherine Belsey, *The Subject of Tragedy: Identity and difference in Renaissance drama* (London and New York: Metheun, 1985), 1–10, 149–91.
8. Traub, *Desire and Anxiety*, 1–15.
9. Gregory W. Bredbeck, *Sodomy and Interpretation: Marlowe to Milton* (Ithaca: Cornell University Press, 1991); Jonathan Goldberg, *Sodometries: Renaissance Texts, Modern Sexualities* (Stanford: Stanford University Press, 1992).
10. Monique Deveaux, "Feminism and Empowerment: A Critical Reading of Foucault," in *Feminist Interpretations of Michel Foucault*, ed. Susan J. Hekman (University Park: Pennsylvania State University Press, 1996), 250.
11. Goldberg, *Sodometries*, 1–50, 122–23; Bredbeck, *Sodomy and Interpretation*, 75–78.
12. Stephen Orgel, *Impersonations: The Performance of Gender in Shakespeare's England* (Cambridge: Cambridge University Press, 1996); Valerie Traub, "The Psychomorphology of the Clitoris," in *Feminist Approaches to Theory and Methodology: A Reader*, ed. Sharlene Hesse-Biber, Christina Gilmartin, and Robin Lydenberg (New York and Oxford: Oxford University Press, 1999), 302–7.
13. Michael C. Schoenfeldt, *Bodies and Selves in Early Modern England: Physiology and Inwardness in Spenser, Shakespeare, Herbert, and Milton* (Cambridge: Cambridge University Press, 1999), 12.
14. Schoenfeldt, *Bodies and Selves*, 17, 37, 36.

Body Problems

Dympna Callaghan

THE MEANING OF THE BODY that has come to dominate literary criticism over the past few years is not the idealized aesthetic body of Marlowe's Leander or Shakespeare's Adonis, but instead the body as viscera—heart, lungs, entrails. This is the body seen from the perspective of Renaissance medical texts, from the point of view of the anatomist slicing into a fresh cadaver on the slab before him in plain view of interested onlookers. That this perspective has come to dominate our ideas about the early modern body is itself, I propose, worthy of examination. Why should it be that we are all rushing to examine the multifarious meanings of early modern innards?

Certainly, Gayle Kern Paster offers a partial answer when she asserts in an important contribution to a recent book, *The Body in Parts,* that the fascinating thing about organs is that they are the same now as in the Renaissance, but their meanings are different. I scratch my head over the profundity of this proposition, though it is without question worthy of some consideration. For what Paster suggests is the importance of historicizing the body, which otherwise seems like a constant, a given of history. As students of the Renaissance, we have come to learn that nothing is constant and that there are no unchanging facts or objects to cling to on the oceans of our inquiries. The point is one familiar to cultural materialists. And yet I wonder if analysis of the body-as-entrails is indeed materialist.

Bodies as such (not to mention their entrails) are of little interest to me because no matter how carefully they are handled and historically situated, they are mere objects. They are a postmodern version of brute fact, that most empirically reductive (mis)understanding of matter. To posit the brute facticity of matter is not materialism (though it is widely believed to be so) but reification. This is so because whenever we attribute brute facticity to anything, we make it seem as if it stands alone beyond its interactions with human consciousness and therefore beyond history in any meaningful sense. We are guilty of a sort of historicist idolatry; that is, we have placed our faith in the thingness of things in order to avoid the messy interactions of matter and consciousness. To say that human consciousness and its intercourse with the material environment is the dynamic force of human history sounds antimaterialist only because Marx's own complex theorization of dialectical materialism has been ignored in favor of the profoundly erroneous belief that matter has a life of its own and that human consciousness is irrelevant to the course of human history. Such views constitute what I regard as the political misuse of materialism; so that analysis of any old dead matter—nothing short of souped-up antiquarianism—gets paraded as "materialist" analysis in a manner that is in no way allayed by the qualification that the object of inquiry is "discourses about" lights, livers, and entrails, for example, as distinct from the organs themselves. These misuses are not, of course, confined to the analysis of the body (but in relation to print, jewelry, embroidery, and to any other object you might care to name), though they are to be found there in particularly egregious concentration.

My contention, then, is that the current vogue for bodies is neither truly historicist (and not just in the Marxist sense) and certainly not materialist. In fact, certain aspects of the body have been so pointedly overlooked in the overly literal anatomical studies that now pervade our field that far from being (despite all claims to the contrary) *not* materialist, they are quietly reactionary. The body marked by and animated by labor, for instance, is regarded as pretty much an irrelevant category of analysis at present. The fundamental (and thoroughly corporeal) dynamic engagement with matter that concerned Marx was, of course, labor—and it is labor more than Galenic versus Aristotelian theories of sexual difference that produces gender difference. Labor constructs gender (along with other aspects of social and ideological formation) not because this is where gender difference "comes from" (its archeological origins, so to speak) but because the practices of human labor fundamentally produce and sustain sexual difference.

At this point, I probably should make it clear that I do not regard the body as insignificant (I have written too much about it myself to be of this opinion). The earlier trend of treating minds as if they existed in the realms of human history without bodies was every bit as erroneous as the view that early modern conceptions of the lights and liver hold a long-forgotten key to Renaissance knowledges. Bodies equipped with minds, active in the processes of history, are important. The body as anatomized object, as dead meat, is not. My complaint, then, is that inquiries about the body represent criticism's furtive return to empiricism. We are interested in the body (especially the innards, at least when surgically displayed for our convenience) because it is reassuringly (in this, our anti-essentialist moment) something we can see. I believe further that there are at least two methodological pitfalls in the business of body myopia—either that we assume the necessary superiority of our own worldview and its categories of analysis, or simply (and at the moment, more fashionably) regurgitate the period's own categories, its own theories of entrails.

Perhaps unfortunately for us, who live in what is arguably the most visual culture that has ever existed, early moderns were more interested in things unseen than in matter visible, in which they simply did not share our faith. It is not just that we live in the age of television and the computer screen, it is that we are uniquely gullible in the face of commodities, the idols of the market, believing them to exist independently of the labor that produces them, in a way that even the majority of characters who go to Jonson's *Bartholomew Fair* do not. We are so smug about advances in medical science since the Renaissance that we forget our own blind spots (especially the invisibility of labor)—which are, of course, precisely the result of the scientific way of thinking that brought about those "advances" in the first place. For the anatomists were more like us in their thinking (we are, conceptually speaking, their direct descendants after al) than someone like John Donne. No matter how well-informed he may have been of the new developments of his era, when Donne implores God to batter his heart, he is not worried about his circulation but is rather concerned to grasp the concrete reality of the divine presence. My point is that in our myopic obsession with Galenism and anatomy, we have forgotten what the major motivating issues of our period really are, and that these might be usefully understood as an attention to things unseen, or at least not completely susceptible to postmodern empiricism.

My final gripe about the body as it is currently manifested in Renaissance literary criticism is that it is not much concerned with literature at all. Now from the perspective of cultural criticism this may be all very well. We have long been told that it is just as appropriate to apply our critical acumen to the entire range of early modern texts and that we need not necessarily privilege literary ones. I believe, on the contrary, that commitment to literature is politically distinct from merely privileging literature, and that now, more than ever, in a world where the humanities is increasingly regarded as irrelevant, we need such a commitment. While literature's meaning and function must necessarily be established in the context of non-literary texts, we should not abandon literary objects. For we are far from having exhausted the meanings of the literary, both specifically textual and more broadly cultural. When I read yet another essay on the early modern body, I fear we have abandoned our political commitment to literature in favor of medical texts and an ahistorical literalism that constitutes those aspects of knowledge that our own world deems more valuable and less troublesome than poetry. Call me old-fashioned, but I'd rather spend my time with Leander and Adonis.

ARTICLES

The Need for Lavinia's Voice: *Titus Andronicus* and the Telling of Rape

Emily Detmer-Goebel

In act 2 of Shakespeare's *Titus Andronicus*, Lavinia refuses to name rape; she refers to an impending sexual assault as that which "womanhood denies my tongue to tell" and as a "worse-than-killing lust" (2.3.174, 175).[1] Lavinia's chaste refusal to say the word "rape" reminds the audience that even to speak of rape brings a woman shame. As feminists have pointed out, an environment that makes it shameful to speak of rape disallows a critique of rape and the culture that sustains it.[2] And yet, while the world of the play suggests how early modern culture's construction of gender "denies" a woman the "tongue" to talk of rape, the play also feeds on the unrest that such silence creates.

Feminist critique of rape representations often explores "telling" as a question of authorship or subjectivity. For example, the first question that many feminist critics ask of various early modern representations of rape is: Who is really doing the talking; who is telling this story of rape?[3] Such questions are particularly useful when pursuing the cultural politics of lines such as Lavinia's quoted above. Feminist scholars have rightly pointed to the myriad ways that patriarchal culture silences women, but it is too simple to say that silence always serves (and is preferred by) patriarchal culture. Sometimes patriarchal culture needs and wants female speech—of a certain kind, under certain conditions.

Few have considered the way these texts also reveal patriarchy's discomfort with silence about rape.[4] For many feminist critics of *Titus Andronicus*, for example, Lavinia's enforced silence is posed as simply an oppressive requirement of patriarchal culture.[5] No doubt the mutilation of Lavinia is brutally oppressive, yet Lavinia's silence is troubling to some men in her world. Speaking may be threatening, but so is silence. Revealing rape may be dangerous for some men (the rapists), but it is necessary for others (the father, the current or future husband). Until Lavinia is able to testify about her rape, it goes undetected and unpunished. Lavinia's family depends on her willingness and ability to tell that she has been raped if they are to revenge it.

Just as the play illustrates the cultural need for both a raped woman's silence *and* her testimony, statutory laws of rape and abduction reflect a legal tradition undergoing change with regards to a woman's non-consent and accusation of rape. While statute law represents legal principles that may or may not line up with practice, I read both the legal and dramatic discourses as evidence of how power is assigned to raped women's claims, and how, in turn, that powerful speech is perceived, represented, and contested. By exploring the relationships between statutory law and the play, I argue that *Titus Andronicus* dramatically registers the culture's anxiety over men's increased dependence on women's voices and, in doing so, shapes and sustains early modern England's contradictory attitude toward a woman's accusation of rape.

" 'Rape' call you it"?

Rape is the centerpiece of Shakespeare's fictional history of Rome.[6] More than any other early modern English play, *Titus Andronicus* has the "pattern, precedent, and lively warrant" (5.3.42) of rape hovering throughout. References to the legendary rape stories of Philomela, Lucrece, and Virginius are used as shorthand for understanding character and motive in four of the most important actions in the play: Aaron's tutorial in rape, Lavinia's revelation of the crime, Titus's revenge against the rapists, and his killing of his own daughter.[7] Even the play's "precedent," Ovid's *Metamorphosis*—the grandfather of rape stories—is literally brought onto the stage.

These heavy-handed references to rape suggest an interest in rape as rape rather than just as a convenient metaphor for chaos or disorder.[8] In a like manner, Lavinia's silence elucidates more than just an oppressive gendered ideal of feminine decorum. Shakespeare's play calls our attention to the act of revealing rape; suspense builds as each character responds to the spectacle of the mutilated and raped Lavinia. The variety of responses to her—from the laughter of the rapists and the poetry of her uncle, to the fear of young Lucius and the budding madness and bloody revenge of

Titus—suggests how Lavinia's telling of rape can be seen as dramatizing the culture's multifaceted stance regarding a woman's claim of rape.

Examining the actual moment of telling in several other early modern dramas reveals the culture's ambiguous attitude towards a woman's revelation of rape. On the one hand, Lucrece honorably postpones suicide until she reveals her rape in Heywood's *Rape of Lucrece* (1607), and Jacinta's struggle to tell her father is dramatically crucial in Rowley's *All's Lost by Lust* (1622). On the other hand, Castiza's confessors instruct her *not* to tell her husband that she was raped in Middleton's *Hengist, King of Kent* (1619). Clara in Middleton's *The Spanish Gypsie* (c. 1614–23) asks for a promise of silence from her rapist, and the play's "happy ending" seems to condone her own silence. Increasingly, early modern dramas that feature rape build on the dramatic tension created when a woman must decide if she should (or can, in Lavinia's case) reveal her rape; I suggest this might be due, in part, to relatively recent changes in the law of rape.

Early statutory law dating from the late thirteenth century conflated sexual assault with abduction, blurring the distinction between the two. Long understood as a property crime, "rape" either by physical abduction (which would often include a forced marriage and sexual consummation) or by "defilement against her will" fell into the same category of wrong. Based on how men experience the "rape" of a woman in whom they have ownership, the law suggests that men apparently found the loss from sexual assault and abduction to be more similar than different.

During the sixteenth century, however, the definition of rape came to exclude abduction. Although no single statute was written precisely to distinguish sexual assault from abduction, a 1558 statute (4&5 Philip & Mary, cap 8) addressed the abduction of heiresses without reference to sexual assault and a later statute in 1576 (18 Elizabeth cap. 7) addressed rape without reference to abduction.[9] According to the historian Nazife Bashar, these acts of law taken together "had the indirect effect of establishing rape and abduction as separate offenses."[10] Thus, early modern culture began to understand rape and abduction as distinct kinds of wrongs.[11]

With benefit of hindsight, modern readers see this as the evolution of rape into a crime against a person (assault, as opposed to theft).[12] Lorraine Helms points out that *Titus Andronicus* "maps both the residual and emergent ideas of rape," helping to distinguish "bride theft" from sexual assault.[13] The play certainly does register the differences between abduction and sexual assault, but it does more. Shakespeare's play powerfully dramatizes how the evolving rape laws were also changing the role of women's authority in the new version of "rape."

Before the definition of rape excluded abduction, a woman's voice was subsumed under her father's or husband's authority. In other words, in medieval law, the right to accuse a person of rape/abduction did not rest with the victim but with her male relatives such as her father, husband, or guardian. As the historian J. B. Post argues, the earlier, medieval statutes were written precisely in such a way as to take the "legal remedies" (the appeal) away from raped or abducted women themselves.[14] Several legal historians conclude that the laws were often used to address consenting relationships that were against the parents' wishes; a woman might "elope" with a husband of her own choice or escape an abusive husband.[15] The conflated rape/abduction laws marginalized a woman's speech acts, be it her consent or her accusation; the father's authority far outweighed the woman's in either case of "rape." As the definition of rape came to exclude abduction, men's authority narrowed.

When rape became a separate offense, the status of a woman's voice, meaning her consent, her accusation, and her right to appeal in her own name gained authority. While men retained their authority in abduction cases, some women gained the exclusive right to charge a man with rape. While a married woman still required her husband's consent to bring an appeal, an unmarried woman (single or widowed) had the right to bring the appeal of rape in her own name.[16] Although changes in the law theoretically increased women's authority to claim rape, it should not be assumed that women began prosecuting rape without male relatives. On the contrary, what I am considering is how this legal change left male relatives, who were still very much involved in the legal process, dependent on women's voices and their knowledge.

Whose Claim of "Rape" Is It?

As if dramatizing these recent legal maneuverings, when both forms of "rape" take place in *Titus Andronicus,* the play interrogates the different sources of authority in both kinds of crimes. When Bassianus seizes and flees with Lavinia in the first act of the play, Saturninus claims "rape," which reflects the older legal definition of the term.[17] Early modern readers/audience members would likely find Saturninus's first reference to abduction as "rape" an increasingly rare usage, but certainly not unknown.[18] Significantly, the drama clearly illustrates how the competing claims of "rape" are represented as disagreements between men. Titus's parental claim is a customary and legitimate source of authority; after all, we just saw Titus consent to Saturninus, the newly crowned king. In contrast, Bassianus's ambiguously "lawful" claim, which is specifically not based on prior sexual activity, gains authority only when other members of Lavinia's family support him. When the rest of Lavinia's family take arms against their sovereign and father in "Lavinia's cause" (1.1.377), the reader/audience member must give some credence to Bassianus's claim. *Who* raped Lavinia from *whom* is unclear, but it never becomes a question of "he said, she said."[19] The ambiguities surrounding the first rape/abduction of the play accentuate the fact that it is a question of men's authority.

Shakespeare's display of men's competing claims of authority in cases of abduction also highlights the marginalization of a woman's claim. All of the men in the play believe their own interpretation of rape (and lawful possession), but none consults Lavinia. Unlike Desdemona, who is called to speak of her free choice of Othello, Lavinia's past promise, consent, or her present feelings play no part in defining this first rape nor is she asked to identify which is the real rapist. By calling Lavinia's abduction "rape," the play illustrates women's customary lack of authority to define rape in the medieval form of the law. In the second and increasingly modern understanding of "rape"—that is, a form of rape that excludes abduction—the role her voice plays increases, as Shakespeare's play powerfully explores. Even though Lavinia's silence in the first rape/abduction scene is presented as appropriate, it becomes vexed in the second rape.

"And strike her home by force, if not by words"

In many early modern rape scenes, the rapist first tries to seduce the woman into consenting to him; however, Chiron and Demetrius never address Lavinia. She learns of their plans as they explain to their mother that instead of killing Lavinia, they propose to "First thresh the corn, then after burn the straw" (2.3.123). Lavinia's nonconsent is assumed. Although she does not need to say "no," Lavinia depends on her voice to plead against the rape: yet Shakespeare makes Lavinia a poor pleader. When Demetrius tells his mother to listen, to "see her tears," but not to relent (2.3.140), Lavinia chides Tamora's son for attempting to teach his mother: "When did the tiger's young ones teach the dam?" (2.3.142). On the heels of this remark, which might insult both mother and sons, she taunts "the boys" about their masculinity with images of nursing: "The milk thou suck'st from her did turn to marble; / Even at thy teat thou hadst thy tyranny" (144–45). Most critics agree that Lavinia speaks the "wrong argument to the wrong audience," as Clark Hulse puts it.[20]

Shakespeare undoubtedly makes Lavinia's verbal defense against rape less persuasive (emotionally moving) than, say, Lucrece's, and this suggests, I think, the limitations of the authority vested in Lavinia's voice. Shakespeare does not use eloquent language to capitalize on Lavinia's feminine vulnerability. But neither logical nor eloquent arguments against rape necessarily save victims; they did not save Lucrece, after all. For many, the absence of an eloquent plea against rape heightens the persuasive force of Lavinia's mutilated body after the rape. For instance, Carolyn Asp notes that for many readers "she persuades through the pathos of sufferings, through non-linguistic means."[21] Significantly, Lavinia needs to do more than evoke pity; she needs to reveal the rape.

Thus the play explores the limitations of the power of a woman's voice and various men's relationship to that power. While her voice is not needed at all in abduction, it has a limited need and power at the scene of rape; where it becomes crucial is after the rape. The specific mutilations of Lavinia's hands and tongue (as opposed to breasts or nose, which women often suffered in war crimes) illustrate how her rapists needed to silence her powerful voice, not just disfigure or humiliate her.[22] While her assailants need a woman to be silenced and unauthorized to name rape, the Andronici men need Lavinia's testimony if they are to know the damage their family has suffered and avenge it.

"Speak, gentle niece"

The importance of the raped woman's voice is immediately underscored when Lavinia's silence is mocked; at the first sight of her, the rapists jeer and joke that she can no longer tell "Who 'twas that cut thy tongue and ravished thee" (2.4.2). They mock her inability to speak, write, wash, or even hang herself. While these jokes function in several ways, the brutality of the rape is somehow intensified by their grotesque satisfaction with Lavinia's enforced silence. This immediately infuses the reader/audience member with the sense that Lavinia needs to tell.

Even though the audience knows she has been raped, the play builds on the tension created by the fact that Titus and Marcus do not know.[23] At the first sight of Lavinia, Marcus immediately calls to mind Philomela's story, which suggests that her mutilations would somehow "speak" or hint of rape. He says to her: "But sure some Tereus hath deflowered thee, And lest thou shouldst detect him, cut thy tongue" (2.4.26–27). But two acts later, Marcus is surprised when Lavinia reveals that she has been raped. A great deal of critical interest has been generated about the nature of Marcus's Ovidian speech.[24] Less speculation has been made regarding why Marcus first thinks of rape when he sees her and then forgets it. A recent exception is Coppelia Kahn, who argues that "Marcus's amnesia" creates for the audience an irony that serves to "dramatize and thematize the erasure of the feminine in patriarchy."[25] While Kahn sees this as suppression of knowledge linked to censoring female experience and complaint, my point is that the effect of Marcus's remarks about Philomela tease the audience with the idea that the men should know that she has been raped. Rather than simply the erasure of gendered authority, it highlights men's ultimate reliance on Lavinia's words.

Although she has the opportunity, Lavinia does not immediately "admit" the rape. When Marcus first mentions rape, she blushes and turns away instead of giving him nods of recognition ("Ah, now thou turn'st away thy face for shame; / And notwithstanding all this loss of blood, / . . . Yet do thy cheeks look red" [2.4.28–29, 31]). Lavinia's silent blushes again underscore how the cultural prescription of silence "denies" women "the tongue to tell." While her shameful turning away assures Marcus of her innocence, it also registers the need for her willing confirmation of the rape.

At this point, the play begins to play out the cultural drama of the raped woman's need to tell. Lavinia's first impulse was to hide her shame, but she misses the chance to confirm her rape. What the audience sees enacted is that a woman's silence protects the rapists and harms the family of the victim. When the new law takes the authority to make the claim of rape out of the father's hands, it makes him dependent on her cooperation in ways that were not previously necessary. A father may still speak for her in court, but his authority is limited to the role of advocate. The play registers this cultural anxiety over losing male authority by dramatizing the Andronici family's dependence on her words.

After reading her reaction of shame to the question of rape, Marcus offers to speak for her:

> Shall I speak for thee? Shall I say 'tis so?
> O, that I knew thy heart, and knew the beast,
> That I might rail at him to ease my mind!
> Sorrow concealed, like an oven stopped,
> Doth burn the heart to cinders where it is.
>
> (2.4.33–37)

Marcus recognizes the need to "rail," but his railing quickly conflates with hers; to "rail at him" will "ease [his] mind." Their suffering (it too is conflated) appears to be the inability to tell; railing will relieve the "burn"—not of rape, but of a rape "concealed." After Marcus's poetic outburst and lament, he seems sated. Without Lavinia's needful confirmation and testimony, Marcus seems to feel the truth will never be known. He deals with his powerlessness and lack of authority in the situation by forgetting about the rape entirely; he does not even mention the possibility to Titus.

Shakespeare creates a situation where the audience watches missed opportunities for the men to know about Lavinia's rape; her mutilated yet muted presence keeps the rape in mind for the audience while the repeated attempts to "read" Lavinia foregrounds the men's need for her words. Like Marcus, who thinks of literary rape at the sight of her, Titus's impulse in seeing Lavinia is to compare her to a picture:

> Had I but seen thy picture in this plight,
> It would have madded me; what shall I do
> Now I behold thy lively body so?
>
> (3.1.103–5)

This repeated impulse to compare Lavinia to a text suggests the men's discomfort with dealing with the actual raped woman on her own terms. When Marcus depends on the authority of the classical rape story of Philomela to discuss rape with his niece, few can miss the initial disparity between the men's knowledge of literary precedents and their knowledge of Lavinia's situation.

While a discussion of Shakespeare's critique of the efficacy of literary representations of rape is beyond the scope of this current project, the degree in which the play questions these texts as

The Need for Lavinia's Voice

sources of men's knowledge seems apt. Aaron's knowledge of the classics incites the rape, but the same text fuels Titus's method for revenge. Thus, the texts of Lucrece and Philomela seem to operate as cultural scripts for action. The classic tales of rape, however, are initially less reliable when it comes to helping men recognize the rape. The play shows the men confused by the intersection of two different sources of authority: the real woman and the literary text that her situation mirrors.[26] Richard Brucher argues that this disparity dramatizes how "the reality is more savage than the legend" while Gillian Kendall suggest it adds to the play's exploration of "how language itself is fragmented."[27] Both of these explanations read the references to classic stories of rape as in some way blinding, either to the horror of "real" rape or just to the existence of it. For me, the repeated evocation of classic precedents illustrates men's unfamiliarity of needing to rely on women as authorities, even as the authority of their own experiences of rape.

In contrast to Marcus, who unconsciously censors or misrecognizes the reality of what he sees, Titus is shown to be too confident an authority of Lavinia's experience. He is an unreliable, although sincere, interpreter of Lavinia's raped body, which again emphasizes their dependence on her words. As many critics have discussed, Lavinia becomes an emblem, a cipher, a mirror, a text, or, in the words of Titus, a "map of woe" to read (3.2.12).[28] Yet, when Titus claims "I understand her signs. / Had she a tongue to speak, now would she say / That to her brother which I said to thee" (3.1.143–45), he still does not know about the rape. We in the audience remain disturbed by what the men do not know. If Lavinia could speak, she would first tell them of the rape.

Shakespeare emphasizes the significance of Titus's role as sympathetic but flawed translator in the "fly-scene," a late addition to the play according to many editors. While many consider it a stock scene that provides "additional testimony to (and witty performance of) the protagonist's madness," it also allows for a repetition of Titus's claims to be the interpreter of Lavinia.[29] After Lavinia is called "a map of woe, that thus dost talk in signs" (3.2.12), Titus has his epiphany:

> Hark, Marcus, what she says—
> I can interpret all her martyred signs—
> She says she drinks no other drink but tears,
> Brewed with her sorrow, mashed upon her cheeks.
> Speechless complainer, I will learn thy thought;

> In thy dumb action will I be as perfect
> As begging hermits in their holy prayers.
> Thou shalt not sigh, not kneel, nor make a sign,
> But I of these will wrest an alphabet,
> And by still practice learn to know thy meaning
>
> (35–45)

There is no doubt that Titus expresses the desire to be his daughter's translator, but the play also questions how reliable or complete can his knowledge ever be without his daughter's words. Titus waxes poetic about the source of Lavinia's tears, but still does not know all about why she weeps. As Karen Cunningham points out, Titus's claims and promises of access to Lavinia's thought and knowledge "dissolve in the face of Lavinia's actions."[30] Titus may be like a "begging hermit" in that he must make do with what he has; but his claims to perfection actually highlight just how flawed his interpretation is.

While in the first rape/abduction in *Titus,* the men do not require Lavinia to speak, but until Lavinia reports the second rape, it remains hidden, unknown, and unpunished. Lavinia's physical inability to define what has happened to her as rape and to identify her attackers is posed as a problem in the play and illustrates a family's dependence on the rape victim's ability and willingness to claim rape. Titus can confidently claim to "wrest an alphabet" (3.2.44) from Lavinia and to interpret her "signs," but without her knowledge and her authority, he remains ignorant of the rape.

Lavinia as a Source of Knowledge

Since Lavinia is deprived of the ability to speak, to write, or even to weave, most of her male relatives stop asking her questions after their initial inquiries; they give up thinking she can tell them anything of importance. Heaven and the will of God will bring revelation, not Lavinia (4.1.36, 73–74). But Lavinia's ability to be a source of knowledge is underrated; her disabilities do not render her incapable of communication. These men are so used to being the "generator" of meaning and interpretations that they fumble when Lavinia tries to convey meaning. When she holds up her arms, Marcus cannot tell if she is reporting the number of her assailants or swearing revenge (4.1.38–40). Even when Lavinia tries to communicate using the familiar texts of rape, her message is not immediately intercepted. Lavinia "busily" "turns the leaves" (45) and "tosses" Ovid's *Metamorphoses* with her stumps, but Marcus does not consider the book as a means for her to reveal rape; rather he suggests her action is in remembrance of a loved one (44). Marcus, who immediately spoke of Philomela when he first saw her, fails to read Lavinia's use of the same source. Mary Fawcett calls this scene "a charade of the interpretation process," but it also reveals how the men are unaccustomed to seeing Lavinia as an authority and as a source of knowledge.

Dramatic tension increases as the men have trouble understanding Lavinia's "reading" of Ovid. In the play, books are presented as a source of comfort for Lavinia, not as sources of knowledge. Titus thinks reading "sad tales" of misery will ease their minds: "Lavinia, go with me. I'll to thy closet, and go read with thee / Sad stories chanced in the times of old" (3.2.80–82). Even though she is "deep[ly] read and better skilled" than the present book's young owner, Lavinia is understood more as a receiver of texts than an author of meaning (4.1.33). When she tries to tell them of her rape by pointing to the book, they assume she uses the book to comfort and "so beguile [her] sorrow" (4.1.35). It's not that men refuse to recognize Lavinia as a "generative source" of knowledge. Instead, as Karen Cunningham argues, "Shakespeare is careful to point out that the [men's] reconstitution is ambiguous and untrustworthy."[31] In this way, the play accentuates men's anxiety about their dependence on women's authority in cases of rape.

Several critics suggest that the play's depiction of Titus as interpreter illustrates men's desire for control over language, reading, and interpretation (e.g., Fawcett and Wynne-Davies). In this line of argument, Lavinia cannot report the rape without relying on men, such as her father and Marcus (as interpreters) and Ovid (as author/text). As Emily Bartels argues, she can only tell her own story by aligning herself with Philomela and "inscribing herself within 'the texts of the fathers.'"[32] Reading the marks on her body and, eventually, her scratches in the sand might seem to uphold men's power as interpreters, but first Titus's interpretation of Lavinia's body is shown to be limited and unreliable. Thus, Lavinia may be dependent on men to tell her story, but at the same time, the men are positioned as dependent upon her; without her authorship, they cannot know, let alone revenge, the rape.

The men come to know of the rape when Lavinia scratches her deposition in the sand. Her language and word choice, "Stuprum—Chiron—Demetrius" (4.1.77), are provocative. Just as Lavinia's relatives have trouble seeing her as a source of knowledge, editors of the play fail to look closely at Lavinia's words. Critics have paid more attention to the sexual overtones of her scratching in the sand than what she says. Some have discussed the significance of her use of Latin, but little has been said about her choice of the word "Stuprum."[33]

Editors of the play gloss the term "stuprum" as Latin for rape without further comment (e.g., see Bate; Hughes; Waith). Interestingly, when Lavinia writes "Stuprum" in the sand, she uses the term for rape not found in Philomela's story. According to the *Concordance of Ovid,* this term for unchastity (possibly through rape, in the context of the fable) is used only once in *Metamorphoses,* in book 2, the story of Callisto.[34] Callisto, a member of Diana's chaste group of women, was raped by Jove, who had assumed the form of Diana. Callisto does not tell anyone of her rape, but her "uncleanliness" is revealed by her pregnancy. With this unquestionable evidence of the loss of her chastity, she is driven from Diana's group. As the story goes, Juno, the wife of the rapist, becomes enraged by the injury done to her bed, and calls Callisto "Stupri" as if calling her "whore."[35] Early modern Latin-English dictionaries do indeed define "stuprum" as rape.[36] Yet, in a play that examines the use of the English term "rape," Shakespeare's use of "stuprum" rather than "raptus" calls the reader's attention to yet another Ovidian rape and allows us to surmise that Lavinia does more than identify the crime. Lavinia's "Stuprum" is suggestive not only of her sense of shame; it also testifies to the consequence of her defilement.

Like Lavinia's word choice, Marcus's idea of scratching in the sand could have been inspired by another rape story from Ovid, which Maxwell first noted in the second edition of the Arden Shakespeare. After being raped and transformed into a cow, Io uses her hoof to scratch her own name onto the ground. According to Bate, "Io writes her own name; Shakespeare adapts the device into a substitute for Philomel's revelation of her rapist's identify in her 'tedious sampler.' "[37] I want to speculate about the way that Lavinia writes to identify, not just the rapists, but also herself; not who she was (as Io does) but who she has become. Just as Io's father could not recognize her, neither Titus nor Marcus recognize Lavinia for what she is, a rape victim. "Stuprum" might be read as naming her "transformation" as much as it names what was done to her.

When Lavinia finally reveals the full extent of her injuries and her transformation, her family's reaction is revealing. Lavinia is never consoled for this newly revealed source of pain and humilia-

The Need for Lavinia's Voice 87

tion. Titus asks, "Lavinia, wert thou thus surprised, sweet girl? / Ravished and wronged, as Philomela was?" (4.1.51–52). After they "see" that this is so, both Titus and Marcus respond by shifting the focus away from Lavinia and onto the forest and its poetic description as "By nature made for murders and for rapes" (4.1.57). By blaming the forest, they suggest that Lavinia is a victim of being in the wrong place; cold comfort indeed. Although they lament that such a place exists, they find no words to acknowledge Lavinia's deeper source of pain.

Instead of comfort, knowing the names of her attackers becomes of greater importance. As soon as Lavinia dutifully writes in the sand the names of her attackers, she is not addressed or consoled, but told to kneel down with the others present and swear revenge; Marcus simply says, "Lavinia, kneel" (4.1.86). Lucrece, "that chaste dishonored dame" (89), and her father get a word of consolation—not Lavinia. Titus does not address Lavinia directly other than to say "Lavinia, come" (4.1.119). But like Philomela's story, once the rape is disclosed, the focus of the story shifts to the revengers. Lavinia's telling of rape is valued because men need to know and not because her experience counts. In other words, telling is constructed as enabling men's revenge rather than authorizing women's experience.

Titus clearly values the words that motivate men's actions, so much so that he plans to rewrite them in brass. Lavinia's writing in the sand is too temporary; it seems to speak too much of Lavinia's experience. He calls for a more permanent remembrance and says that he will "go get a leaf of brass, and with a gad of steel will write these words, and lay it by" (4.1.101–3). Yet he cannot bear another remembrance of the rape—his daughter's "lively body"; this account of the crime needs to be silenced, while its record, as precedent for revenge, needs to be engraved by him onto brass. Titus says he kills her out of pity, but also to bury his sorrows: "Die, die, Lavinia, and thy shame with thee, / And with thy shame thy father's sorrow die" (5.3.45–46). Once Lavinia is able to inform them of the particular details that they needed, they prefer to "bury" her specificity. In other words, the men will save her reappropriated words in brass and bury the real woman.

While the play registers the problem of the rape remaining hidden, it constructs the problem as limiting the agency of male relatives rather than that of the victim. Lavinia is a witness for the men's revenge rather than for herself (or her experience).[38] Significantly, Lavinia tells her family and leaves the decision of action to them. No one asks if Lavinia wants to pursue a bloody revenge or seek another form of legal remedy. Thus, while the play registers increasing cultural anxiety over men's dependence on women's willingness to tell through Lavinia's silence, it represses the women's new authority in terms of deciding on a response.

Just as the plot and structure of the play seem to parallel the development of the legal definition of abduction and rape, the play also interrogates the increased authority granted to women by relatively recent changes in the law. While Lavinia's silence in the first rape scene is constructed as appropriate, it becomes vexed in the second rape. Where Ovid allows Philomela her outrage and her lament before her tongue is cut out, Shakespeare silences Lavinia. Rather than reading this as a signal of female oppression, what follows in the play highlights the culture's need for the rape victim's voice as informer/witness. While *Titus Andronicus* acknowledges the need for women's voices, this limited agency is hardly something for feminist to celebrate.

Notes

1. William Shakespeare, *Titus Andronicus,* ed. Eugene M. Waith (Oxford: Clarendon, 1984); further citations will be in the text.

2. Susan Brownmiller (*Against Our Wills: Men, Women and Rape* [New York: Simon & Schuster, 1975]) and Susan Griffin ("Rape: The All-American Crime," *Ramparts* 3 [1971]: 26–35) first ignited the feminist exploration of the politics of rape. Brownmiller, for example, argues that rape legitimizes patriarchy and women's subordination; it functions through fear, whereby women limit their own behavior and freedom. Patriarchy benefits from rape when women perceive they need men's protection from *other* men. See also Sharon Marcus's discussion of rape "as a question of language, interpretation, and subjectivity" ("Fighting Bodies, Fighting Words: A Theory and Politics of Rape Prevention," in *Feminists Theorize the Political,* ed. Judith Butler & Joan W. Scott [London: Routledge, 1992], 387). Much has been written on the intersections of rape, silence, and shame—for example, see Anna Clark, *Women's Silence, Men's Violence: Sexual Assault in England 1770–1845* (New York: Pandora, 1987); Angela Davis, *Women, Race, and Class* (New York; Vantage, 1981); Susan Estrich, *Real Rape* (Cambridge: Harvard University Press, 1987); and Diane Russell, *Rape in Marriage,* rev. ed. (Bloomington: Indiana University Press, 1990).

3. Coppélia Kahn, "*Lucrece*: The Sexual Politics of Subjectivity," in *Rape and Representation,* ed. Lynn A. Higgins & Brenda R. Silver (New York: Columbia University Press, 1991), 142.

4. For an exception, see Christina Luckyj, " 'A Moving Rhetoricke': Women's Silences and Renaissance Texts," *Renaissance Drama* ns 24 (1993): 33–56. Luckyj argues that various early modern texts problematize such silence and "invest feminine silence with considerable power and danger" (34). While Luckyj proposes

silence as a space for subversion, I am interested in the play's complex representation of a woman's troubling and powerful silence in relation to disclosures of rape. For those who have discussed the act of telling in literary texts, see Patricia Klindienst Joplin, "The Voice of the Shuttle Is Ours," in *Rape and Representation*, ed. Lynn A. Higgins and Brenda R. Silver (New York: Cambridge University Press, 1991), 35–66; and Carolyn D. Williams, " 'Silence, like a Lucrece knife': Shakespeare and the Meanings of Rape," *Yearbook of English Studies* 23 (1993): 93–110. For historians of the early modern period who have profitably explored this area, see Miranda Chaytor, "Husband(ry): Narratives of Rape in the Seventeenth Century," *Gender & History* 7 (1995): 378–407; and Garthine Walker, "Rereading Rape and Sexual Violence in Early Modern England," *Gender & History* 10 (1998): 1–25. For feminist literary criticism on representations of rape and the erasure of women's experience of violence, see the wide variety of essays in *Rape and Representation*, ed. Lynn A. Higgins and Brenda R. Silver (New York: Columbia University Press, 1991).

5. See Mary Fawcett, "Arms/Words/Tears: Language and the Body in *Titus Andronicus*," *ELH* 50 (1983): 261–77; and Marion Wynne-Davies, " 'The Swallowing Womb': Consumed and Consuming Women in *Titus Andronicus*," in *The Matter of Difference: Material Feminist Criticism of Shakespeare*, ed. Valerie Wayne (Ithaca: Cornell University Press, 1991), 129–51. While Fawcett claims that Shakespeare characterizes Lavinia as simply "a mute body to be disputed over" (267), to Wynne-Davies her muteness signals the culture's need to control the female subject (136). See also Douglas E. Green, "Interpreting 'her martyr'd signs': Gender and Tragedy in *Titus Andronicus*," *Shakespeare Quarterly* 40 (1989): 317–26. Green finds Lavinia's "muteness" complex; while it signifies powerlessness, her voice must be silenced because it has the power to critique not only the "the premeditated violence of the rapists" but also her father's "thoughtless cruelty" (323).

6. Discussions of rape in *Titus* include Jonathan Bate, "Introduction," *Titus Andronicus*, Arden Shakespeare (London: Routledge, 1995); Lorraine Helms, " 'The High Roman Fashion': Sacrifice, Suicide, and the Shakespearean State," *PMLA* 107 (1992): 554–65; Gillian Murray Kendall, " 'Lend me thy hand': Metaphor and Mayhem in *Titus Andronicus*," *Shakespeare Quarterly* 40 (1989): 299–316; Sid Ray, " 'Rape, I fear, was root of thy annoy'': The Politics of Consent in *Titus Andronicus*," *Shakespeare Quarterly* 49 (1998): 22–39; Catharine R. Stimpson, "Shakespeare and the Soil of Rape," in *The Woman's Part: Feminist Criticism of Shakespeare*, ed. Carolyn Ruth Swift Lenz, Gayle Green, and Carol Thomas Neely (Urbana: University of Illinois Press, 1980), 56–64; Ann Thompson, "Philomel in *Titus Andronicus* and *Cymbeline*," *Shakespeare Survey* 31 (1978): 23–32; David Wilburn, "Rape and Revenge in *Titus Andronicus*," *English Literary Renaissance* 8 (1978): 159–82; Williams, "Silence, like a Lucrece knife"; and Wynne-Davies, " 'The Swallowing Womb.' "

7. Aaron suggests his plot of rape by claiming that Lavinia is another Lucrece: "Lucrece was not more chaste / Than this Lavinia" (2.1.109–10). Aaron also uses Philomela as shorthand to explain his revenge plot to Tamora: "His Philomel must lose her tongue today, / Thy sons make pillage of her chastity, / And wash their hands in Bassianus' blood" (2.3.43–45). Lavinia is able to convey that she was raped by literally using the text of Ovid (4.1.). When Titus enacts his revenge, he calls attention to the precedent found in Ovid: "For worse than Philomel you used my daughter, / And worse than Procne I will be revenged" (5.2.194–95). Virginius's story is used as justification and "warrant" for Lavinia's murder (5.3.35–51).

References to legends of Lucrece and Philomela are also made throughout (2.4.26–27, 38–39; 4.1.47–48, 62–63).

8. Traditionally, rape in the play has been read as a symbol of the overall chaos in Rome; for example, see Eugene M. Waith, "The Metamorphosis of Violence in Titus Andronicus," *Shakespeare Survey* 10 (1957): 26–35; and Robert S. Miola, "*Titus Andronicus* and the Myth of Shakespeare's Rome," *Shakespeare Studies* 14 (1981): 88.

9. *A Collection of Sundry Statutes,* ed. Fardinando Pulton (London, 1640). The 1558 statute (4&5 Philip & Mary, cap 8) deals with the "disparagement" of propertied women under the age of sixteen, who are "secretly allured and wonne to contract matrimony with the said unthrifty and light personages, and there upon either with slieght or force, oftentimes be taken and conveyed away from their said parents" (*A Collection,* 997); punishment was increased if the maid was also "deflowered." In 1576, Statute 18 Elizabeth cap. 7 addresses rape ("unlawfully and carnally know and abuse") as a felony without benefit of clergy.

10. Nazife Bashar, "Rape in England between 1550 and 1700," in *The Sexual Dynamics of History: Men's Power, Women's Resistance,* ed. The London Feminist History Group (London: Pluto, 1983), 41. For additional discussion of rape law, see J. B. Post, "Ravishment of Women and the Statutes of Westminster," in *Legal Records and the Historian,* ed. J. H. Baker (London: Royal Historical Society, 1978), 150–60; and his "Sir Thomas West and the Statutes of Rapes, 1382," *Bulletin of the Institute of Historical Research* 53 (1980): 24–30. Detailed discussion of accusations of rape can be found in Chaytor, "Husband(ry)," and G. Walker, "Rereading Rape."

11. Classical and medieval Latin texts used "raptus" for both abduction and rape; however, legal treatises such as *Bracton* (c. 1220–30) utilized "raptus" in the narrower definition, to mean forced coitus (Bracton, *On the Laws and Customs of England,* trans. Samuel E. Thorne, 4 vols. [Cambridge: Harvard University Press, 1968]). Thus, the first English statutes (Westminster I [1275] and II [1285]) codify the conflation of the meanings. Two important early modern sources regarding rape in legal terms include T. E., *The Lawes Resolution of Womens Rights* (London, 1632); and Matthew Hale, *Historia Placitorum Coronae: The History of the Pleas of the Crown,* 2 vols., 1736 (London: Professional Books Ltd., 1971).

12. Cf. Wynne-Davies who claims, too optimistically I think, that the 1597 act "tacitly accepts the crime committed as one against the corporal person of the women, rather than one of theft against her family" (" 'The Swallowing Womb,' " 131). Chaytor's work also suggests that this change did not take hold until the mid to late seventeenth century.

13. Helms, " 'The High Roman Fashion,' " 557.

14. Post, "Ravishment of Women," 150.

15. Sue Sheridan Walker, "Punishing Convicted Ravishers: Statutory Strictures in Medieval England," *Studies in Medieval Culture* 4 (1974): 237 and 245; see also Post, "Ravishment of Women", 160. One further statute, written in 1382 (6 Richard 2), made clear the priority of family interests: women who consented to their abductors were disinherited. T. E. succinctly says that this statute punishes women for their consent (382).

16. T. E., *The Lawes Resolutions,* 390.

17. For brief discussions of the two kinds of rape in *Titus,* see Helms, " 'The High Roman Fashion,' " 557; Williams, " 'Silence, like a Lucrece Knife,' " 99–100; and Wynne-Davies, " 'The Swallowing Womb,' " 130–31.

18. In *The Lawes Resolutions of Womens Rights,* T. E. acknowledges the long confusion over the two terms, and notes that the terms "rape" and "ravishment" are often used interchangeably. In an effort to be clear, T. E. suggests using "ravishment" for abduction; in practice, he often refers to rape as ravishment and to abductors as "takers for lucre" or "covetous ravishers" (402). That T. E. returns to the confusion over terms twenty pages later suggest that ambiguity over the terms persists. In contrast, Michael Dalton, in *The Country Justice: Containing the Practice of the Justices of the Peace out of their Sessions* (London, 1618), consistently uses the verb "to ravish" to mean rape and "to take" to mean abduct (248).

19. Cf. Ray, who argues that Lavinia has clearly given her hand to Bassianus, and Titus disregards her prior consent, an act that leads to disastrous ends, which he finds akin to disregarding the people's right to political consent.

20. Clark Hulse, "Wresting the Alphabet: Oratory and Acting in *Titus Andronicus,*" *Criticism* 21 (1979): 109. Critics have long noted the problem of Lavinia's voice in the first part of this scene: when she opens her mouth, critics find her unappealing; see for example, Green, "Interpreting 'her martyr'd signs,' " 322; Alan Sommers, " 'Wilderness of Tigers': Structure and Symbolism in *Titus Andronicus,*" *Essays in Criticism* 10 (1960): 286; and A. C. Hamilton, *Titus Andronicus*: The Form of Shakespearean Tragedy," in *Titus Andronicus: Critical Essays,* ed. Philip Kolin (New York: Garland, 1995), 143; and most famously, Dover Wilson, in the 1948 Cambridge edition of the play, calls her an "insulting hussy" and approves of Arthur Symond's judgment that "her punishment becomes something of a retribution" (lvii, lix; qtd. In Hamilton, 143).

21. Carolyn Asp, " 'Upon her wit doth earthly honor wait': Female Agency in *Titus Andronicus,*" in *Titus Andronicus: Critical Essays,* ed. Philip Kolin (New York: Garland, 1995), 229. See also Karen Cunningham, " 'Scars can witness': Trials by Ordeal and Lavinia's Body in *Titus Andronicus,*" *Women and Violence in Literature: An Essay Collection,* ed. Katherine Anne Ackley (New York: Garland, 1990), 149; Fawcett, "Arms/Words/Tears," 266).

22. Other examples are available, but Milton's *History of Britain* (which reworks Dion Cassius) is interesting in comparison with the grisly mutilations and murders of *Titus*: "The Roman Wives and Virgins [are] hang'd up all naked, had their Breasts cut off, and sow'd to thir mouthes; that in the grimness of Death they might seem to eat thir own flesh" (*The Works of John Milton,* ed. Frank Allen Pallerson, 20 vols. [New York: Columbia University Press, 1932], 10:67). Might this tale, in whatever source Shakespeare might have found it, suggest the troubling moment where Titus places his own mutilated hand into Lavinia's mouth as they march offstage?

23. See Peter Stallybrass, "Patriarchal Territories: The Body Enclosed," in *Rewriting the Renaissance: The Discourses of Sexual Difference in Early Modern Europe,* ed. Margaret Ferguson, Maureen Quilligan, and Nancy Vickers (Chicago: University of Chicago Press, 1986), 126. Stallybrass shows how according to patriarchal ideology surrounding women's bodies, the violation of a woman's mouth would have sexual overtones in early modern culture.

24. Waith's essay began the twentieth-century inquiry into the issue of the dissonance created by the Ovidian poetry and the "crude violence." See also Richard Brucher, " 'Tragedy, Laugh On': Comic Violence in *Titus Andronicus,*" *Renaissance Drama* ns 10 (1979): 71–91; Helms, " 'The High Roman Fashion,' "; Hulse, "Wresting the Alphabet,"; Kendall, " 'Lend me thy hands,' " D. J. Palmer, "The Unspeakable in Pursuit of the Uneatable: Language and Action in *Titus Androni-*

cus," *Critical Quarterly* 14 (1972): 320–39; and Albert H. Tricomi, "The Aesthetics of Mutilation in *Titus Andronicus*," *Shakespeare Survey* 27 (1974): 11–19.

25. Coppelia Kahn, *Roman Shakespeare: Warriors, Wounds, and Women* (London: Routledge, 1997), 58.

26. See Kendall, " 'Lend me thy hands,' " where she argues that the "problem is that Lavinia's plight so mimics the Philomela story that her own story is hidden" (309). See also Brucher, " 'Tragedy, Laugh On,' " and Katherine A. Rowe, "Dismembering and Forgetting in *Titus Andronicus*," *Shakespeare Quarterly* 45 (1994): 279–303.

27. Brucher, " 'Tragedy, Laugh On,' " 88; Kendall, " 'Lend me thy hand,' " 309.

28. Numerous critics have persuasively detailed the interest in "writing, reading, quoting, and deciphering;" for an overview of this line of argument see Philip Kolin, "Performing Texts in *Titus Andronicus*," in *Titus Andronicus: Critical Essays*, ed. Philip Kolin (New York: Garland, 1995), 249–60; see also Kendall, " 'Lend me thy hand,' " 305, and Rowe, "Dismembering and Forgetting," 295.

29. Bate, ed., *Titus Andronicus*, 118.

30. Cunningham, " 'Scars can witness,' " 150.

31. Cunningham, " 'Scars can witness,' " 150.

32. Emily Bartels, "Making More of the Moor: Aaron, Othello, and Renaissance Refashioning of Race," *Shakespeare Quarterly* 41 (1990): 444.

33. On Lavinia's use of Latin, see Palmer, "The Unspeakable in Pursuit of the Uneatable," 335.

34. *A Concordance of Ovid*, ed. Roy J. Deferrari, M. Inviola Barry, and Martin R. P. McGuire, 2 vols. (Washington, DC: Catholic University Press, 1939).

35. Cf. Jonathan Bate, *Shakespeare and Ovid* (Oxford: Clarendon, 1993), 224–25, for his discussion of Shakespeare's use of the Callisto myth in *The Winter's Tale*.

36. See, for example, *A Copious and Critical English-Latin Dictionary*, ed. William Smith and Theophilus D. Hall (New York: American Book Co., 1871.)

37. Bate, ed., *Titus Andronicus*, 215.

38. While some critics point to Lavinia's participation in the revenge, I question how much agency is located Lavinia's actions surrounding the murder. When Titus cuts off their heads, Lavinia holds a basin to catch the blood. Titus's command, "Lavinia, come, / Receive the blood" (5.2.196) is an image that eerily evokes the "stained" blood her culture believes that she has already received by the rape; it also parallels Tamora's punishment, who will unknowingly "receive" her sons' blood in her dinner.

Controlling Clothes, Manipulating Mates: Petruchio's Griselda

Margaret Rose Jaster

ONE OF THE MOST HILARIOUS—or hideous—scenes in Shakespeare's *Taming of the Shrew* occurs in act 4, when Petruchio, with the aid of Grumio and Hortensio, symbolically addresses Katherina in apparel he chooses for her. Throughout the scene, Petruchio in effect *un*dresses his new wife by contradicting enough of her sartorial desires to the delight of the assembled males, and to Katherina's manifest discomfort. Editors and playgoers have usually relished the banter among the men and Katherina's resultant frustration; they have often been relieved that Petruchio chooses to tame his new wife in so innoculous a manner.[1]

But apparel is too potent a tool in any power dynamic to dismiss its manipulation as a benign taming game. In early modern England, as today, any contention about apparel raises issues of personal and social identity. Although Petruchio employs less physical abuse than traditional tamers, we cannot blithely disregard any attempts by one party to control another's identity through this most intimate device, even if those attempts are made by Shakespeare's "humane" husband.

"Dress defines not only *who* one is, but *how* one is: that is, how one fits into a culture's moral and religious value system."[2] Female dress was complicated for early modern women by legal and social codes that, when they mention women at all, subjected wives to the personal taste and generosity of their spouses. This essay will examine the potency of apparel as a battle-site in gender relations in early modern England through an analysis of texts that retell the Griselda story. We can then return to Shakespeare's *Shrew*—perhaps to re-vision the controversial tailor scene.

Christiane Klapisch-Zuber has characterized the economic and social implications of nuptial arrangements in early modern Italy as the "Griselda Complex."[3] The term derives from Boccaccio's tale of the Marquis who chooses to wed a poor peasant girl and proceeds to rest her worthiness through a series of emotional ordeals that rival Job's. Her image in *cassone* (wedding chest) paintings popularized her for patrician Italians; and the early modern English public would have been familiar with the tale through versions by Boccaccio, Chaucer, and Petrarch, as well as contemporary ballads, prose pamphlets, and plays.[4]

Klapisch-Zuber appropriates the fictional character to illustrate a social system that bridled women in an increasingly complicated pattern of trafficking in women.[5] The exclusion of daughters as heirs in favor of their brothers effectively subjected wives to husbands—who managed, then, to control the entire conjugal estate. The considerable expenditure on apparel in this time period had the very real effect that the lady sported her husband's estate on her person; he was also responsible for her dressing within her class.

The very fact that the husband presents his bride with gifts of expensive clothing suggests a pecuniary one-upmanship between the father of the bride, who dowers his daughter, and the new husband, who expensively clothes her. The effect of this counter-trousseau is to restore the economic imbalance (of giver over recipient) that occurs when the wife's father establishes his superiority by paying the dowry. That the new bride's clothing might have been rented or borrowed by the husband for the wedding[6] points up the symbolic character of the exchange, even as it reminds us of the material considerations.

A husband's investment in clothing his wife has resonances far beyond its significance as a fact of material culture. Indeed, the present study is most interested in Griselda's betrothal as a ritual act that uses apparel to mark her transformation from daughter of one male to the wife of another. This transformation, her *vestizione*, places the husband's gifts of apparel in the symbolic sphere where we can best analyze their use by Griselda's Walter and Katherina's Petruchio.

I noted above that a woman's garb defines her place in society's moral and religious value system, and that as the early modern bride dons her husband's gift of apparel, she is symbolically integrated into her husband's household and lineage. By accepting her husband's gift of wedding apparel, a bride assumes a new social identity, one that is, to a great extent, manipulated by her new spouse.

Thus, Griselda's plight emblematizes early modern women's sartorial subjugation; while Griselda's story is admittedly extreme, and fictional, we may learn something of the constraints on early modern women from an analysis of these presentations of Griselda. Though the edifying principle of an obedient wife accounts for a certain amount of the tale's popularity,[7] its use of the ritualized exchange of clothing, a shared code among the various versions, may also be significant in the reception and dissemination of the story. Similarities among the accounts of Griselda's transformation also suggest that the tale's several audiences recognized in the depiction their own attitudes toward marriage, clothing, and identity.

Because the tale of Griselda is so salient to an understanding of how apparel figured in early modern gender relations, I will summarize her story here. In most versions, Griselda's dilemma derives from the commonplace in a patriarchal society that it is an aristocratic male's duty to provide an heir to rule after his death: Walter, the Marquis of Salusa, is prevailed upon by his court to many, and so produce an heir. Walter agrees to marry if his nobles agree to his choice, sight unseen. They do. Walter then chooses to wed Griselda, the daughter of the poorest man in his region. She bears him a daughter, then a son. Though in all versions Griselda is an exemplary spouse, Walter tests his wife's loyalty by removing each infant from its mother. He fabricates the children's deaths, with the explanation that Griselda's low birth makes her an unfit mother. These horrors, and her eventual replacement by a younger aristocratic woman, are borne by Griselda with resilient patience. The tale ends happily ever after when Walter reveals that Griselda's replacement was, in fact, his own daughter, and the family is reunited.

In all versions of the tale, there are three occasions in which apparel figures significantly: the moment of Griselda's metamorphosis from peasant girl to noble lady; the point when Walter returns her to her father's house; and finally when she is reinstated as Walter's wife. For the sake of clarity, I will anglicize the names to Griselda, Walter, and Janicola (her father) though they vary in the different versions; for the sake of brevity, I will concentrate exclusively on Griselda's first transformation—from peasant to "princess."[8]

In Boccaccio's tale (1353), Griselda's garments have been made for her long before the wedding, before she is aware of her destiny. Walter has

> made . . . readie most riche and costlie garments, shaped by the body of a comely young Gentlewoman, who he knew to be equall in proportion and stature, to her whom hee had made his election.[9]

Walter is the sorcerer who effects a magical metamorphosis: "Presently he took her by the hand, so led her forth of the poore homely house, and in the presence of all his company, with his owne hands, he took off her meane wearing garments, smocke and all, and cloathed her with those Robes of State which he had purposely brought thither for her, whereat every one [stood] amazed...."[10]

Walter's actions here are particularly significant for an understanding of Griselda's predicament. He removes her garments with his own hands, and in the presence of his company. Walter's direct intervention heightens the dramatic moment. Singularly, Boccaccio insists that Walter takes off "smocke and all," emphasizing her vulnerable nudity. He then clothes her in Robes of State: Griselda is no longer a peasant girl, her father's daughter—she has become her role as Walter's consort, and a refection of his status, not her own.

After Walter finishes her, we are told, everyone stood amazed—that their new mistress has been created from such coarse material? They need not have worried. Shortly after this, Boccaccio asserts the power of apparel to affect one's personality: "And the young bride apparently declared, that (with her garments) her mind and behavior were quite changed." Boccaccio's Griselda is an example of how apparel contributes to the erasure of a peasant woman; the Griselda everyone knew has been subsumed into one who can more acceptably fill the shoes of "her whom he had made his election."[11] Walter's confidence in the relieved response of his court suggests a society in which the ceremony of investiture symbolically transforms an inadequate individual into a suitable public servant; Walter's attitude would have been approved by the courtly readers of Boccaccio, Chaucer, and Petrarch, as well as by Shakespeare's audience.

While Boccaccio's Walter personally fashions Griselda by stripping off her old apparel and providing her with a new identity with his new clothing, Chaucer's Walter seems threatened by contamination through contact with Griselda's personal possessions. Chaucer's version of the betrothal scene[12] offers hints at Griselda's future humiliation:

> And for that no thyng of her old geere
> She sholde bryng into his hous, he bad
> That wommen sholde dispoillen hire right theere;
> Of which thise ladyes were nat right glad
> To handle hir clothes, wherinne she was clad.

> But nathelees, this mayde bright of hewe
> Fro foot to heed they clothed han al newe.
>   Hir heris . . . they kembd, that lay untressed
> Ful rudely, and with [their] fyngres smale
> A corone on hire heed they han ydressed,
> And sette hir ful of nowches grete and smale.
> Of hir array what sholde I make a tale?[13]
> Unnethe the peple hir knew for hir fairnesse
> Whan she translated was in swich richnesse.
>
> (372–85)

Griselda is "despoillen." Glossed as "undressed" by the Riverside editor, the word is used elsewhere by Chaucer in its other Middle English usages: "to strip of possessions by violence"; and "to spoil or plunder, especially the arms or clothes of an enemy, or the skin of a beast."[14] Although modern readers might not figure Griselda as enemy or beast, we cannot ignore these implications present to earlier audiences, which implied violence or deprivation."[15]

Chaucer himself seems unsure about Griselda's worth: despite the courtly ladies' scorn, Griselda is "a maid bright of hue" before she is "clothed all anew." However, following Boccaccio, the people know her fairness only after she is translated into such richness.

Griselda alludes to this mutation of her identity later in the poem, when Walter rejects her:

> "For as I lefte at hoom al my clothyng,
> Whan I first cam to yow, right so," quod she,
> "*Lefte I my whyl* and al my libertee,
> And took youre clothyng; wherfore I yow preye,
> Dooth youre plesuance; I wol youre lust obeye...."
>
> (653–58; my emphasis)

Griselda's assertion reinforces the link between clothing and social identity—she relinquished her will, a part of her previous social role—when she accepted Walter's apparel.

That this scene of transformation is depicted on early modern *cassone* may help to emphasize the resonances of the literary Griselda in the lives of early modern women. Cristelle Baskins, in a study of images of Griselda on *cassoni* argues that any interpretation of these artifacts "must be located . . . in the strategic interconnections between textual narrative, pictorial narrative and the construction of gender difference."[16] She notes that the chests formed part of society's acknowledgement of the couple's new status in the community: a circumstance that is as public as the chest, and as private as the trousseau it contained. Baskins also reminds us that in the newlyweds' living quarters, the *cassoni* served as a "permanent reminder of the physical, material, and familial transformations produced by that marriage."[17]

Explications of these *cassoni* as texts categorize them as either allegorical (relying on conventional readings and authoritative texts) or descriptive (considering the depictions as culturally and socially accurate). The paintings Baskins discusses render only the betrothal scene—a nude Griselda—and Baskins notes that her redressing—the transformation—is never depicted, but that "the thematics of dress and undress continue in the text and affect our understanding of her as a 'bare bride.'"[18]

The choice of Griselda as a subject to decorate *cassoni* lays bare the power dynamics of early modern marriage. In these paintings, Walter suggests the complete submission that occurs with Griselda's advancement to her new role: he offers the spectacle of his nude wife to the court; this action foreshadows his later truculence when he will insist that Griselda return to her father's house in her smock. The paintings also operate outside the accepted discourse by displaying Griselda's nakedness—portraits of early modern women normally celebrate the wealth of their families, not the nude accessibility of their women.[19] Furthermore, the familiar image of Griselda would have been a chronic reminder of the darker side of marriage: the depiction of Griselda's compulsory nudity recalls Walter's tyranny during the marriage, which, though it provided an exemplum for the new spouse, was problematic, as both Boccaccio and Chaucer conceded.[20]

Griselda's shadow over the English stage projected forcefully into the cultural conversation on matrimonial matters. Although we know of only two plays that claim to tell her tale—both designated as "comedies" in their print versions—Griselda's image impacts a number of tormented female characters. Shakespeare's Hermione, Imogen, Helena, Hero, Julia, Desdemona, and Marina among the females who shared Griselda's fate of waiting patiently as "the injustices done to them by their menfolk are painstakingly resolved."[21]

Let us look more closely at the betrothal scene in the two Griselda plays, observing the role of apparel in these theatrical versions. We can then return to Shakespeare's *The Taming of the Shrew,* examining Katherina's transformation, with attention to the use of apparel in Shakespeare's treatment of marriage, women, and identity.

Unfortunately we have no record of any performance of John Phillips' 1565 play *The Commody of Pacient and Meeke Grissill*, though the printed text carefully instructs would-be directors how "eight persons maye easely play this Commody."[22] Griselda's transformation from peasant to princess takes place after Walter is convinced of his need for a wife; he falls in love with the grieving Griselda, whose mother has just died.

Although the dramatic convention of boy-actors playing women's parts precludes the stripping of Griselda in the stage versions of this tale, the betrothal scene remains pivotal. In this version, both Janicola and Griselda resist Walter's sartorial metamorphosis. Griselda uses their peasant attire to prove their unworthiness for the great honor women intends to bestow—and, one could argue, to avert imminent tragedy. Early in the play, Griselda argues:

My poore estate my missery, the tyme doth forth unfould,
What better profe can be here of, than these our ragges so torne,
These pante and shoe our penurie, which wee to bide were borne. . . .
(671–73)

But Walter argues that humble raiment signals noble virtues:

Thy ragged clothes the[y] argue not, in poore estate to lyve,
Thy vertues noble doe the[y] make, such Fate doth Fortune give. . . .
(694–95)

Walter's flattery reimagines the fantasy of reciprocity implicit in every fairy tale wherein the peasant girl is actually a princess by birth; but unlike Shakespeare's Marina or Perdita, Griselda is only a princess because Walter makes her one. Walter's praise renders her a metaphorical princess, made noble by virtue, but society will recognize only the princess created when his clothes transform her.

Soon Walter tells his ladies to dress Griselda; when Griselda returns with the ladies, she protests that she is uncomfortable with the new finery:

O noble Lord, these costlye Robes,unfittly seeme to bee:
My ragged weed much more then this, doubtles contented mee.
(822–23)

Walter's contradiction reminds us that, in all of these versions, Griselda discards her earlier social role—and her contentment—when she exchanges her ragged weeds for his costly robes:

> These garmentes nowe to thine estate belong, my lady deare,
> Disdaine them not, but for my sake refuse them not to weare.
>
> (824–25)

Walter reminds Griselda that the garments belong to her estate, another reminder of the elevation in status wrought by marriage. In addition, the use of the word "disdaine" betrays his apprehension that by elevating Griselda's status, he has rendered himself vulnerable to rejection. So these lines also illustrate that while the changes in Griselda accommodate the needs of Walter and his domain, the alterations in both characters are not due entirely to Walter's decision to marry out of his class but are, rather, the expected result of entering into the state of matrimony.[23]

Although in all versions of this tale Griselda gracefully acquiesces to her new station, it is also true that she seemed content in her poverty. That Walter has the most to gain from plucking Griselda from her peaceful penury is admitted in the betrothal scene from the 1599 play *The Pleasant Comodie of Patient Grisill* by Thomas Dekker, William Haughton, and Henry Chettle.[24] In the betrothal scene, this Walter says:

> Ile gild that pouertie, and make it shine,
> With beames of dignitie: this base attire,
> These Ladies shal tear of, and decke thy beautie
> In robes of honour, that the worlde may say,
> Vertue and beautie was my bride today.
>
> (1.2.270–75)

Significantly, Walter boasts that he is wedding the embodiment of womanly qualities, virtue and beauty, and Griselda is defined by those personifications. As her base attire is torn off and replaced with Walter's robes of honor, Griselda becomes a reflection of her husband's wealth, status, and interests.

While in Phillip's play the betrothal transformation occurred offstage, in the 1599 version we witness the betrothal, but our attention is deflected by the shenanigans of Janicola's servant, Babulo. Babulo trenchantly metonymizes his objections to social intercourse between the classes:

> Its hard sir for this motley lerkin, to find friendship
> with this fine doublet.
>
> (1.2.304)

When Babulo verbalizes the impossibility of a friendship between Walter and himself, and advises Walter that he himself would make a better consort for Griselda (line 315), he underscores Griselda's double indemnity: she is distanced from Walter by the impediments of gender as well as status.

In act 2, scene 1 of Shakespeare's *Taming of the Shrew* (1593?), Petruchio promises the world a second Griselda, linking Griselda's hapless image to the fate of his betrothed. The allusion occurs in Petruchio's boast to Baptista and his guests that, despite what they know of Katherina, and what the audience has just observed of her, he has won the consent of the recalcitrant Katherina. As Petruchio's lie incorporates the figure of the unfortunate Griselda, his false narrative of the events of the "courtship scene" (2.1.177–267) presages his manipulation of the rhetoric of apparel through the rest of the play. In the only reference to Griselda in the entire Shakespeare canon, Petruchio declares to the assembled males that "For patience she will prove a second Girssel . . ." (2.1.284). with that telling allusion, Petruchio alerts the attentive interpreter to the shaping of Shakespeare's Griselda which occurs when Petruchio exploits apparel to realize his boast.

So we return now to the dilemma with which I opened this essay: how is one to react to the tailor scene (4.3)? In order to address that question, we must recognize that the signals Shakespeare sent to his original audience do not suggest a sympathetic Katherina, one who is worthy of the reward of a humane husband. The play's title arouses the expectations of his early modern audience, and the playwright does not disappoint: from our first view of her through her wedding scene, Katherina is the very caricature of a "shrew." She threatens violence to Hortensio (1.1.63–65) and is physically abusive to her sister, Bianca, whose hands she ties while she verbally attacks her (2.1.1–22); she even strikes Petruchio at their initial meeting (2.1.213).

As other interpreters have noted,[25] Shakespeare's audience would understand her unbridled speech as "shrewishness"; in order for Petruchio to prove to an early modern audience that he has tamed Katherina, he must silence her. He begins that process shortly after the "wooing scene" (2.2.177–267), when he convinces her father that he speaks for the two of them; he continues it at the wedding, where he cuts off Katherina's protestations by claiming her as his "goods" and "chattel" (3.2.219), and finally silences her in the tailor scene (4.3).

Although I realize, as I mentioned earlier, that this scene is admired for its good-natured humor, let us consider it anew in relation to the figure of Griselda, which Petruchio has introduced. First, the scene occurs immediately after Grumio, a servant, then Petruchio, with Hortensio's aid, bait Katherina with food. Are we constrained to laugh along with the Gentlemen as Katherina, apparently fasting since the wedding, begs for food (4.3.1–60)?

The tantalizing that Petruchio began with victuals continues with clothes, when Petruchio promises Katherina that they will return to her father's house

> And revel it as bravely as the best,
>   With silken coats and caps, and golden rings,
> With ruffs and cuffs and farthingales and things,
> With scarves and fans and double change of brav'ry,
> With amber bracelets, beads and all this knav'ry.[26]
>
> (4.1.54–58)

Petruchio had already pulled a sartorial bait-and-switch before the wedding. He promised that for the wedding he and Katherina "will have rings, and things, and fine array" (2.1.312), only to arrive at the wedding in a mockery of wedding attire that even the obtuse Baptista noted was "a shame to your estate, / An eyesore to our solemn festival" (3.2.90–91).

In the tailor scene, Petruchio employs apparel to continue his mockery of Paduan society that had begun in the wedding scene, and he further humiliates his spouse. The leering courtiers who scrutinized the nude Griselda are replaced by an audience of servants and salesmen. Alone in the presence of these males, Katherina must endure slurs to her social position and her chastity, comments that provoke Katherina's final speech of resistance.

As in the Griselda tales, the solicitous husband has already ordered his wife's postnuptial apparel; by this action Petruchio reasserts his right to control his wife's image, the embodiment of his estate to the world.[27] In his denunciation of the new hat, Petruchio taunts Katherina with food words as well as sexual innuendoes. He says,

> Why, this was moulded on a porringer—
> A velvet dish! Fie, fie, 'tis lewd and filthy . . .
> A knack, a toy, a trick, a baby's cap.
>
> (4.3.64–67)

"Porringer" and "dish," and "knack" remind her of her empty stomach, while "lewd," "filthy," and "trick" have sexual connotations. Linking the images of sex and food reminds Katherina and the audience that in his role as husband, Petruchio controls the necessities of Katherina's life. Petruchio's behavior throughout the play insists on his right to "husband" the goods and chattels of his household, including his wife, in whatever manner he sees fit.

But Katherina *likes* the hat, insisting that it is both fashionable and fitting for a gentlewoman (line 70)—to which Petruchio retorts that when she is a gentlewoman, she shall have one, too. Petruchio's play on Katherina's words slights her social position and intimates that she thwarts her master with her supposed recalcitrance.

In the next short speech (lines 73–80) Katherina pleads to be heard; she reminds Petruchio that his "betters" have endured her speaking her mind (line 75). Her tongue, she says, will tell the anger of her heart—or else it will break. Unfazed, Petruchio returns to a linguistic maneuver he has used frequently in the play: he pretends to misunderstand her, agreeing with her *dis*like of the hat, telling her he loves her more because she hates it.[28] Katherina appears to win this round. She retorts,

> Love me or love me not, I like the cap
> And it will have or I will have none.
>
> (84–85)

But he ignores her remarks and moves to the gown:

> Thy gown? Why, ay . . .
> What's this—a sleeve?
> 'Tis like a demi-cannon.
> What, up and down carved like an apple-tart?
>
> (86–89)

Again, Petruchio's words suggest bawdy connotations ("sleeve," "cannon," "carved," and "tart") and remind her of her hunger. Katherina's plea for this dress reminds us of a woman's spousal subjection in matters of her wardrobe. She asserts,

> I never saw a better-fashioned gown,
> More quaint, more pleasing, nor more commendable.
> Belike you mean to make a puppet of me.
>
> (101–3)

When Petruchio contradicts her, asserting that it is the *tailor* who tries to make a puppet of her, Katherina is silent.[29] She stands by while the men discuss her raiment—at one point her chastity is impugned again when the dress is described as "a loose-bodied gown," a term for prostitutes' dresses, which allow easy access and conceal the results of the women's labors.

Finally, Petruchio decides that they will proceed to her father's house in their old clothes:

> For 'tis the mind that makes the body rich,
> And as the sun breaks through the darkest clouds,
> So honour peereth in the meanest habit.
>
> (166–68)

In the light of his previous manipulations, Petruchio's proselytizing seems a yet another strategy in the subjugation of the mind through the subjugation of the body. In adding this sartorial humiliation to the traditional shrew tale, Shakespeare is surely drawing upon the tale of Griselda. In both stories, reshaping the body is imperative before one can reshape the mind.

At the same time, Petruchio's insistence on humble apparel at this point is yet another blow at the social status of Katherina and her family: as newlyweds, Petruchio and Katherina were entitled to demonstrate their elevated marital status through sartorial display. To return to Padua dressed in "garments poor" may not be the exact equivalent of sending Katherina naked to her father's house, but Petruchio *does* strip Katherina of her social position, and the sartorial slight is an attempt to demonstrate to all that Katherina's identity and will are now subject to her husband.[30] The gesture is, at the least, an echo of Petruchio's "eye-sore to [the] solemn festival" that was their own wedding.

The connection between apparel and social identity is again apparent in act 5, and contributes to the image of a Katherina who has completely capitulated to her husband. When Petruchio needs to prove his wife's subservience, he orders her to publicly destroy her cap. His behavior is unnecessary; she has already obeyed him—she has come at his call, and has left and returned with the less-compliant wives. But Petruchio persists, again masking his tyranny under solicitousness:

> Katherine, that cap of yours becomes you not:
> Off with that bauble—throw it underfoot!
>
> (5.2.121–22)

Whether or not this cap is the same one that Petruchio denied her in act 4, scene 3, it is the cap she chose to wear on this special occasion. The jubilant tone of the remaining comments from the males suggests that Katherina divests herself of the cap and tramples it underfoot, extinguishing her own desires in favor of her husband's.[31]

It is significant, I think, that in act 5, the *other* man who knew Katherina well expresses astonishment at this Katherina who has responded to her master's call, and mouthed his dictates. In her father's praise of Petruchio, we may discern Katherina's fate:

> Now fair befall thee, good Petruchio!
> The wager thou hast won, and I will add
> Unto their losses twenty thousand crowns,
> Another dowry to another daughter,
> For she is changed, as she had never been.
>
> (5.2.111–15)

Baptista voices the relief of all the men: the shrew has disappeared as though she never was. Like Janicola, Baptista has acquiesced to the superiority of the new husband; like Griselda, Katherina is now a woman nobody knows.

In conclusion, Shakespeare's introduction of the image of Griselda recollected Griselda's ritual sartorial submission, which emphasized Katherina's eventual compliance—absolutely essential to the comic ending. Petruchio's behavior can then be understood in the light of a husband's duty to transform a headstrong woman into an obedient wife, a transformation that required control of his wife's sartorial desires.[32]

But Shakespeare's use of the Griselda tale also complicates the connection between clothes and matrimonial dominion in early modern England. While Petruchio, following Walter, controls his wife's public persona through her apparel, by emphasizing the clothed body (rather than Griselda's nude or smocked body), Shakespeare's character suggests that clothing forms the essential being. Instead of proffering his unclothed wife to ogling courtiers, in 4.3 Petruchio invites the audience of merchants and servants to fantasize Katherina's nudity and her marital relations with him by sexualizing Katherina's wardrobe. His dominance in marriage is more obvious and more subtle than Walter's: Petruchio dispenses with the redressing that signals Griselda's reentry into society. At the play's end, Katherina is appareled in whatever "mean habiliments" (4.3.167) Petruchio permitted. Echoing early modern sumptuary regulations and marriage homilies, Shakespeare maintains that the clothed person matters most, and that marital authority supersedes society's expectations of the well-dressed wife. From the moment that Petruchio conceives of the notion to take a wife, he asserts his rights as a husband, including especially his prerogative—and duty—to dress his wife as he will. He does not submit to the expectations of the wedding guests at his own or Bianca's celebration: his complete sartorial control in both instances authenticates his dominion. Once she dons her husband's chosen apparel, Katherina mouths his words—the words of a patriarchy in whose interest it was to transform stubborn women into submissive wives. As he boasted in act 2, Petruchio has created a second Griselda, her existence powerfully proven by Katherina's complete sartorial submission.

Notes

This paper was originally delivered at the March 1993 Symposium on Women and the Arts in the Renaissance, under the auspices of the National Museum of Women and the Arts, Washington, DC. I am grateful to Jane Donawerth, Theresa Coletti, Ann Rosalind Jones, Peter Stallybrass, Elizabeth Welles, and Linda Woodbridge for their helpful comments on various revisions of that paper.

1. In her New Cambridge edition of the play (New York: Cambridge University Press, 1984), Ann Thompson comments that critics frequently defend Petruchio's methods, which are "positively kindly when compared with what happens in most of the other medieval and Renaissance versions of the shrew-taming plot where violence is commonplace" (28). Elsewhere, Thompson herself admits to being "less sanguine" than feminist apologist critics ("The Warrant of Womanhood: Shakespeare and Feminist Criticism," in *The Shakespeare Myth*, ed. Graham Holderness [Manchester: Manchester University Press, 1988], 74–87, 78).

2. Ruth Barnes and Joanne B. Eicher, *Dress and Gender: Making and Meaning* (New York: St. Martin's, 1991), 2.

3. Christiane Klapisch-Zuber, *Women, Family, and Ritual in Renaissance Italy*, trans. Lydia Cochrane (London: University of Chicago Press, 1985), 228.

4. The most comprehensive treatment of the impact of the Griselda tale from Boccaccio until the present is Judith Bronfman's *Chaucer's "Clerk's Tale": The Griselda Story Received, Rewritten, Illustrated* (New York: Garland, 1994).

5. Klapisch-Zuber, *Woman, Family, and Ritual*, 214, and passim.

6. Klapisch-Zuber, 224, 227–28.

7. See, for example, Linda Woodbridge, *Women and the English Renaissance* (Urbana and Chicago: University of Illinois Press, 1984), who utilizes the Griselda myth as an exemplum of the formal controversy about women; Edward Pechter also recognizes the use of Griselda in homiletic domestic dramas ("*Patient Grissil* and the Trials of Marriage," *The Elizabeth Theatre XIV: Papers Given at the International Conference on Elizabethan Theatre held at the University of Waterloo in Ontario in July 1991* [Toronto: P.D. Meany, 1996], 83–108, especially 84 n. 4).

8. I will limit the study of nondramatic versions to those by Boccaccio and

Chaucer, which enjoyed greatest dissemination in their own century and in ours. Three other nondramatic texts—Petrarch's *De insignia obedientia et fide uxoria* (1374), which directly influenced Boccaccio's version; Thomas Deloney's ballad "Of Patient Grissell and a Noble Marquis" (1586?); and an anonymous English pamphlet of 1619—also utilize apparel to signal the changes in Griselda's status. The ritual of sartorial transformation is handled similarly in these texts.

9. Giovanni Boccaccio, *The Decameron*, translated into English 1620, vol. 4, ed. Edward Hutton (New York: AMS Press, 1967), 295–312, 298.

10. Boccaccio, *Decameron*, 299.

11. Boccaccio, *Decameron*, 229.

12. Geoffrey Chaucer, *The Riverside Chaucer*, ed. Larry D. Benson, 3rd ed. (New York: Houghton Mifflin, 1987), 137–53.

13. As Carolyn Dinshaw illustrates, the clerk *does* spend an inordinate amount of time on Griselda's apparel (*Chaucer's Sexual Politics* [Madison: University of Wisconsin Press, 1989], 134, 144, and *passim*). Also see Kristine Gilmartin Wallace, "Array as Motif in the Clerk's Tale," *Rice University Studies* 62.2 (Spring 1976): 100, and *passim*.

14. *Oxford English Dictionary*, s.v. "despoil."

15. William Caxton also links undressing with despoiling in *The Golden Legend*: "He . . . wold not relece hir obdeyence til that she was destroyed to hir smocke." While this linguistic linkage might seem to normalize the activity, we should note that being stripped to one's smock is, once again, connected to a woman's submission.

16. Cristelle Baskins, "Griselda, or the Bride Stripped Bare by Her Bachelor in Tuscan *Cassone* Painting," *Stanford Italian Review* 10.2 (1991): 153–75, 156.

17. Baskins, "Griselda," 160.

18. Baskins, "Griselda," 161, 164, 175.

19. In "Women in Frames: The Gaze, the Eye and the Profile in Renaissance Portraiture," Patricia Simons discusses early modern portraiture as a cultural event participating in the construction of gender rather than a naturalistic reflection of its society (*History Workshop* 25 [1988]: 4–30).

20. See Lee Bliss, "The Renaissance Griselda: A Woman for All Seasons," *Viator* 23 (1992): 301–43, for a comprehensive study of the tale's influence and controversy. Laura Lunger Knoppers persuasively links a woman's nudity and her ritualized degradation in "(En)gendering Shame: *Measure for Measure* and the Spectacles of Power," *English Literary Renaissance* 23 (1993): 450–71.

21. Lisa Jardine, *Still Harping on Daughters: Women and Drama in the Age of Shakespeare* (Totowa, NJ: Barnes and Noble, 1983), 184.

22. John Phillip *The Play of Patient Grissell* [1565], ed. Ronald B. McKerrow (London Malone Society Reprints, 1909), Ai,r. The title page suggests the multiple parts each actor can play, including Griselda doubling as the midwife.

23. As Wallace points out, Chaucer also emphasizes that Griselda and Walter assign different symbolic significance to her changed clothes: while she obviously sees her transformation as perfect acquiescence to his will, Walter sees only that she has been raised to his high estate ("Array as Motif in the Clerk's Tale," 102).

24. *The Dramatic Works of Thomas Dekker*, ed. Fredson Bowers, vol. 1 (New York: Cambridge University Press, 1953). The title page, dated 1603, states "it hath beene sundrie times lately paid." The play was owned by the Admiral's Men and performed at the Fortune in 1600 (Andrew Gurr, *The Shakespearean Stage*, 3rd ed. [New York: Cambridge University Press, 1980], 240).

25. See Barbara Hodgdon, "Katherina Bound; or, Play(K)ating the Strictures of Everyday Life," *PMLA* 107.3 (May 1992): 538–53; Lisa Jardine, *Still Harping on Daughters,* esp. 121–33; and Karen Newman, *Renaissance Family Politics and Shakespeare's The Taming of the Shrew,*" *English Literary Renaissance* 16.1 (Winter 1986): 86–100, among others.

26. All citations from New Cambridge edition of *The Taming of the Shrew.* The play was owned by the Lord Chamberlain's Men, and performed at the Globe, Blackfriers, and possibly the Theatre (Gurr, *Shakespearean Stage,* 241).

27. In scene ten of the anonymous play *The Taming of the Shrew* (1594; ed. Stephen Roy Miller [New York: Cambridge University Press, 1998], Kate has chosen her own clothes, to which her husband objects, piece by piece; this dissension typifies that play's theme of the perpetual battle of the sexes. In contrast, as Katherina admires the new clothes, Petruchio objects to the clothes that he himself has chosen; his petulance demonstrates his belief that within matrimoney, he is entitled to determine his wife's appearance.

28. Karen Newman details the devastating effects of Petruchio's deliberate misunderstanding. She reminds us that Katherina has established the connection between the use of language and one's independence during the altercation over staying for the wedding dinner ("Renaissance Family Politics," 94). Newman continues, "Kate is figuratively killed with kindness, by her husband's rule over her not so much in material terms—the withholding of food, clothing, and sleep—but the withholding of linguistical understanding" (95).

29. Carolyn E. Brown ("Katherine of *The Taming of the Shrew*: 'A Second Grissel,' " *Texas Studies in Literature and Language* 37.3 [Fall 1995]: 285–313) comments that Katherina is quite *un*shrewish in this scene, clearly pleased with the tailor's work (303).

30. Patricia Cramer notes the connection between ritual stripping and destruction of the will in "Lordship, Bondage, and the Erotic: The Psychological Bases of Chaucer's *Clerk's Tale, Journal of English and Germanic Philology* (October 1990): 505.

31. Petruchio's expectation that his wife will relinquish her sartorial preferences to his is echoed in spiritual conduct books of the time. Consider, for example, William Gouge's dictum on the matter in *Of Domesticall Duties: Eight Treatises* (1620):

> For as it well beseemeth all women, so wives after a peculiar manner, namely, in attiring themselves, to respect rather their Husbands place and state, then their own birth and parentage, but *much rather then their own minde and humour.* . . .
>
> On the contrary, *such proud dames as must have their owne will in their attire,* and thinke it nothing appertaineth to their husbands to order them therein, who care not what their husbands ability, or what his place and calling be, they show little respect and reverence to their husbands. . . . (Third Treatise, 164; italics mine)

While the main concern here is that the wife choose apparel appropriate to her husband's status, his command, desire, and example must clearly take precedence over her "minde and humour."

32. In her powerful discussion of the predicaments of Griselda and Katherina, Carolyn E. Brown cites linguistic and sartorial proof that Katherina's future looks bleaker than Griselda's. Chaucer's Walter, she reminds us, has at least admitted "this is ynogh" (line 1052); Petruchio offers no such guarantee.

More or Less: Editing the Collaborative

Jeffrey Masten

> In this work a broad distinction is made between *natives* and *denizens* (naturalized foreigners) on the one hand, and *aliens* (non-naturalized foreigners) on the other. *Natives* are words of Old English origin, *denizens* are borrowings from foreign languages which have acquired full English citizenship, *aliens* are words that retain their foreign appearance and to some extent their foreign sound.
> —*The Shorter Oxford English Dictionary on Historical Principles* (1933)[1]

> The worst [work of the disintegrators], however, amounts to an alien invasion.
> —E.K. Chambers, "The Disintegration of Shakespeare," Annual Shakespeare Lecture (1924)[2]

> Shall strangers rule the roost?
> —Clown, *Sir Thomas More* (2.1.2; 69.2)[3]

A.

WHEN WE WANT *More* in a Complete Works edition of Shakespeare, what do we want? I refer to *The Booke of Sir Thomas More,* the complexly collaborative, revised, possibly Shakespearean, and therefore controversial manuscript that has been on the margins of the canon since the first decades of the twentieth century. Wanting *More* in these editions is linked to our desire for more and more Shakespeare; thus the seemingly escalating race to add to our volumes: more *Lear* in the Oxford and still more in the Norton; the "Funeral Elegy"; the arrival of *The Two Noble Kinsmen* in the updated fourth edition of Bevington's Longman edition; *Edward III* in the second edition of the Riverside, and so on.

But with *The Booke of Sir Thomas More,* it is also clear that less is taken to be more: more Shakespeare, but less of his apparent collaborators. The stance of the editions that include the play—(currently the prominent one-volume editions that do so are the Oxford, the Norton on which it is based, and the Riverside) is to include not all of *More*, but less: the parts of the manuscript that are Shakespearean; the part of the manuscript, that is, written in Hand D, or, in the case of the second included bit, a part that seems more Shakespearean, even though it is written in another hand, C.[4]

I point this curious fact out in part because it seems to have gone largely unremarked: unlike the other possibly collaborative texts printed by these editions *(The Two Noble Kinsmen,* for example), part of *More* is all we (and our students) get. While *The Two Noble Kinsmen* has been aggressively divvied up between writers at least since Cyrus Hoy's linguistic tabulations of the 1950s,[5] and there are confident attempts to do the same with *Pericles* and *Henry VIII*, no one has apparently yet decided to publish *only* those scenes deemed Shakespeare's in volumes comprising his "complete works." But with *More,* we read in the Riverside only *"The Additions Ascribed to Shakespeare,"* and in the Oxford and the Norton only "Passages Attributed to Shakespeare."[6] (Even the Passages disappear from the Norton's second table of contents, arranged "by genre," though "Lost Plays" are nonetheless included.)[7] *More,* already excluded in the Longman edition because "Shakespeare's contribution to it is fragmentary,"[8] is in the other editions made *incomplete* (is editorially *incompleted*) in order to produce a Works that is Complete. Though it does not exist incompletely[9] (McMillin and Gabrieli/Melchiori argue that the play is complete and performable), *More* is nevertheless *presented as* a less-than-complete work—no work, in the conventional sense of the term, because not completed by Shakespeare, or not completely by Shakespeare.

The first and (thus far) last one-volume complete-works edition to include all of *More* was Sisson's in 1954;[10] the only recent full (and teachable) text, Gabrieli and Melchiori's Revels edition of 1990, is apparently now so far out of print that St. Martin's and Manchester University Press were unable to determine who owned the rights the last time I taught the play. If one wants to read more *More* than is currently published in the Riverside or Norton, and seeks to reassemble it from the pieces scattered in complete-works editions, there are thirty-one more lines to be found (only thirty-one lines, Hand E's) in the first volume of Bowers's *Dramatic Works of Thomas Dekker*.[11]

The anomalous treatment of the *More* manuscript in Complete-

Works editions (and its absence thus far from multivolume series like Arden, Cambridge, and Oxford[12]) is rooted in the historical vicissitudes of New Bibliography's emergence in the early twentieth century. Reproduced in facsimile in Farmer's Tudor Facsimile series in 1910,[13] edited by W. W. Greg in his indispensable edition for the Malone Society in 1911, coinciding with the paleographer Edward Maunde Thompson's review of the extant Shakespeare signatures in a three-hundredth death-anniversary collection in 1916,[14] its canonical claims given a strong boost by a 1923 collection in the Pollard/Wilson Cambridge "Shakespeare Problems" series, a collection that included essays by Greg, Pollard, Wilson, and Thompson,[15] the manuscript's ascendancy is contemporaneous with, and, I would argue, inextricably intertwined with, the development of Pollard's theory of good/bad quartos, and the development of Greg's theories of foul papers/promptbooks, those now largely discredited hypotheses that frame New Bibliographic editions of Shakespeare in the twentieth century and now beyond. If the *More* manuscript does not exactly correspond with either "foul papers" or a "promptbook," as Paul Werstine has skillfully demonstrated,[16] it nevertheless has fulfilled a central and crucial role in Shakespearean editing. If, as Fredson Bowers influentially articulated it, the goal of editing is to strip away "the veil of print" from the text to reveal the manuscript,[17] and if, as Werstine's articles have shown, the tendency of New Bibliographic textual "narratives" has been to smooth the assumed road from authorial manuscript to printed text,[18] then *More* provides a manuscript of totemic—if not fully rationally explicable—significance. In the descent of text from Shakespeare to print, it stands in for the missing link. Moreover, as Pollard argued explicitly in the anniversary year 1923,[19] the manuscript can function not only to link Shakespearean printed texts with Shakespearean manuscripts but could also serve as a trump card in the larger controversy over authorship (apparently by proving that Shakespeare had in fact existed and had written plays): "if Shakespeare wrote these three pages the discrepant theories which unite in regarding the 'Stratford man' as a mere mask concealing activity of some noble lord . . . come crashing to the ground."[20]

This may explain the apparatus of the *More* edition in the Riverside and the anomalous treatment of Hand D in the Oxford edition. Riverside follows and supplements its facing-page transcript and modernized text of the Hand D pages with photographs of extant Shakespearean signatures (directly below, almost as if to suggest visually that the transcript of the play is itself signed by Shakespeare).[21] The Oxford editors (with a corresponding effect on the Norton) self-consciously depart from their admirable editorial practice in the rest of the volume, where they "have generally regarded the more 'theatrical' text as a better embodiment of Shakespeare's final intentions," and edit the work "in the final form which Hand D gave to it, before it had been massaged by Hand C." This entails "accept[ing] all Hand D's own revisions to the text, but . . . ignor[ing] Hand C's."[22]

More's exceptional, totemic status may also help to explain the handwriting now appearing on the covers of one-volume complete-works editions that lack *More*. Though neither includes the play in part or entirety, both the Longman and the recent one-volume *Arden Shakespeare Complete Works* reproduce the aura of the missing manuscript link. The updated Longman (fourth edition) now features a secretary-hand-esque "Shakespeare" on its cover, superimposed over an illustration of the Globe. I call this apparently handwritten or signed word "secretary-hand-esque," because it is not a facsimile of an extant signature, and features of the word's calligraphy (not to mention its spelling) have been modified—signs, I would argue, that the sheer alterity and multiplicity of the Shakespearean signature works at odds with the transparency and unity it is being deployed to exhibit here in a marketing context. The complete Arden is illustrated by a version of the First Folio portrait, underlaid with a ghostly manuscript in italic hand that is not *More* and is almost certainly not Shakespeare's.[23] Without reproducing *More*, each of these editions nevertheless deploys the trope for which More stands: the authorial hand signing or writing by itself in a manuscript.

In our editions, then, we clearly want *More*, but we want more of what *More* has come to signify, which is actually (to correct or emend the grammar of my title) *More* and fewer: fewer hands, fewer agents, fewer functions performed by those few; Hand D unmassaged by C, ideally a hand that keeps to what we persist in thinking of as itself (original authoring rather than copying or revising or playhouse-functioning),[24] one hand and one mind going together.

B.

It would be wrong to take *Sir Thomas More* as the template of playwrighting practice in the early modern English theater, or even of a collaborative playwrighting practice. As Werstine has shown, a significant problem of twentieth-century bibliography in this area has been to reduce the multiplicity of diverse practices to fit our singular theories,[25] and I am loathe to generalize on the basis of this manuscript. What I want to do instead is to take *Sir Thomas More* as an impetus to raise theoretical or methodological questions about the way we edit collaboration, or the way in which we have largely failed to re-imagine editing in relation to the collaborative.

If the fact that collaboration was the "dominant mode of textual production" in the early modern theater[26] has been widely recognized now as a thread of theatrical/literary history, it has largely not altered our editions of the plays thus produced. To be sure, Shakespeare editions have in general become more tolerant of collaborative plays,[27] and the new Oxford Middleton is likely to be the most collaboration-friendly single-author edition ever published. In his important essay "The Renaissance and the End of Editing," Gary Taylor has pointed out that "Middleton provides us with an inescapably collaborative model of textual production."[28]

Nevertheless, I think we have not yet fully confronted the implications of such models: our concentration on the production of single-author editions has deformed our treatment of *both* the collaborative and singularly written texts produced in a generally collaborative context. Setting out to produce single-author volumes and series, we see collaborative texts as aberrant productions of multiple, discrete persons; simultaneously, we view the *minority* of plays apparently produced by one person "writing alone" as if "writing alone" were not itself crucially inflected, in ways we are only beginning to see, by writing in conversation, consortium, contention—writing together.[29]

The problem—both at the level of the large-scale editorial projects we imagine for ourselves and at minute levels of editorial practice (modernizing, punctuating, emendation, etc.)—is that we have thought of ourselves as editing persons rather than editing plays. In general, I could not agree more with, and I urge us all to act on, Taylor's point that "we should not be editing Shakespeare because we should be editing someone else,"[30] but even here *someone,* not *something,* is the object of our analysis, and that *someone* continues to be conceptualized as singular.

Thinking singular authorship on a modern model, rather than collaborative textual production on its (multiple) early modern models,[31] has led us to think we must "establish authorship," as we say, before we start editing. This is required not only at the outset by the single-author volume/series model, which requires a determination of authorship before a play is allowed into the volume or series, but also inflects the production of our text. This inflection extends from relatively small editorial decisions (if Fletcher is said to be writing this scene, how are the horizons of potential emendation and modernization contracted by that assumption?), to questions of dating on which we rely in various ways (emphasis on *a* "date of composition" obscures the possibilities of diachronic collaboration), to relatively large questions of format, like, for example, the upfront placement of sections on authorship and biography in critical introductions.[32] These are decisions that often have an inordinately large effect on our students and their horizons of reception and interpretation; they are also reflected strongly in our curricula and syllabus design.

I do not think that the *establishment* of authorship (itself a performative, and not simply empirical, process)[33] indispensably precedes editing and interpretation, and, even if it did, I think the methods used in attribution study are seriously faulty, susceptible to both historical and logical critique. I have argued the particulars elsewhere and attempt further to expand that critique in the forthcoming Oxford *Middleton,* in work on the 2- or 3-way collaboration *The Old Law.*[34] So I want here to generalize about some larger principles.

First, these attributional methods, like a number of mid-twentieth century New Bibliographic methods for isolating ostensibly discrete agents, have an overall tendency to mark or produce difference at the expense of continuity (or the unrationalized coexistence of difference). D. F. McKenzie calls this the danger of "division as a function of analysis"[35]—the danger, for example, posed by Charlton Hinman's insistence, in analogous compositor studies, on discarding nonvariant spellings as "non-significant" and continuing to search for more and more evidence that will support the discovery of difference.[36] We have yet fully to theorize, I think, the culturally variable meaning of variation, especially when it occurs within a non-standardized linguistic system.[37]

Second, in their attempt to reify difference as individuation, attributional methods mistake identity as a fact for a process that we might better call "identification." Although I think that the processes of identity formation through identification are likely to have varied remarkably across time, I have in mind here the kind of model of "identification-*through*"(identity as a process, rather than as a fact) that is summarized succinctly by Diana Fuss in her instructive re-reading of/against Freud on identification:

In perhaps its simplest formulation, identification is the detour through the other that defines the self. This detour through the other follows no predetermined developmental path, nor does it travel outside history and culture. Identification names the entry of history and culture into the subject, a subject that bears the traces of each and every encounter with the external world.[38]

In attribution study's terms, however, textual "habits" are taken more simply to convey or express individual identities, and, in practice, these identifications are largely conceptualized as preexisting, unmarked by "external" factors. At the same time, attribution study typically fails to register the ways in which "habits," however seemingly concrete in a given text, can be broken, emulated, adopted, adapted, thrown off, unintentionally lost, and contextual. To think about this through the words of Stuart Hall, then, identification is

> a process never completed—always "in process." It is not determined in the sense that it can always be "won" or "lost," sustained or abandoned. Though not without its determinate conditions of existence, including the material and symbolic resources required to sustain it, identification is in the end conditional, lodged in contingency.[39]

In this sense, any theory that wants to account for the relation of writing habits to "identities" (which is to say identifications-in-process) would want to consider, among the "determinate conditions of existence," not only the plasticity and emulation of style and articulation in the world of Erasmian *copia,* but also the "indivisibility" that, according to Raymond Williams and Peter Stallybrass, was a characteristic of individuality in early modern culture.[40] To return to *More,* the hand, as McMillin has argued, has been taken to be a synecdoche for the *writer,* while it's actually a metonymy for the *writing* (that is, the *process,* a point furthered in Werstine's analysis of hands in the manuscript)[41]: hands are functions (actions, habits) rather than persons. Jonathan Goldberg's work on early modern handwriting and the signature further unwrites any easy linkage of hand and identity, seeing instead the hand as the organ of emulation and identification.[42]

Looked at along these axes of analysis, collaboration, in current editorial work, seems to be deployed largely in a mode we might call "old historicist." Though such a label is not entirely adequate, it does capture the way in which editing has admitted the *prevalence* of collaboration but has allowed it only in a recognizably modern, "disintegrationist" way (to use Chambers's famous term). That is, such an approach literally dis/integrates the play in an effort to differentiate authorial agents. (This is accomplished in a number of ways, small and large—for example, by marking a given scene at its outset as ostensibly "by" one playwright in textual notes or commentary, by citing parallels only or largely to that playwright's work in the glossarial notes, etc.). Another option, however, would be "new historicist" in looking not only to historicize the text itself (in all its editorially resistant materiality, a point made strongly by Margreta de Grazia and Peter Stallybrass[43]) but also to historicize our models of "agency," "individuality," "style," corporate effort, contention, influence, and so forth—the complex production not only of the text in the realm of the social (following Jerome McGann[44]) *but also* of "individual" agents within the realm of the discursively social. (To do so may well require the invention of new kinds of editorial apparatuses, criteria for and modes of emendation, etc.).

Someone like Chambers, and perhaps someone like you, might find this viewpoint even more disintegrationist in its tendencies,[45] since this position sees the "individual" playwright not as the modern agent (dividual from the social) but as an "individual" in Williams's etymological sense (undividable)[46]—and not as an identity "disclosed" by habits, but as a Bourdieuian creature of the *habitus*.[47] The challenge of such an approach is to bring scholarly editing into conversation more closely with a *critical* practice that has, at its best, become increasingly attuned to the interpenetration of texts syn- and diachronically, but also to the history of the subject, the agent, the author (so-called). Editing must become more attuned, in the words of Stephen Greenblatt, to the "collective making of distinct cultural practices"[48]—where collective making includes the making of the play-makers. This would mean *Collaborative* Negotiations: less reading for ostensibly distinctive, identitarian difference, and more reading across hands, for even across hands there are *identifications.* Again, Hall is instructive: "[identification] obeys the logic of more-than-one. And since as a process it operates across difference, it entails discursive work, the binding and marking of symbolic boundaries, the production of 'frontier-effects.' It requires what is left outside, its constitutive outside, to consolidate the process."[49] While such a process forces us to review the identificatory traces within collaborative texts, such identifications-*through,* as a "logic of more-than-one," will also inflect those plays that we now assign, however confidently, to a single hand.

C./D.

the writing has a quality of urgency increased by D's compulsive use of conjunctions.[50]

"Hands off proud stranger," says Doll Williamson in the first scene of *Sir Thomas More* (1.1.55–56, Greg 3.44), setting up the grievances between lower-class English and foreigners that will become an anti-alien riot later to be quelled by not-yet-Sir Thomas. "Whatsoever is mine scorns to stoop to a stranger. Hand off then when I bid thee" (6–7, Greg 1.7–8). The play is nothing in its opening scenes if not attentive to protecting private English property, and keeping separate the hands of "strangers" and native English.

And yet—and I want to be clear that I am reading across the hands now—the later scenes of this play present a massive complication of such rhetoric and such boundaries, even as the play continues to negotiate the demands of English nationalism. First, there is of course More's speech quelling the riot, which turns on a turning of natives into strangers:

> Say now the king,
> As he is clement if th'offender mourn,
> Should so much come too short of your great trespass
> As but to banish you, whither would you go?
> What country, by the nature of your error,
> Should give you harbour? Go you to France or Flanders,
> To any German province, Spain or Portugal,
> Nay, anywhere that not adheres to England,
> Why, you must needs be strangers.
> (2.3.133–41, Greg 78.245–53)

Though this seems a simple and transparently conservative move, the speech is, I think, a radical denaturalization of some complexity, for in its very rhetorical strategies around the notion of the stranger, the speech places its hearers (onstage and off) in a position of cross-identification that resonates throughout the play: "Grant [the strangers] removed," says More to the rioters, and

> Imagine that you see the wretched strangers,
> Their babies at their backs, with their poor luggage
> Plodding to th' ports and coasts for transportation,
> And *that you sit as kings in your desires,*
> Authority quite silenced by your brawl,

>   And you *in ruff of your opinions* clothed:
>   What had you got?
>   (78, 80–86, Greg 76.195, 197–203, emphases added)

The speech may work by reversing the place of the stranger and the native, but this structure of replacement and rhetorical cross-identification also enables or produces a transgression of the sumptuary laws (Doll Williamson in a ruff) and a crowd sitting as (plural) kings in its (plural) desires. The cross-class-dressed "ruff" comes back to redress itself a few lines later, as More argues that part of what the natives-turned-kings will have got through their efforts is a pattern under which they will themselves be inevitably quelled,

>   For other *ruff*ians, as their fancies wrought,
>   With selfsame hand, self reasons and self right
>   Would shark on you. . . .
>   (90–92, Greg 76.207–9, emphasis added)[51]

Hands, reasons, rights, even ruffs and ruffians become exchangeable in this rhetoric. Does one hand know what the other is doing? It is impossible to say, in the selfsameness this rhetoric encourages.

I will not elaborate here a potentially important strand of this argument, the link between cross-identification, theatricality, and clothing, in a play that dresses More's servant Randall in More's "shift" (meaning "suit of clothes," but also "jest" [3.1.25, Greg 80.4, 26.757]) to fool Erasmus, and places More, first, in a play-within-the-play as the character "Good Counsel," among other jests or shifts, and then has him say on the scaffold that he had been made "of a state pleader a stage player" (5.4.73, Greg 64.1933). These and other substitutions, or traversals, (and again, I am reading across the hands), can be traced here through the persistent rhetoric of *strangeness*—indeed, More's final journey is on a scaffold he calls "this strange wooden horse" (5.4.60, Greg 63.1924)—and the way in which More (put in the place of the other by his failure to subscribe the vague "articles," "liv[ing] estranged," as he says, "from great men's looks" [4.4.107, Greg 50.1528], exiled within his own country) is made in the play to replay his own rhetoric. "He bears himself most strangely," says More's son-in-law, Roper (4.2.60, Greg 45.1346), and Lady More too comments on More's exile from his prior persona, narrating the "strangest dream" (4.2.8, Greg 43.1290) she has had, of their boat unmoored from the king's on the Thames: "What strange things live in slumbers!" (4.2.14, Greg 43.1296).[52] More later calls her commentary on their "strange point / In time's new navigation" a "strange discourse" (4.4.24–25, 31; Greg 48.1439–40, 1449).

If the play's impetus (across hands) is for More to live out an estrangement or cross-identification produced through the rhetoric of his early speech, it is only more so in his very name, a signifier that migrates (floats, we might say, engaging Lady More's strange dream) in its progress through the play. Stripped of his titles and banished from court to his house in Chelsea, More tells his wife "my title's only More" (4.3.71, Greg 45.1360), a line that signifies a cross-identification between lack and excess, reduction and expansion, a self defined as a supplement.[53] This cross-identification might have been even more accentuated in the speech of an early modern actor, since the word *only* contained within it, as it no longer does for us, the sound of the number *one* (routinely pronounced "own" into the eighteenth century) and was often spelled *onely*, and thus bore more insistently the trace of its etymology.[54] In the utterance "my title's only More," then, the play quite literally engages identification's "logic of more-than-one," and More's name, thus entered into the play's rhetoric, moves in more and more directions—introducing into the play, indeed, the strange hand of the foreigner Erasmus, through the familiar pun on More's name as Folly, a character pointedly mentioned as not represented in the play-within: "we have no Folly in our play" (3.2.158, Greg 34.1018).

The name of the self that is the selfsame name as the supplement joins with the rhetoric of the stranger at the moment of More's final arrest. Speaking to the *place* on his removal/estrangement from it ("Chelsea, adieu, adieu"), More bids "Strange farewell, thou shalt ne'er more see More true, / For I shall ne'er see thee more" (4.4.163–64, Greg 52.1591–93).[55] Speaking of himself as a third person, a grammatical stranger, More is reduced to "only More," the bare name that only signifies More (capital M) and yet—given the name's introduction into/as rhetoric, given the historical surround, given the English language, given the hand of Erasmus in the strange tongue of Latin in a text outside but drawn inside this one—signifies *still more*.[56]

My point by now is perhaps more than obvious. I mean first to notice that our editorial work on *More,* so attuned to the ostensibly discrete hands of the texts, has stopped us from readings its continuities and theirs. The rhetoric of strangeness is engaged by at least

Hands S, B, and D;[57] and Hand C (whose revision is also a reading and an editing of the text and thus a writing) lets it stand and thus reinscribes it. These hands we think of as separable draw on this rhetoric, write and are written by it, and it is only Tilney who cannot abide its lack of specificity (the vague estrangements it permits), insisting that the word *stranger* be written "lombard."[58] Losing this sense of through-line—a thread we need not necessarily imagine as "unity" or "coherence" but rather as engagement, contention, "massage" (to use the Oxford edition's term)—we lose site of a collective enterprise.

By choosing to follow out this word *stranger* (and the closely related terms *self* and *more*), I also mean to point out that our insistence on the distinction of the hands—as if one could say, "hands off, proud stranger" to the hand that interposes/revises on a given page, to mark it as out of bounds—fails to notice the way in which these hands (and the "identities" we take them to stand for) are already themselves marked by the discourses of strangeness and self-sameness.

This is not to say that there is not a conception of "the alien" in early modern culture, as James Shapiro and Emily Bartels, among others have helped us to understand.[59] But, as Shapiro begins to suggest, the potential overlap between *alien* and related terms in sixteenth- and early seventeenth-century culture is extraordinary and complicated. While the three main categories of what we would call "nationality" or "citizenship" (but largely understood here as relative "obeisance" to the monarch) were the *subject* (native born, or naturalized by act of parliament), the *alien* or *stranger* (meaning "foreigner"), and the *denizen* (an alien granted certain rights by royal letters patent), the meanings of these terms were often ambiguous, overlapped significantly, and were often contested. Throughout this period, *stranger* could refer to a person from outside the nation, or the town, or the household, or the family/ bloodline; *stranger* was additionally the routine term used in parish registries to denote "a person not belonging to the parish"[60] (playwright Philip Massinger, for example, was so denoted when he was buried in the church at St. Mary Overies with John Fletcher). While *foreigner* could denote someone from outside the nation, or the parish, or the county, or the guild, it was also, as Shapiro points out, the term by which Londoners routinely referred to immigrants to the city from the English countryside. George Unwin notes in his monumental study of London guild culture that a major component of London expansion in the fourteenth and fifteenth centuries was "a constant stream of immigrants from the country, the 'foreigners' from Hertfordshire, Essex, Kent, Surrey, Middlesex, or more distant counties." William Shakespeare was, of course, one of many such foreigners.[61] Throughout the period, *denizen,* likewise, could refer to *both* the seemingly mutually exclusive categories of a native inhabitant of a country *and* "an alien admitted to [partial] citizenship by royal letters patent."[62] The history of "stranger" legislation under Henry VIII could be seen as a continuing struggle to address the proliferation of terms, to scale back the privileges of denizenized aliens, and to regulate the number of strangers/denizens in the trades—even as the legislation resorts repeatedly to supplementarity and to profusion of terms in its attempts to do so:

> The King our moste dradde Souveraine Lord calling unto his blissed rememberaunce the infinite nombre of *Straungers and aliens* of *foren countries and nations* whiche daily doo increase and multiplie within his Graces Realme and Dominions in excessive nombres, to the great detriment[,] hinderaunce [,] losse [,] and empoverishment of his Graces naturall true *lieges and subjectis* . . .
> . . . in the xiiijth & xvth yere of [his] reign . . . , it was enacted that noo *straungier* borne out of his Graces obeisaunce were he *denisen or not denisen* . . .
> . . . And furthermore be it enacted by thauctoritie aforesaid that no *alien or Straungier denisen or not denisen* using any handy crafte, being borne out of the Kinges Graces obeisaunce. . . .[63]

What or who, then, was an alien, stranger, foreigner, denizen? An emigrant to London from the country? The nationless Jew, as Shapiro asks in a brilliant reading of the "alien" Shylock in *The Merchant of Venice?* Since the Lombards had a London street named for them, could they be considered denizens (inhabitants) or were they denizens (aliens with rights to practice business by patent)? Asked another way: where—in general discourse, in London usage, in legislation, in plays—will the boundary of strangeness be drawn? At the threshold of the household, in the rolls of the parish, at the boundary of "countries and nations"?

These intersecting striations in definition and usage, as I have already suggested, inflect not only the strangers or denizens or aliens: *all* hands are marked by "the discourses of strangeness and self-sameness." It is perhaps then no surprise that Tilney works in the *More* manuscript to rewrite the meaning of both the "stranger" (substituting "lombard") *and* the "English" (substituting "man").

Returning to *More,* then, and attuned to these marking and remarkings, we might notice, as unsettling to the notion of "the alien," and within identification's "logic of more than one,"

- that the rhetoric of this play instigates potentially transgressive and overlapping slippages between the native and the stranger, the clown and the king, the lord chancellor and the stranger, and, in the play's last line, Sir Thomas and the king;[64]
- Or that there are marks of an Italian (if not "Lombard") hand in *The Booke of Sir Thomas More;* and that, increasingly, literate male persons in this culture could write with the native *and* the stranger hand. (The ways in which our readings of the manuscript have already been inflected by intersecting discourses of nationalism and modern individuality are evident in Greg's description of Hand A: "an English hand, almost devoid of Italian intermixture, clear and legible with a good deal of individual character."[65] But if a hand can sign with/as/in two hands, as Goldberg would ask, how can a hand locate an identity? What are the acceptable parameters of intermixture?
- Or that, at about the time this play was apparently first begun, Thomas Kyd—a playwright, incidentally, who wrote in at least two hands;[66] the writer, apparently, of a tragedy set in a strange land and culminating in a play of diverse strange tongues— was arrested and tortured apparently in connection with a libel posted against "strangers," a controversy also connected in some way with Christopher Marlowe, writer of a play (most recently) about a monarch who seeks to "share the kingdom with his dearest friend" (a French stranger with an interest in Italian masques);
- Or that, as McMillin has persuasively argued, *Sir Thomas More* was probably first written for Lord Strange's Men;
- Or that at least one of the persons involved in the production of *Sir Thomas More* (Munday) made himself a stranger before writing this play by living "in the Catholic English College in Rome from February to May 1579" and writing about the experience in *The English Romayne Lyfe* (1582);[67]
- Or, lest we imagine this playwright's experience to lie somehow unmediated at the root of the play, that Munday's peregrinations may in part follow a trajectory imagined by Thomas More in *Utopia,* where, on an embassy in Flanders, More is introduced by Peter Giles to a "certeyne straunger" Raphaell

Hythlodaye, the (Portuguese) narrator of his experiences as a foreigner in Utopia.[68]
- Or that, as is recognized by every reader of *Utopia,* the very production of its text is explained through the primary structure of More's identification through, and ventriloquism of, the stranger Hythlodaye.
- Or that, further, travel and its traces on "identity" form an itinerary imagined retrospectively *for* More by Erasmus, who wrote in his commendatory letter to *Utopia:* "What would this wonderful, rich nature [of More's] not have accomplished *if his talent had been trained in Italy . . . ?*"[69] This, in a letter that returns repeatedly to the question of More as native and stranger.
- Or that the word *stranger* may have continued to be closely linked to More in later contexts, for example the play *Thomas Lord Cromwell,* published in 1602 and roughly contemporaneous with one possible date of the *More* play's revisions; there, the entrance and naming of the character Thomas More in a speech seems immediately to prompt, or coincidentally produces, the word *strange* in the playtext, with a meditation by Wolsey on national difference: "Come and sit downe, sit downe sir *Thomas Moore:* / Tis strange, how that we and the Spaniard differ, / Their dinner, is our banquet after dinner...."[70]
- Or that the word *stranger* is itself something of a stranger to English, having arrived from France in the late fourteenth century. If not one of the "strange and inkhorne tearmes" of Ascham's denunciation in *The Scholemaster* (1570),[71] it is perhaps at the time of the *More* play somewhere between an "alien" and a "denizen."[72]
- Or that Hand D's spelling "straingers," cited by Dover Wilson in his 1923 attempt to identify Shakespeare in the manuscript on the basis of spelling,[73] is itself potentially a *stranger* again removed, according to the *OED:* a Scottish spelling of the word (also used, for example, by the stranger monarch who may have been on the throne at the time of the play's revision).[74]

In such contexts—and there is no play for which there are *not* such contexts; that is, no play which is not itself inscribed by subjects inscribed by the complex languages they in turn inscribe; no "self" in this culture free and clear of its synonym "same," to use the words of Hand D [or is it C?]—it is difficult to see why we would want to continue to think of our work on collaborative plays as what Chambers called, back now in the previous century, "the quest for alien hands."[75]

Notes

A version of this essay was first presented on the panel "Editing Shakespeare Revisited" at the Shakespeare Association of America annual meeting in Montréal (2000). I'm grateful to James Shapiro for inviting me to participate in the panel, to Leeds Barroll, Margreta de Grazia, Jay Grossman, and Marion Trousdale for comments on the essay, to the Northwestern English department faculty colloquium, and to undergraduate and graduate students in my courses over the past decade at Northwestern and Harvard Universities for questions and comments that have contributed to my understanding of this play and the issues it raises. I take pleasure in, and instruction from, Paul Werstine's similarly titled essay "Shakespeare, More or Less: A.W. Pollard and Twentieth-Century Shakespeare Editing," *Florilegium* 16 (1999): 125–45, which came to my attention after the present essay was titled. Thanks to David Hacker for research assistance.

1. William Little et al., eds., rev. C. T. Onions, *The Shorter Oxford English Dictionary on Historical Principles*, 2 vols., (Oxford: Clarendon Press, 1933), 1:vii.

2. E. K. Chambers, "The Disintegration of Shakespeare," Annual Shakespeare Lecture (12 May, 1924), *Proceedings of the British Academy* (1924–25), 89–108, at 94.

3. Anthony Munday and others, Revised by Henry Chettle, Thomas Dekker, Thomas Heywood and William Shakespeare, *Sir Thomas More*, ed. Vittorio Gabrieli and Giorgio Melchiori, The Revels Plays (Manchester and New York: Manchester University Press, 1990). Citations of the play are to this modern-spelling edition and appear parenthetically in the text, together with cross-references to page and line numbers in W.W. Greg's indispensable transcript of the manuscript: Greg, ed., *The Book of Sir Thomas More*, Malone Society Reprints (Oxford: Oxford University Press for the Malone Society, 1911). As the ensuing lines in this scene suggest, the Revels edition's modernization of the manuscript's "Roste" as "roost" is probably anachronistic; see OED *roost* (1e.) and *roast* (1b.), which suggest that the phrase "rule the roast" long predates the earliest recorded use of "rule the roost" (1769). All dictionary references are to *The Oxford English Dictionary*, 2nd edition on CD-ROM.

4. This is complicated by Scott McMillin's argument that Hand C may be more like Hand D than scholars have allowed themselves to see; see his "Hand D," chapter 7 of *The Elizabethan Theatre and The Book of Sir Thomas More* (Ithaca and London: Cornell University Press, 1987), 135–59. This persuasive and revolutionary perspective on the manuscript has greatly influenced my thinking in the present essay.

5. Cyrus Hoy, "The Shares of Fletcher and his Collaborators in the Beaumont and Fletcher Canon (I–VII)," *Studies in Bibliography* 8–15 (1956–62).

6. G. Blakemore Evans, et al., eds., *The Riverside Shakespeare*, 1st edition, (Boston: Houghton Mifflin, 1974), 1683; Stanley Wells and Gary Taylor, et al., eds., *William Shakespeare: The Complete Works* (Oxford: Clarendon, 1986), 889; Stephen Greenblatt, et al., eds., *The Norton Shakespeare Based on the Oxford Editioin* (New York and London: W.W. Norton and Company, 1997), 2011.

More or Less 125

7. Greenblatt, ed., *Norton Shakespeare* (ix–x).

8. David Bevington, Preface, *The Complete Works of Shakespeare,* David Bevington, ed., Updated Fourth Edition, (New York: Longman, 1997), n.p. Bevington's comment that Shakespeare "was evidently called in to supply a new scene for a play written by another playwright who had run into trouble with the censor" seems to indicate another set of implicit principles for inclusion in a Complete-Works edition: 1) Shakespeare's work must be both original and voluntary (not "*called in* to supply a new scene" in a play thought of as someone else's) and perhaps 2) Shakespeare (though himself free of the crime) must not aid and abet.

9. I.e., with some allowances for the deterioration of the manuscript.

10. C. J. Sisson, ed., *William Shakespeare: The Complete Works* (New York: Harper, 1954). *More* in this volume (pp. 1235–66) was edited by Harold Jenkins. In the volume's table of contents, *More* is listed in a separate subsection (within "Plays," before "Poems") as a "PLAY IN PART AUTHORSHIP"; the volume does not, however, include *The Two Noble Kinsmen,* suggesting again the anomaly of *More's* editorial treatment or perceived value in ways explored further below. The complete play was first printed in the nineteenth century; Alexander Dyce, ed., *Sir Thomas More, A Play; Now First Printed,* in *Shakespeare Society of London Publications* 23 (London: for the Shakespeare Society, 1844), and rpt. in *Shakespeare Society of London Publications,* Vol. 3, Old Plays (Nendeln, Liechtenstein: Kraus Reprint Ltd., 1966).

11. Fredson Bowers (ed.), *The Dramatic Works of Thomas Dekker,* 4 vols., (Cambridge: Cambridge University Press, 1962; first edn. 1953), 1: 4–5. *More* is also treated exceptionally here: "For these few lines from a Dekker manuscript the apparatus takes the Malone Society form [Bowers follows Greg's 1911 edition], not that found subsequently for the critically edited text in these volumes" (1:3). See also Cyrus Hoy, *Introductions, Notes, and Commentaries to texts in 'The Dramatic Works of Thomas Dekker',* 4 vols. (Cambridge: Cambridge University Press, 1980) 1:1–6.

12. The Arden edition intends to commission an edition in its third series.

13. John S. Farmer, ed., *The Book of Sir Thomas Moore* (The Tudor Facsimile Texts, 1910).

14. Sir Edward Maunde Thompson, "Handwriting," *Shakespeare's England: An Account of the Life and Manners of his Age,* 2 vols., (Oxford: Clarendon Press, 1916), 1:284–310. The volumes are prefaced by an "Ode on the Tercentenary Commemoration of Shakespeare" by Robert Bridges, Poete Laureate, a poem that makes clear the centrality of Shakespeare (and scholarship devoted to him) within a larger English nationalist ethos in time of war.

15. *Shakespeare's Hand in The Play of Sir Thomas More: Papers by Alfred W. Pollard, W.W. Greg, E. Maunde Thompson, J. Dover Wilson, and R.W. Chambers, with the text of the Ill May Day Scenes edited by W.W. Greg,* Shakespeare Problem series, ed. A. W. Pollard and J. Dover Wilson, vol. 2, (Cambridge: Cambridge University Press, 1923). On the importance of the assembly of this team, see Werstine, "Shakespeare, *More* or Less."

16. See Paul Werstine, "Plays in Manuscript," *A New History of Early English Drama,* ed. John D. Cox and David Scott Kastan (New York: Columbia University Press, 1997), 481–97, esp. 490–92.

17. Fredson Bowers, "A Search for Authority: The Investigation of Shakespeare's Printed Texts," in *Print and Culture in the Renaissance: Essays on the Advent of Printing in Europe,* ed. Gerald P. Tyson and Sylvia S. Wagonheim (New-

ark: University of Delaware Press; London and Toronto: Associated University Presses, 1986), 32.

18. See Werstine, "Plays in Manuscript" and Werstine, "Narratives about Printed Shakespeare Texts: 'Foul Papers' and 'Bad' Quartos," *Shakespeare Quarterly* 41 (1990): 65–86.

19. That is, the four hundredth anniversary of the Folio text his good/bad quarto distinction helped resuscitate.

20. A. W. Pollard, Preface, *Shakespeare's Hand in The Play of Sir Thomas More*, v. For a historically detailed version of this argument, see Werstine, "Shakespeare, *More* or Less," 126–27.

21. This is the case in both editions: *Riverside Shakespeare,* 1st edition, 1696; *Riverside Shakespeare,* 2d edition, 1790. Additionally, Riverside includes an engraved alphabet of secretary hand, and photographs of the Hand D manuscript pages.

22. Stanley Wells and Gary Taylor, with John Jowett and William Montgomery, *William Shakespeare: A Textual Companion* (New York and London: W. W. Norton, by arrangement with Oxford University Press, 1997), 461–62.

23. I have not yet been able to identify this manuscript. As of mid-2000, the unidentified manuscript was also in prevalent use on the ardenshakespeare.com website. It is perhaps worth noting that even the older Pelican edition includes a secretaryish font on its binding.

24. On the multiple functions of the hands, see Paul Werstine, "Close Contrivers: Nameless Collaborators in Early Modern London Plays," *The Elizabethan Theatre* XV, ed. A. L. Magnusson and C. E. McGee (Toronto: P. D. Meany, forthcoming 2001); and McMillin, "Hand D," 152–59.

25. Werstine, "Plays in Manuscript." See also Marion Trousdale's acute commentary on regularity, order, and method in critical bibliography ("A Second Look at Critical Bibliography and the Acting of Plays," *Shakespeare Quarterly* 41 [1990]: 87–96): "Stage procedures and their importance, as embedded in the texts that remain to us, have yet to be looked at outside of the rubric of the assumptions about method that we inherited from the Enlightenment" (95). This logic can undergo some perverse twists in the treatment of this play, however—as when Grace Ioppolo argues that the *More* manuscript should not serve as a model of playtext revision because the revisions are not singlehandedly authorial enough: "[*More* and *The Spanish Tragedy*] should not, as they very frequently have, stand as primary examples of the ways in which *all* plays were revised, precisely because they contain mainly nonauthorial revisions. The handling of these two plays proves to be exceptional not because, as E. K. Chambers argued, they *were* revised, but because they present no clear evidence of revision *performed by or with the permission of the original author*" (*Revising Shakespeare,* [Cambridge: Harvard University Press, 1991], 55-56, final emphasis added).

26. Jeffrey Masten, *Textual Intercourse: Collaboration, Authorship and Sexualities in Renaissance Drama* (Cambridge: Cambridge University Press, 1997), 14; G. E. Bentley, *The Profession of Dramatist in Shakespeare's Time, 1590–1642* (Princeton: Princeton University Press, 1971); Stephen Orgel, "What is a Text?," *Research Opportunities in Renaissance Drama* (1981), 2–4.

27. Longman and the 3d generation Arden have added *The Two Noble Kinsmen,* for example.

28. Gary Taylor, "The Renaissance and the End of Editing," *Palimpsest: Edito-

rial Theory in the Humanities, ed. George Bornstein and Ralph G. Williams (Ann Arbor: University of Michigan Press, 1993), 121–49 at 135.

29. Carol A. Chillington's essay, "Playwrights at Work: Henslowe's, Not Shakespeare's Book of Sir Thomas More," ELR 10 (1980): 439–79, has been largely dismissed in the wake of her controversial attribution of Hand D to Webster, leading attribution-minded critics to miss her larger, important contribution: that the play is the production of a "syndicate," and tells us much about playwrights working together.

30. Taylor, "The Renaissance and the End," 143.

31. On the importance of recognizing the multiplicity of collaborative modes of playwriting for the early modern English theater, see Masten Textual Intercourse, 20–21, a point emphasized by Heather Hirschfeld: "the simultaneously competitive and communal milieu of the Renaissance theater fostered among the playwrights a variety of specific, evolving models of dramatic authorship"; "Collaborating across Generations: Thomas Heywood, Richard Brome, and the Production of The Late Lancashire Witches," Journal of Medieval and Early Modern Studies, 30.2 (2000): 340.

32. See, for example, the Introductions to plays in the New Mermaids Series, which routinely begin with a section called "The Author," a mode of organization that has implications in all cases and seems particularly ill-suited to a play like The Knight of the Burning Pestle (Michael Hattaway, ed., [London: A&C Black; New York: Norton, 1991]), which is reduced in this series to one author, despite the fact that it was attributed first to no one, and then to two playwrights.

33. This is a process that began at least with the First Folio, as Margreta de Grazia's reading of that volume's instrumental performance of authorship demonstrates: "The 1623 Folio and the Modern Standard Edition," chapter 1 of Shakespeare Verbatim: The Reproduction of Authenticity and the 1790 Apparatus (Oxford: Clarendon, 1991), 14–48, esp. 41.

34. Masten, "Seeing Double," chapter 1 of Textual Intercourse; "Playwrighting: Authorship and Collaboration" in Cox and Kastan (eds.), A New History of Early English Drama; "Canon and Chronology: The Old Law" in The Complete Works of Thomas Middleton, gen. ed. Gary Taylor, (Oxford: Oxford University Press), forthcoming 2001.

35. D. F. McKenzie, "Stretching a Point: Or, The Case of the Spaced-out Comps," Studies in Bibliography 37 (1984): 116–17.

36. See Charlton Hinman, "Principles governing the use of variant spellings as evidence of alternate setting by two compositors," The Library, 4th ser., 21 (1940–41): 78–94.

37. I offer a critique of compositor studies' assumptions about spelling and individuation in "Pressing Subjects; Or, the Secret Lives of Shakespeare's Compositors," in Jeffrey Masten, Peter Stallybrass, and Nancy Vickers, eds., Language Machines: Technologies of Literary and Cultural Production (New York: Routledge, 1997).

38. Diana Fuss, Identification Papers (New York: Routledge, 1995), 3.

39. Stuart Hall, "Introduction: Who Needs 'Identity'?" in Questions of Cultural Identity, ed. Stuart Hall and Paul du Gay (London: Sage, 1996), 2–3. I would add to Hall the caveat that such sustenance and abandonment may take place both within and beyond/outside the agency of the individual, this being a part of its conditionality and contingency.

40. See Raymond Williams, Keywords: A Vocabulary of Culture and Society, re-

vised edition (New York: Oxford, 1983), 161–65; Peter Stallybrass, "Shakespeare, the Individual, and the Text," in *Cultural Studies,* eds. Lawrence Grossberg, Cary Nelson, and Paula Treichler, with Linda Baughman, and with assistance from John Macgregor Wise (New York: Routledge, 1992), 593–610. For some discussion of "identity" from this perspective in a signed manuscript roughly contemporaneous with *More,* see Jeffrey Masten, "The Interpretation of Dreams, circa 1610," in Carla Mazzio and Douglas Trevor, eds., *Psychoanalysis, Historicism and Early Modern Culture* (New York: Routledge, 2000), 157–85.

41. McMillin, "Hand D," 158; Werstine, "Close Contrivers."

42. Jonathan Goldberg, *Writing Matter: From the Hands of the English Renaissance* (Stanford: Stanford University Press, 1990).

43. See Margreta de Grazia and Peter Stallybrass, "The Materiality of the Shakespearean Text," *Shakespeare Quarterly* 44 (1993): 255–83; also David Scott Kastan, *Shakespeare After Theory* (New York and London: Routledge, 1999), 67.

44. "[A] textual history is a psychic history only because it is first a social history"; Jerome J. McGann, *A Critique of Modern Textual Criticism* (Chicago: University of Chicago Press, 1983), 62.

45. Though I have called the old historicist approach to collaboration "disintegrationist," I should make clear that the alternative I've identified as new historicist is not antidisintegrationist, but rather an attempt to loosen the hold of this unhelpful binary. Chambers's own position against disintegration in his lecture is something of a know-nothing stance, in the sense that it is predicated on a certain faith in the Shakespearean canon as an unchippable monolith composed (nonetheless) of episodes of experimentation and difference (96).

46. Williams, *Keywords,* 161.

47. In a passage I find useful for thinking about writing practices and textual production, Bourdieu writes: "Because the *habitus* is an infinite capacity for generating products—thoughts, perceptions, expressions and actions—whose limits are set by the historically and socially situated conditions of its production, the conditioned and conditional freedom it provides is as remote from creation of unpredictable novelty as it is from simple mechanical reproduction of the original conditioning." See *The Logic of Practice,* trans. Richard Nice (Stanford: Stanford University Press, 1990), 55.

48. Stephen Greenblatt, *Shakespearean Negotiations: The Circulation of Social Energy in Renaissance England* (Berkeley: University of California Press, 1988), 5.

49. Hall, "Introduction," 3.

50. Carol A. Chillington, "Playwrights at Work," 456.

51. In original spelling, the manuscript reads "with sealf same hand sealf reasons and sealf right" (Greg 78.208).

52. The manuscript has a question mark (Greg 43.1296).

53. Patricia Parker's remarkable excavations of networked "puns" around *moor/more* (and more specifically her emphasis on inter- and intra-linguistic play on More's name in several kinds of texts) suggest the extension of meaning in even more directions; see "Mulberries, Moors, and More" (unpublished essay, 1–9). I'm indebted to Parker for sharing with me her work in progress.

54. See *OED one* (a., pron.) and *only* (adv.) Here the manuscript reads: "my title's only Moore" (Greg 45.1360). On the variability of the word *one* in this period, see de Grazia and Stallybrass, "Materiality," 262 n. 26, and their essay's section on "Word."

55. Manuscript: "*Chelsey,* adiewe, adiewe, / straunge farewell, thou shalt nere more see Moore true, / for I shall nere see thee more:" (Greg 52.1591–93).

56. To take this in another direction that I will not pursue here but that potentially intersects with the rhetoric of strangeness, the title "only Moor(e)" may also resonate with a rhetoric of racial otherness—in which *only* might signify not singularity but lack, or reduction in value. On "Moor" rhetoric in unexpected places (especially when obscured by modern spelling and editing), see Patricia Parker, "Murder in Guyana," in *Shakespeare Studies* (September, 2000). In the Hand D pages alone, More is spelled "moor" (8 times), "moore" (twice), and "more" (once). These figures do not include speech prefixes: "moo" (once), "moor" (7 times). See Thomas Clayton, *The "Shakespearean" Addition in the Booke of Sir Thomas Moore: Some Aids to Scholarly and Critical Shakespearean Studies,* vol. 1 of *Shakespeare Studies Monographs Series,* ed. J. Leeds Barroll (Dubuque: Wm. C. Brown Company Publishers for Vanderbilt Center for Shakespeare Studies, 1969), 30–31, 23. The adjectival spelling is "more" (five occurrences), though, as my argument suggests, this distinction (Clayton's) is difficult to maintain.

57. In Greg's edition, see Hand B at p. 69 ("strangers," "alians," "audatious strangers," "outlandishe fugetiues"); Hand D ("stra<ingers>" [73], "stra<raungers>" [74], "strainghers" [76–78]). Though without apparently using "stranger" and related words, Hand C writes the Erasmus and Falkner scenes (which contain Latin, refer to Erasmus as "thou reverent germaine" [84.145], and present the "Ruffian" Falkner who has been too long away from the "Barbars" (= barbers, [82.72–74], but this spelling may be revealing, given More's reference soon after to his servant Randall as "foole painted Barbarisme" [84.139] and given D's description in the crowd scene of "a nation of such barbarous temper" [78.254]). Hand E writes that Faulkner is potentially "ma[d]e a Sarcen" (87.219). Though it is part of my point that such discursive borders are hardly discrete or impermeable, it might be said that Hand A's only inscription of this discourse occurs in the phrase "my exile from the court" (66.21).

58. While it's clear that Tilney is most bothered by the term "strangers" (marking over a dozen instances in the part of the manuscript he saw), he also crosses out "ffrencheman." Jame Shapiro cogently argues that Tilney wishes to substitute "a largely fictive minority population that was an easy target" (because associated with moneylending and usury) and "peripheral to the real object of [1590s] anti-alien sentiment." See *Shakespeare and the Jews* (New York: Columbia University Press, 1996), 185–87. For a nuanced account of Tilney's interventions, see William B. Long, "The occasion of *The Book of Sir Thomas More,*" in T. H. Howard-Hill, ed., *Shakespeare and Sir Thomas More: Essays on the play and its Shakespearean interest* (Cambridge: Cambridge University Press, 1989) 45–56.

59. Shapiro, *Shakespeare and the Jews,* esp. chapter 6, "Race, Nation, or Alien"; Emily C. Bartels, *Spectacles of Strangeness: Imperialism, Alienation, and Marlowe* (Philadelphia: University of Pennsylvania Press, 1993).

60. *OED, stranger, n.,* 1a., 2a., 2b., 3a.

61. Shapiro, *Shakespeare and the Jews,* 181; George Unwin, *The Gilds and Companies of London* (London: Methuen, 1908), 245. For an account of London's complex "social space" in this context, see Garrett A. Sullivan Jr., "The Beleaguered City: Guild Culture and Urban Space in Heywood's 'I Edward IV' and Shakespeare's '2 Henry VI,' " chapter 6 of *The Drama of Landscape: Land, Property, and Social Relations on the Early Modern Stage* (Stanford: Stanford University Press, 1998), 197–229, esp. 210–12.

62. See *OED*, denizen, n., 1a., 2a.

63. 32 Henry VIII c. 16, "Concerning Strangers," in *The Statutes of the Realm*, vol. 3 (1817), rpt. (London: Dawsons of Pall Mall, 1963), 765–66, abbreviations silently expanded and emphases added.

64. The last line has More "tend[ing] progress to the state of states" (5.4.122); More's identification with the King of Kings (as opposed or in addition to Henry VIII) may resonate further in the manuscript's spelling "prograce" (Greg, 65.1986).

65. Greg, ed., *Book of Sir Thomas More*, viii. In this context, it is perhaps unsurprising that Greg presents Hand D as "a purely English hand" (ix). Though D's purity in this regard is aberrant when compared with the other hands in the manuscript, Greg faults Hand S for insufficiently distinguishing secretary and italic hands: "the writer's intention [in writing one hand or the other] [is] usually clear though the two styles, particularly as regards majuscules, *are not always kept clearly apart*" (vii, emphasis added). In Hand E, Greg sees the styles as "adequately distinguished" (ix). The miscegenation of hands (as we might call it, and this is not the same thing as a writer's ability to write two hands separately) has implications that require further study and analysis.

66. For more on Kyd's hands and Marlowe's, see Masten, "Playwrighting."

67. See Gabrieli and Melchiori's introduction, 14–15.

68. *A fruteful and pleasaunt worke of the beste state of a publyque weale, and of the newe yle called Vtopia: written in Latine by Syr Thomas More knyght, and translated into Englyshe by Raphe Robynson Citizein and Goldsmythe of London, at the procurement, and earnest request of George Tadlowe Citezein & Haberdassher of the same Citie* (London: by Abraham Vele, 1551) sig. Bii^v. Giles says of Hythlodaye: "there ys no man this daye lyuynge that can tell you of so manye strange and vnknowne peoples and contreis as this man can. And I know well that you be verye desyrous to heare of suche newes" (sig. Biii). For an edited Latin text and modern translation, see Thomas More, *Utopia*, in *The Complete Works of St. Thomas More*, vol. 4, ed. Edward Surtz, S. J., and J. H. Hexter (New Haven and London: Yale University Press, 1965), 48–49. I'm grateful to Margreta de Grazia for suggesting this connection.

69. "Erasmus of Rotterdam to John Froben [printer]," in More, *Utopia*, 4:3, my emphasis. ("Quid tandem non praestitisset admirabilis ista naturae felicitas, si hoc ingenium instituisset Italia?" [2].)

70. W. S., *THE True Chronicle Historie of the whole life and death of Thomas Lord Cromwell* (London: for William Iones, 1602) sig. D2^v. Some additional connections between the texts have been noted; see Gabrieli and Melchiori's introduction (44 n. 29, 45 n. 39).

71. Roger Ascham, *The Scholemaster* (London: by Iohn Daye, 1570), book 2.

72. For a fascinating study of the frequency of "loan-words" in sixteenth-century scholarly prose (a study that includes in its sample prose of both More himself and Ascham), see Matti Rissanen, " 'Strange and Inkhorne Tearmes': Loan-Words As Style Markers in the Prose of Edward Hall, Thomas Elyot, Thomas More and Roger Ascham," *Style and Text: Studies Presented to Nils Erik Enkvist*, ed. Hakan Ringbom, et al., (Stockholm: Sprakforlaget Skriptor, 1975), 250–62.

73. J. Dover Wilson, "Bibliographical Links Between the Three Pages and the Good Quartos," in Pollard (ed.), *Shakespeare's Hand*, cited above, 127–28.

74. See *OED* entries for *strange, stranger*; for James I's use, see *OED ceremony*, 1b. The difficulty of linking spelling and "identity" is suggested by the fact that nearly a fifth of the words Hand D writes more than once are spelled in more than

More or Less 131

one way (Clayton, *The "Shakespearean" Addition,* 39). My favorite line in this regard is a line spoken by the crowd ("all") and written out by Hand D: "Shreiue moor moor more Shreue moore" (Greg 75.168). Its six word-forms contain what we would consider two words, one spelled two ways and another spelled three ways. Philip Gaskell writes of one Hand D passage: "Note that the word 'sheriff' appears five times in . . . five lines in five different spellings" (*A New Introduction to Bibliography* [New York and Oxford: Oxford University Press, 1972] 359 n. 37).

75. Chambers, "Disintegration," 99.

Assessing "Cultural Influence": James I as Patron of the Arts

Leeds Barroll

Recent cultural history has seemed inclined to foster a concept of King James and his English court based on seemingly contradictory but interdependent views. On one hand, many essays have depicted James I as a royal patron of the arts. We are often reminded, for example, that his first act in the literary realm was to take the theaters under his patronage because as part of his entertainment James demanded court performance of plays. He cared enough about public drama, it seems, to have assumed Shakespeare's own company under the new name of "the King's Men," and even to have assigned the remaining London troupes to other members of the royal family. Although these changes in the status of theater companies are of themselves unreliable indices of James's preoccupation with the London stage,[1] such evidence has encouraged scholars to make related assumptions about the role of the new king in other important initiatives—such as furthering the brilliant and fruitful collaboration of Inigo Jones and Ben Jonson in their series of opulent masques at court, appointing the poet John Donne Dean of Paul's, and, to be sure, ordering the translation project that resulted in the King James Bible.

The other side of this particular conceptual coin, curiously, is a concomitant view of the new king as somewhat incompetent—as lax, self-indulgent, and even slightly unsavory. An extreme example of such an attitude may be found in the observations of Roy Strong, who describes James as "the bloated, pedantic middle-aged father [of Prince Henry], careless of affairs of state, prepared to accept appeasement at any price, bent on the pleasure of the chase, totally unaesthetic, whose penchant for handsome courtiers was hardly becoming." Earlier, G. P. V. Akrigg's book on the Jacobean court, still popular with literary scholars, viewed James as a spendthrift king, always absorbed in his current male favorite to the detriment of the state, and concerned with losing status if he did not maintain himself as the generous benefactor to his supporters, a practice which depleted the royal budget.[2]

Interestingly, this dualistic construction of James—as royal, generative patron of the arts or cultural icon, on the one hand, and as corrupt dawdler, on the other—has not been understood as troublingly inconsistent because indifference to politics and personal indolence in a learned king seem to many commentators to augur well for the arts—presumably, they flourish in such compost. It is almost as if absorption in the affairs of "high culture" is incompatible with the practice of statesmanship, or vice versa (at least in the case of James).

This essay, part of a larger effort to determine the structure and purpose of high cultural practices at court during the first decade of the Stuart reign, would interrogate the implications of James's dual image for our construction of the early court scene. In undertaking this limited analysis, I think it important to view James's situation not solely from the vantage point of his investment in *belles lettres,* but also in terms of the kinds of regnal problems to which he addressed himself at his accession. In other words, in order to reconfigure the misleading premises in so many portraits of the king, it is important here to assess James's relationship to the development of the arts in England in terms of his parallel assumption of monarchal responsibilities.

Accordingly, in what follows I shall be arguing two points. First, I would like to challenge the narrative of James's self-indulgent political ineptness, focusing primarily on representative activities surrounding the accession. Second, I hope to counter the view of King James as the primary instrument of high culture in the Stuart court by identifying the parameters of his intellectual interests, and by suggesting his own relative remoteness from contemporary currents of change in the arts.

There are, however, important caveats that need to be established in connection with both these points at the outset. It is clearly not feasible here, nor is it my intention, to offer an extensive analysis of James's style of governing, although recent revisionist studies have begun this task.[3] Instead, I have deliberately chosen to concentrate on events surrounding the first year of James's reign in order to demonstrate his political acumen and decisiveness—so reminiscent of his Scottish monarchal style. Although the framework of a single year may indeed seem limited in the context of a twenty-two-year reign, I would argue that James's activities in 1603 established a structure for governance in England that would function effectively for a decade. Significantly, this is the decade in which the arts burgeoned at the Stuart court, particularly the masque for which the court is renowned. Further, in describing James as a person with narrowly defined intellectual interests, I am hardly subscribing to popular caricatures of the King. On the contrary, although fundamentally unmoved by the artistic innovations that we might associate with the great accomplishments of the early Stuart period, he appears to have been excited by a traditionally academic form of intellectuality rooted in mid-sixteenth-century culture.

Any assessment of the new Stuart monarch at the turn of the century is best framed, in my view, in terms of his preceding *persona* as James VI of Scotland. There James was challenged by at least three critical problems: the political opposition of powerful Scottish earls to the entente generally beginning to prevail between the Crown and the other magnates who were indispensable to it; the efforts by the Kirk to gain autonomy and then political power through an elected internal hierarchy responsible in theory not to the King but only to God; and the threat of destabilization continually posed by blood feuds among the nobility, revenge patterns often bereft of any broad political goals.[4]

On the whole, James seems consistently and effectively to have managed these formidable threats to the stability of his Scottish kingdom. He dealt with hostile nobles by eventually destroying or neutralizing such threatening figures as Bothwell and the Gowries, even cooperating for a time with the implacable Bothwell.[5] Meanwhile he worked to stabilize Crown authority by creating or maintaining offices that functioned as lightning rods to absorb attack: Maitland's chancellorship, for example, and, after Maitland's death, the "Octavians" onto whom James displaced antimonarchist resentments. He outmaneuvered the Kirk by eventually pushing it from the political arena through counterpolemic or by carefully chosen confrontations.[6] And finally, he controlled blood feuds through deploying agents of court power in those localities where feuding was chronic. Having also (and usually in response to these initiatives) endured many assassination attempts in Scotland, the new English king was, in 1603, after many Scottish regnal years, hardly a political innocent, naively self-absorbed and sometimes destructively self-indulgent.

Yet as a consequence of the prevalence in some quarters of viewing James as politically foolish, many literary accounts have incompletely contextualized or even ignored significant activity surrounding his 1603 accession, omitting in the process important illustrative texts.[7] Yet it was 1603 that saw the formation of King James's inner circle of advisors, an important event to attend to here, if only because the James of English literary chronicles is also characterized as exclusively cultivating young favorites whom he presumably advanced to positions of power over the heads of more experienced and wiser nobles.[8] Through reference to well-known though seldom-invoked texts dealing with first decade of the Stuart reign, however, it is possible to shape a narrative somewhat different from the conventional one.

Central to this revised narrative is the so-called secret correspondence, well before Queen Elizabeth's death, between James VI and Robert Cecil, the queen's First Secretary. This correspondence demonstrates James's skilled instrumentality in the cooperative effort to work out the political details of his quiet and assured succession to the English throne. The succession effort principally involved Robert Cecil, but others also contributed to it, including Henry Lord Howard, younger brother of the Duke of Norfolk (Norfolk's letters to James's mother, Mary Queen of Scots, as well as other activities, had led to his execution in 1572 in the Tower). Northumberland, whose earldom was situated closest to Edinburgh, and who was married to Dorothy, one of the two sisters of the lately decapitated Earl of Essex, was also a party to the correspondence.[9] But Henry Lord Howard, the future Earl of Northampton, and Robert Cecil, the future Earl of Salisbury, were the principal figures, and James's initial actions with the English nobility—deliberate and, it would seem, well planned—reflected the Cecil and Howard view of the English situation.

Their dominance of this intrigue excluded those whom they regarded as enemies: Sir Walter Ralegh, Captain of Queen Elizabeth's Guard, and Henry Brook, 11th Lord Cobham, Warden of the Cinque Ports.[10] Cobham's position, especially, was a strong one because England, much to the admiration of some foreigners, was able to exercise control over its boundaries far more stringently than could a partially land-bound area such as "France." The Warden of the Cinque Ports supervised the bureaucracy that administered the seaports, and his authority extended even to the nobility, who were required to show passports when entering or leaving England. Thus Ralegh, official guard over the monarch's body, and Cobham, controller of access to England by sea, might jointly have proved formidable if anarchy had edged into the immediate power vacuum resulting from the death of the heirless Queen Elizabeth. But by presumably acquiescing in Cecil's and Henry Lord Howard's view of things, James of Scotland gambled that *these* nobles and their associates could deliver the English throne to him—and of course they did. On 31 March, only a week after the Queen's death, and shortly after Charles Percy, brother of the Earl of Northumberland, and Thomas Somerset, son of the Earl of Worcester, Master of the Horse, rode north as the official messengers announcing James's accession, he was proclaimed King, and with scarcely any of the difficulties and obstacles many had feared.[11] The conventional narrative of the quiet beginning of the Stuart reign seems to represent this peaceful transition even as axiomatic, but perhaps this is because James's political adroitness lay just here: in maneuvering to avoid opposition, and thereby presiding over a historical interlude devoid of drama.[12]

The first month after his accession saw the formation of those key associations of James that would dominate the first ten years of the new reign. On 11 April, for example, James wrote the Privy Council of England, summoning Robert Cecil north to Scotland to convey to him their consensus on the timing of the state funeral of Queen Elizabeth, the coronation, and the procession south into England of the royal court of his consort, Queen Anna, as well as various other matters "not fit for paper neither fit for us to resolve of, until we hear from you of our Privy Council." Cecil, riding north with his fellow in the secret correspondence, Henry Lord Howard, met up with James in York where the three talked for an hour before the ceremonial dinner to be given for the new King by the Lord Mayor of that city.[13] Cecil then returned to London while James continued his leisurely progress, attended by Henry Lord Howard, who by 25 April (when Howard wrote Cecil that James had decided upon his new Lord Chamberlain), was already entrusted with overseeing access to the king and inditing letters for him (*Hatfield,* 15:58).

The Chamberlainship was an important and powerful office, coveted by many earls and barons—an anachronistic combination of royal household duties reaching back to the twelfth century and of much wider, seventeenth-century administrative responsibilities involving constant access to the monarch. Thus one contemporary described the Lord Chamberlain as "the greatest governor in the king's house."

> He disposeth of all things above stairs. He hath a greater command of the King's guard than the captains hath. He makes all the [court] chaplains, chooseth most of the King's servants, and all the persuivants.[14]

James had apparently resolved early in his progress to London[15] to maintain the temporary appointment of Thomas Lord Howard of Walden made by Queen Elizabeth (Hunsdon being ill), for on 6 April (James had only reached the border town of Berwick-on-Tweed), the King wrote the Privy Council:

> For as much as for many services necessarily to be attended both about the Queen's funerals, our reception into the cities and towns of this our realm, and our coronation, the use of a Lord Chamberlain is very needful, and that the Lord Hunsdon, who now hath that place, is not able by reason of his indisposition to execute the services belonging to his charge, we have thought good to appoint our right trusty and right well-beloved the Lord Thomas Howard of Walden to exercise that place for the said Lord Hunsdon; and for that purpose we have directed our letters specially to him.[16]

Lord Howard of Walden was, significantly, the forty-one-year-old nephew of Henry Lord Howard who at present was inditing the King's letters.[17] And although all Crown officials at the death of the monarch customarily and ceremonially demonstrated the end of their tenure by breaking their staffs of office at the time of the royal funeral, James, before Elizabeth's funeral on 28 April, commanded Howard that

> after the staff [is] broken at the funerals by the Lord Thomas, he shall notwithstanding bring a white staff to Theobalds [where James was to meet the male nobility of England], and that if it need any express warrant, either you shall use one of the blanks you have, or send hither, and a warrant shall be sent with all speed.[18]

James's action here, coupled with later gestures towards these Howards, further demonstrates his intention to depend on the Howard-Cecil axis, but also his declaration of independence from the memory of Queen Elizabeth, who had executed Henry Lord Howard's brother. For not only did Henry Lord Howard, as Northampton, become a key figure at James's court until Northampton's death in 1614, and not only was a relative that Northampton most valued made Lord Chamberlain, but James went so far as to restore the entire family to its former status.

Sixty-three at the time of James's accession, Henry Lord Howard had never married. But his older brother the Duke of Norfolk had fathered sons before his execution and attainder in 1572, and these fatherless nephews were Henry Lord Howard's closest male relatives. Having made one of these nephews the new Lord Chamberlain, James went on to honor another, now dead. Philip Howard had become 1st Earl of Arundel during Elizabeth's reign, but because of accusations of treason, Arundel, like his father Norfolk, had also been imprisoned and attainted, and died in the Tower in 1595. He too left a son (Henry Lord Howard's great-nephew), another Thomas Howard, who of course had no title to inherit after his dead father's attainder. King James wrote *finis* to the whole situation in a paragraph of activity which also suggests the shape that his political inner circle would take.

Soon after appointing Lord Howard of Walden his Lord Chamberlain, James created him one of the first new earls of his reign as 1st Earl of Suffolk. Then, less than a year later, James created his secret correspondent, Henry Lord Howard, 1st Earl of Northampton.[19] At that time, James also addressed the problem of Henry Howard's great-nephew, the other Thomas. In a definitive gesture, the King restored in blood the nineteen-year-old son of the attainted Arundel, and recreated him as Earl of Surrey and Earl of Arundel.[20] Thus, very significantly, the brother, the son, and the grandson of the executed and attainted Duke of Norfolk, killed for his sympathy to James's mother, were all earls within two years of James's arrival in England.[21]

Illustrative of James's attitude towards this group is the account of a moment at Burleigh-on-the-Hill during James's progress south when Henry Lord Howard arranged an audience for the new Lord Chamberlain's younger brother (William Howard) and William's son.

> My lord Henry Howard at their first coming to Burleigh brought them presently [immediately] unto the king and my lord [William Howard] and he kneeling down, the king gave my young lord his hand and then came unto my lord William in like sort, and willed them to stand up, and, turning unto my lord Henry, said "Here be two of your nephews [*sic*], both Howards. I love the whole house of them." And then turning again unto my young lord [William Howard's son], said, "I love your whole house." And then my lord [William] kissed again his hand, and the king said they should never repent his coming into this kingdom, and so drew my lord Henry along the gallery with him.

In short, James's favors at this early point in his reign were hardly whimsical. Whether proceeding from a strong and vengeful need for a symbolism that redeemed the memory of his mother or from the necessity of political repayment to Henry Lord Howard, the new King's preferments seem to have been intelligent, systematic, and clearly defined. Indeed, Scaramelli, the Venetian Secretary for English affairs, noted wryly at this time that "The King continues to support those houses and persons who were oppressed by the late Queen" (*SPV*, 10:17), and that those who had been members of the Elizabethan Privy Council were now frenetically trying to prove that they had been uninvolved in the execution of Mary Queen of Scots.

The measures James took to assure his physical security at the accession also attest to his political sagacity and to its role in the early configuration of his court. James's fear of assassination has often been treated humorously by historians who themselves, had they suffered James's experiences in Scotland, might have been equally cautious.[22] But James's anxiety, however intense, was nonetheless turned here to the service of his political program. In one stroke, the king combined two objectives: that is, he provided for the security of his person while simultaneously disempowering a foe of his supporters, Sir Walter Ralegh (who several months later would be involved in the conspiracy to seize the King conventionally known as the "Bye [actually the "Maine] Plot").

Prior to the accession, as noted above, Cecil and Henry Lord Howard had made their hostility to Ralegh obvious: his removal had been a condition of their cooperation with James.[23] Thus on 8 May Ralegh was quickly relieved of his position as Captain of the Guard, and James, typically reconfiguring the political situation so as to suit himself, replaced Ralegh with the Scottish Sir Thomas Erskine, a Gentleman of the King's Bed Chamber in Scotland since 1585. Importantly, in the fighting during the Gowry attempt to assassinate James, Erskine was said to have physically protected the King's life, receiving a wound in the hand, and for those services Erskine had been granted a third part of Gowry's former honors. Now he became Captain of the Yeomen of the King's Guard, a post he would hold for James until 1617.[24]

James was no less astute in regard to another important political situation—the composition of the Privy Council of England. At the accession the Council had been composed of fourteen men, but James soon raised the number to twenty-four. Some time before 14 April 1603, Edward Bruce, Abbot of Kinloss, recently (in February) created Baron Kinloss, aware of and instrumental to the King's secret correspondence with Cecil and Henry Howard, had traveled to London carrying orders that he was to be admitted to all future meetings of the Privy Council (*SPV*, 109:10). By 4 May four more

Scottish nobles had been sworn in, including John 7th Earl of Mar, James's closest Scottish advisor.[25] Shortly thereafter, five additional *Englishmen* were appointed (assignments that might well temper our sense of a "flood of Scots" now attaining office in England). The new English members included the new Lord Chamberlain; his uncle (Henry Lord Howard); the Earl of Northumberland (also, we recall, privy to the secret correspondence); Thomas Cecil, 2nd Lord Burleigh, Robert Cecil's older brother and heir to Queen Elizabeth's great Lord Treasurer; and Lord Mountjoy (the future Earl of Devonshire). Having added five Scottish and five English nobles friendly to him, James had also diluted the Council's (Elizabethan) authority in the very process of inflating its numbers.[26]

The pervasive denigration in literary tradition of King James has effectively eclipsed the foregoing events, and thus misses the main political schema of James's early reign: his pattern of consistent allegiance to his own political base. Scottish earls such as Mar and Kinloss and English advisors such as Salisbury and Northampton were the core of James's kingship and the insurers of his safety, and James appears to have treated them appropriately. Indeed, the tone of his later letters to these supporters suggests that here was a special kind of intimacy of interests that others of the court, including any young favorites, simply did not share.

During the time of the secret correspondence, James, Cecil, and Northampton had all identified themselves by numbers rather than by name (that is, James = 30, Northampton = 3, Cecil = 10), and the King continued to refer to his nobles familiarly by these numbers even after he was safely King of England. For instance, during August 1604, when the Spanish Constable of Castile was expected to sign the Peace Treaty, James elected to be out of London, hunting in Royston, while Queen Anna remained in the city to act as the regal representative, attended by Cecil, the Lord Chamberlain, and Northampton, among others. Prior to his own short visit to London to participate in the final ceremonies King James wrote Cecil from the hunting lodge on 5 August (anniversary of the Gowry Plot), calling him, as usual, his "little beagle," teasing him, Suffolk, and Northampton about what was now their involvement with a *second* female court, and making jokes in a tone that suggests the intimacy James seems to have felt with this group:

> Ye and your fellows there are so proud now that ye have gotten the guiding again of a feminine court in the old fashion as I know not how to deal with you. . . . Well, I know Suffolk is married and hath also his

hands full now in harboring that great little proud man [Cecil] that comes in his chair. But for your part, Master 10, who is wanton and wifeless, I cannot but be jealous of your greatness with my wife, but most of all I am suspicious of 3, who is so lately fallen in acquaintance with my wife. . . . But for expiation of this sin I hope ye have all three with the rest of your society taken this day a Eucharistic cup of thankfulness for the occasion which fell out at a time when ye durst not avow me. And here hath been this day kept the feast of King James's deliverance. . . . All other matters I refer to the old knave the bearer's report, and so fare ye well.[27]

This tone helps to define an inner cluster of peers in England who constituted what might be called James's iron circle in the years before Cecil's death in 1612. Indeed, accounts of the early Stuart court that omit reference to this close-knit group and to the Scottish history preceding it cannot adequately encompass the complex matrix of relationships comprising James's political network. Thus the most common portrait in literary studies of the monarchal James is, in my view, severely reductive. In these early years of his reign, impulse seldom, if ever, seems to have interfered with James's political decision-making—he may have been the new king, but he was hardly new to kingship. And it is worth remembering that while a seventeenth-century European king may, from the cradle, have taken his position as "God's Anointed" for granted, James was not born King of England. On the contrary, it was a regnancy for which he had striven and schemed for a considerable period.

But even though the English members of the secret correspondence necessarily held the king's primary political allegiance, James did not cultivate them exclusively. For other and perhaps equally important reasons, he seems to have made a point of honoring—without politically advancing—quite a different group of nobles. This group, associated with the uprising of the Earl of Essex two years previously, had developed as a social faction after his beheading, and would become political playmakers later in the reign. It is important to consider these nobles briefly here, because the followers of the dead hero of this "Essex group," as I shall term it, seem to have enjoyed attention from James, although it differed in kind and purpose from that informing his relationships to those nobles selected to help him govern. James cultivated this group while, at the same time, astutely exploiting the symbolism of his public largesse to them.[28]

The Essex circle had been only incidentally, briefly, and quite incompletely a party of political conspirators. The earl's own wild personality may have plunged those around him into a confrontation that finally had to be defined as "treason," but it was personal loyalty and family ties, not a political platform, which gave coherence (such as there was) to this collection of rebellious nobles. Thus it is not the group's politics *per se* but its social identity as a circle that constitutes its importance to the early Stuart court and to James's monarchal policies.

The group's inspiration or principle of cohesion seems to have been the concept embodied by Sir Philip Sidney, that astonishingly charismatic figure who, himself an almost-member of the highest peerage, became one of its idols. Sidney's premature death led to his secular consecration as the Renaissance *beau ideal* of poet-courtier-warrior: and, indeed, the following verses from a contemporary sonnet illustrate the feelings evoked by—or, at least, thought to be appropriate to—his demise.

> Bewail, I say, his unexpected fall.
> I need not in remembrance for to call
> His youth, his race, the hope had him of aye
> Since that in him doth cruel death appall—
> Both manhood, wit, and learning every way.
> Now in the bed of honor doth he rest,
> And evermore of him shall live the best.

It was King James VI of Scotland who wrote these lines in 1586, appending to them a eulogy in Latin in honor of the dead poet.[29] James, like many English nobles, was thus attuned to Sidney's symbolic stature, and his admiration of Sidney's poetry may have been enhanced by the fact that Sidney himself never made any great headway as a courtier with Queen Elizabeth.

When Sidney died, he left his sword to Robert Devereux, 2nd Earl of Essex, and four years later the earl married Sidney's widow, Frances *née* Walsingham; thus Essex, by a kind of osmosis of identity, himself replicated and magnified the Sidney concept. For by such reincarnation Essex could become not only the flower of chivalry, but also, perhaps, of earldom too—a sphere to which Sir Philip Sidney, no matter his illustrious lineage, had not managed to ascend. Indeed, Essex's image as the *peerage's* avatar of Sidney was put into focus in the 1590s by the dramatist George Peele in an eclogue. He wrote of

> Young Essex, that thrice honorable earl
> Yclad in mighty arms of mourner's hue
>
> . . . .
>
> As if he mourn'd to think of him he missed,
> Sweet Sidney, fairest shepherd of our green,
> Well lettered warrior, whose successor he
> In love and arms had ever vowed to be.[30]

Those earls who were friends of Essex had several points of contact with him and with each other, including an early association as young, fatherless nobles who had been gathered together under the wardship and in the household of William Cecil, 1st Lord Burghley, Queen Elizabeth's architect of policy and also Master of Wards.[31] Essex was an older boy in this household, but he seems to have formed permanent friendships with three earls in particular who had all sat with him at Cecil's table. They were Henry Wriothesly, 3rd Earl of Southampton; Roger Manners, 5th Earl of Rutland; and Edward Russell, 3rd Earl of Bedford. Two of them, Rutland and Southampton, would, in the end, ride with Essex in 1601 at the head of his two hundred men in the ill-conceived attempt at a coup. But prior to this disaster Rutland had married, in 1599, Sir Philip Sidney's daughter, Elizabeth, whose mother was now Essex's wife. In the same year, the young Earl of Southampton, secretly, and without the Crown's permission, had married Elizabeth Vernon, the Earl of Essex's first cousin. Further, Southampton's first child was named Penelope, presumably after Essex's sister, Penelope Rich, the "Stella" of Sidney's sonnets.

It was Southampton, serving with Essex in Ireland, who seems to have been closest to Essex, and these two were the earls most severely punished for the uprising in 1601. While Essex was beheaded, Southampton was granted some leniency. Although his earldom was attainted and he was sent to the Tower, presumably until death, he was at least permitted to live. The other earls in Essex's circle, Rutland and Bedford, were judged to have involved themselves in the conspiracy for Southampton's sake only and thereby escaped the Tower, but they were forced to pay brutally heavy fines: £30,000 for Rutland and £20,000 for Bedford.[32]

Other nobles were connected to the Essex group in various ways. For example, Charles Blount, Lord Mountjoy, as is well known, was the lover of Essex's sister Penelope, Lady Rich, who bore several of Mountjoy's children while still married to Lord Rich. Another noble, Sir Robert Sidney, was Sir Philip Sidney's brother and had long corresponded with Essex, who supported him for the Lord Chamberlainship in the 1590s. Also the brother of Mary Sidney Herbert, Countess of Pembroke, Robert was thus the uncle of her son William, the young Earl of Pembroke, who after 1615 would himself become James's Lord Chamberlain.

At the time of the accession, the most visible symbol of the Essex group and remnant of the previous reign was the young Earl of Southampton in the Tower. With his title attainted and all his possessions seized by the Crown, Southampton, even before Elizabeth's death, had written to King James in Scotland with the consequence that Southampton's case became a topic of discussion in the secret correspondence. Edward Bruce, Abbot of Kinloss ("8") commented on the matter to Henry Lord Howard:

> The earl of Southampton has written to 30 [James] an earnest letter for a warrant of his liberty immediately upon 24 [Queen Elizabeth's] death, which 30 refuses to grant without consent and authority of the [Privy] Council, and what they advise him to do shall be performed with diligence. It is enjoined to you by 30 to speak with 10 [Robert Cecil] and if he find it expedient to enlarge him and that his present [immediate] service may be of any use in the state, he shall be content and assents he be presently [immediately] relieved: otherwise to let him stay till further resolutions be taken for the best course in his business. (Bruce, p. 51)

Responding with characteristic care, James had obviously conditioned his assent on that of the Privy Council of England. It is important to note, however, that elsewhere he showed a definite leaning towards the *idea* of granting relief to Southampton (whom he had never met). For in another secret letter several months before Elizabeth's death, James responded to Northampton's comments on persons faring poorly under Elizabeth, writing:

> Your observing of their names in particular puts me in mind of one of them, poor Southampton, who lives in hardest case of any of them, and if in any sort your means may help to procure him farther liberty or easier ward, pity would provoke me to recommend it unto you. (Bruce, p. 71).

Again the prudence: the request is merely that Southampton be permitted to walk about the Tower grounds more extensively or perhaps to be confined elsewhere. Nevertheless, Southampton's membership in a circle associated with Sir Philip Sidney, for whose death James had written two sonnets, may have been a factor in James's concern. And since Essex had claimed to support James as England's future monarch, James may also have felt he owed Essex (whom James had already mystified as his "martyr") a debt that should be ostentatiously repaid.

Whatever his primary motive, James made Southampton's release one of the earliest official acts at his accession (24 March 1603); the release was ordered on 5 April, along with that of Sir Henry Neville, another member of the Essex conspiracy, even before the King arrived in London (and more than a month before the appearance of a patent for a group of London actors as "The King's Servants").[33] Five Privy Councilors, writing to the King on 10 April about various matters, indicated that the Southampton order had been attended to. Thus, in early April, Henry Wriothesly—technically he was no longer "Southampton"—was free to walk the streets, but still with no home to call his own.[34] It is no wonder then that before reuniting himself with his family, Southampton rode north to meet King James still in progress from Scotland.

On other fronts as well, King James was beginning to publicly elaborate this kindly attitude towards the Essex conspirators and their friends. For several months prior to the accession, Charles Blount, Lord Mountjoy, had secretly corresponded with James to assure him that Essex would indeed support James's claim to the English throne.[35] As Essex's successor in Ireland, Mountjoy in December 1602 had effected the surrender of Tyrone who subsequently acknowledged James as the new King of Ireland. James's response as English king to Mountjoy's initiative was swift: as early as 26 April 1603, he made Mountjoy one of the new Privy Councilors and summoned him home with honor on 26 May.[36]

Four days earlier, on 22 April, James had extended himself to other members of the Essex group, when in his progress south he stopped at Belvoir Castle where he was entertained by Roger Manners, Earl of Rutland, and his wife Elizabeth, daughter of James's youthful ideal, Sir Philip Sidney. Later in the day, James dined at Exton with Sir John Harington, father of the Countess of Bedford, whose husband had ridden in the Essex uprising. He then moved on to spend the night and Easter Sunday at Harington's other house, Burleigh-on-Hill.[37]

This particular visit not only attests to James's self-conscious cultivation of nobles in the Essex group, but also to the mode by which he continually delineated boundaries in his relationships with appropriate members of the peerage. For it was at Burleigh, we recall, that James instructed one of his *political* confidants, Henry Lord

Howard, to inform his nephew, Lord Howard of Walden, of his permanent appointment as Lord Chamberlain. That evening, after this crucial piece of business had been attended to, James gave audience to only two visitors. According to Sir Thomas Lake, James's traveling secretary, in correspondence with Cecil for the King, there "came hither my Lord of Southampton and my Lord of Pembroke, and have been well used" (*Hatfield,* 15.58).

The young Earl of Pembroke, in association with Southampton, was, in fact, to form the core of a new royal circle, distinct from the protective iron band of James's political associates, and in this case well represented by Essex-related nobles. This new group would be composed of younger men, English and Scots, whom James seems to have cultivated, to put it simply, because it pleased him to do so. Significantly, however, James was extremely slow to bestow on such nobles any formal political power, although he did require their company in the alternative lifestyle he subsequently developed in England—a lifestyle marked by the practice of hunting deer and living quasi-rustically at his lodges away from the London area, such as Royston and Newmarket. These younger men, sometimes members of the Bed Chamber, sometimes not (those in the Bed Chamber were at that time generally Scots who did not have baronies or earldoms), were treated as favorites long before Somerset and Buckingham would redefine what a "favorite" could finally attain to.[38]

As the nephew of Sir Philip Sidney and son of the learned editor of the *Arcadia,* as a friend of the Haringtons (he had spent Christmas at Burleigh with members of the Essex group and with his uncle Sir Robert Sidney), and as an attractive, well-titled, and rich twenty-three-year-old earl, William Pembroke obviously interested James early on. On 28 April, only four days after Pembroke had come with the thankful Southampton to Burleigh to meet King James, he was in London to participate in Elizabeth's funeral, bearing, by James's decree, the great banner, assisted by the Earl of Nottingham's son, Lord Howard of Effingham.[39]

Thereafter both Southampton and Pembroke were the recipients of much largesse,[40] and perhaps it was James's treatment of them that gave rise to the speculation by the Venetian ambassador that the King might be intending to pardon all nobles who had been punished for any offenses at all against the late Queen, Pembroke himself having incurred Elizabeth's anger.[41] But James evidently confined himself to a strategic program that combined personal pleasure with political symbology—the cultivation of young favorites with the honoring of the group associated with Sir Philip Sidney and then the Earl of Essex. On 17 May James made both Southampton and Pembroke Gentlemen of the King's Privy Chamber, a position they eventually shared with more than twenty others. These Gentlemen, while lacking the intimate access of the (primarily Scottish) Bed Chamber, had important privileges: a warrant of this same year, 1603, illustrates their access to the King.[42] According to this warrant, only members of the Privy Council and those sworn to the Privy Chamber were to be admitted there—

> Always provided that if any nobleman or gentleman of quality shall desire at any time to speak to the King, the King shall be acquainted therewith by some sworn to his Chamber [i.e., a Gentlemen of the Privy Chamber], and he will thereupon assign a time for audience.[43]

In according further favor to these two earls, James, having earlier given Henry Wriothesly his physical freedom, conferred on him an official Grant of Pardon and Restitution on May 16, thus returning Southampton his title and all his confiscated property. One week later, the King dined in great state, and his carver was, significantly, this same one-time leader, with Essex, of the uprising against Queen Elizabeth.[44] Pembroke, on the other hand, required less aid than Southampton. Young, single, and with few pressing responsibilities, he was now the owner of Wilton although his mother still resided there. James sojourned to Wilton often, and even made it the temporary royal court during the autumn of 1603 when plague gripped London.[45]

Pembroke and Southampton—about ten years apart in age, but joint heirs of the Sidney-Essex legacy—serve as important indicators of James's public posture regarding the Essex-Sidney faction, a posture emphasized in an extremely significant incident that occurred soon after James's first meeting with the two young earls. As the Venetian ambassador wrote to the Doge,

> On his journey his Majesty meantime has destined to great reward the Earl of Southampton and Sir Henry Neville, as I have informed you, and also others, and has received the twelve-year-old son of the Earl of Essex and taken him in his arms and kissed him, openly and loudly declaring him the son of the most noble knight that English land had ever begotten. He has appointed the lad to bear the sword before him on his entry into the city [London], and has destined him to be the eternal companion of his eldest son, the Prince of Wales. (*SPV*, 10:26)

Finally, an even more emphatic and emblematic act occurring in the early summer of 1603 at the annual Feast of the Order of the Garter, held on 2 July, epitomizes James's approach to the political affiliations through which he shaped the ceremonies of his accession. To be inducted as a Knight of the Garter was a significant honor vied for by the most prestigious members of the nobility. Controlled by the Crown, membership never rose above twenty-four, the number of the spaces in the Chapel of St. George at Windsor vacated only at the death of the incumbents (whose names still decorate their individual stalls today).

Six persons were inducted into the Order in the first Feast of King James's reign. First, of course, was James himself, in a private and elaborate ceremony. Next, *in absentia*, was the King of Denmark, Queen Anna's brother. Next, the Duke of Lennox, the ranking noble of both kingdoms as the only duke, cousin to the King, and the peer nearest to the throne in succession during the minority of the two very young princes. Just as significantly, the fourth new Knight of the Garter was the Earl of Mar—so trustworthy that his family hereditarily served as the guardians of the Scottish heir apparent. In such a context, then, the filling of the two remaining vacancies was eloquent statement. And the last two new Knights of the Garter were English: Southampton and Pembroke, as James simultaneously saluted Essex, Sidney, and the new possessors of two long-standing English earldoms.[46]

The foregoing account of James's very early political acumen in England represents only a fragment of the material that could be invoked by a revisionist historian to discredit the notion of an irresponsible and self-absorbed James and to create a counterimage—that of a King with energy and interests appropriate to the record of his accomplishments. Nonetheless, I hope I have suggested on a small scale James's skill in political maneuvering, particularly his ability to separate the substantive from the symbolic—to consolidate power at the same time that he engaged in public acts which defined his monarchal style. Whatever James's faults and vulnerabilities as a ruler (for I certainly do not mean to imply that he had none), and however much they may have worsened in his later years, his political disposition in 1603, at age 37, seems seasoned, sophisticated, and engaged.

Any urging of James's early skills as ruler, however, cannot omit reference to a particular activity which to many commentators has seemed to epitomize his supposed sloth in this sphere, that is, his absorption in the hunt. Indeed, early in his English reign James began locating himself whenever possible at one of several hunting lodges where he would be found for much of his reign. But when "hunting" James observed not a slothful but a demanding routine. He rose before five in the morning and was on horseback until the early afternoon when he returned to his residential quarters to rest and to deal with whatever state affairs required his direct attention. Hardly in fugue or attempting to avoid responsibility, he could assume the presence in London of certain very industrious and judicious nobles, the members of his inner political circle. This group featured, as we have seen, English lords such as Robert Cecil, Earl of Salisbury, Principal Secretary; Henry Howard Earl of Northampton, Lord Treasurer; and Thomas Howard, Earl of Suffolk, Lord Chamberlain; but for James it was also undergirded by the Scots inner circle of Esmé Stuart, Duke of Lennox; George Home, Earl of Dunbar; and Thomas Erskine, Lord Fenton, Captain of the Guard. Additionally, the Earl of Mar, a deeply trusted intimate, provided on-site supervision of Scotland and was in regular correspondence with both Fenton and Northampton.[47]

With such men—perhaps venial but certainly loyal and effective—in place, and with Salisbury working with a Privy Council much enlarged (and diluted) from that of Elizabeth's day, James received in his rural retreats regular packets that kept him abreast of affairs, responding as necessary to Cecil's occasional requests for his presence in London beyond routine annual appearances.[48] Thus the following letter of December 1610 to Cecil from his lodge at Royston is not atypical—here I am interested less in the specific situation than in the evidence of James's concern with maintaining the lines of regnal communication.

> As for this particular that troubleth you, it is true that the first night of Lake's coming to Royston, he did broadly and roundly inform me that ye had told him that there was a worse thing in head than anything whereof ye had advertised me, which was that ye had intelligence that, if the Lower House had met again, one had made a motion for a petition to be made unto me that I would be pleased to send home the Scots if I look for any supply from them. But the next morning, when I urged him to repeat the words again, he minced it in those terms as ye now have it under his hand, which yet is directly contrary to that which ye affirm in your letter. (*Hatfield,* 21:265)[49]

The king often, of course, sent his commands through his officials. Thus, on 8 March 1605, the Earl of Worcester, James's Master of the Horse, writing to Cecil from Thetford, describes James's attention to his duties as well as the problems of his officials who were not, perhaps, so rurally inclined as was their king.

> I enclose the sweet and comfortable fruit of his Majesty's own garden. He willed me to say that when he sat last among you he took on him the office of attorney with the gentlemen then convened, so now he has done the same in writing "postels" upon the copy of Bywater's sweet and charitable collections. His Majesty has sent you by the Duke of Lennox the letters from France, wherein he notes both the King and the Queen with Rosny give him the style of "King of England, Scotland, &c." but the Duke of Guise writes him "King of the Isle of Great Britain." He begins his journey homewards on Tuesday next. He will stay three days at Newmarket and four at Royston. And then I hope to the wished land of two months' rest. (*Hatfield,* 17:88–89)

Relevant to our sense of James's engagement, small details interestingly intermingled with larger ones. Thus on 22 February 1608, Sir Thomas Lake, who often, as we have seen, wrote Cecil for James, sent the following missive from "court at Royston":

> Your packet came about 6 this morning, so I had time to cause some of the letters for alehouses to be made ready before his Majesty's going. Herewith you shall receive six of them. The rest shall be done at Newmarket. I have sent also the two bills and the commission for exemption from juries, concerning which it is to good purpose that which you have written by way of caution; for it was the first news I had at my arrival here, that one came to me in the name of himself and one of his fellows to show me a motion they intended for his Majesty which was for the benefit of thirty of those exemptions. Upon reading of your letters by his Majesty I had a just occasion to tell him of it; but your letter has armed him.
>
> His Majesty willed me also to signify that he is desirous to hear of the success [outcome] of the matter of the fines in the King's Bench, or what the impediment is why it is not put to a point; for except there be any greater [impediment] than he has yet heard, he thinks it should not stay [delay]. (*Hatfield,* 20:79)

This is the description of a king at a hunting lodge, but hardly of a king mesmerized by hunting.

If the activities alluded to so far suggest James's inclination to rule intelligently, albeit in his own style, how does this portrait connect to the question of his relationship to the arts? In the first place, it argues that if James was interested in the arts at all, it was not as a function of his ineptness as ruler. But what of the other issue introduced at the outset of this essay—that is, the influence of James's intellectual interests on court culture? As I suggested earlier, the caricature of James as a lazy and politically indifferent monarch has implicitly reinforced the notion of his supposed interest in the arts, creating, as it were, a critical expectation that the King's influence is to be found at the center of early Stuart artistic achievement. James's putative involvement with Shakespeare's acting company when they became "the King's Servants," Ben Johnson's continual references to him in the poet's many court masques, and James's own publication of a book of poetry are often cited as evidence for this view.

I've argued elsewhere that the designation of Shakespeare's company as "The King's Servants" need not have involved King James directly; indeed, it seems far more likely that this patronage was effected through the efforts of other members of the peerage. More relevant to the immediate context, my own recently published study of Anna of Denmark seeks to demonstrate that it was James's Queen Consort and her own court (comprised primarily of nobility from the Essex circle) that developed the Stuart masque and that constituted the primary network of patronage for the leading poets and dramatists of the time.[50] Thus if any royal figure is to be associated with the artistic productions for which the first decade of the Stuart reign is now primarily valued, it is probably not James who should be cited, but Anna. Any reconstruction of Anna as a powerful presence at court, however, need not deny James his own sphere of influence in the intellectual life of the time. Indeed, for this reason, it seems of great importance to distinguish between the *kinds* of pursuits that engaged James and Anna, and thus between the cultural imprints that each might have made during the reign.

While James's intellectual interests can hardly be denied, the term "intellectual," even as it implies curiosity and erudition, need not involve the arts. Indeed, there is little evidence that James had any nurturing interest in painting, sculpture, architecture, music or what we might term *belles lettres.* Certainly as a young man James wrote verses and, in 1589, he even essayed a short masque for the wedding of the Earl of Huntley to Ludovick Stuart's sister.[51] Moreover, during the last twenty years of his life he continued to write poems from time to time—for example, on the occasion of Anna's death in 1619.

Nonetheless, it does not appear that King James had a serious or abiding interest in verse. Even those poems James wrote after the 1580s demonstrate his interest in examining political and social issues rather than in emulating the verse achievement of the English Renaissance. Verses in this vein include, for example, several sonnets, one in Latin, on the Danish astronomer Tycho Brahe whom James met in Denmark after his marriage to Anna in 1589, and his *Lepanto,* printed in 1590. Both poetical exercises underscore James's concern with politics and in the natural world, apparent in his prose writings. Thus the verses of *Lepanto* demonstrate his lifelong concern with the strategic importance of Venice as a dominant power in the Mediterranean, while the sonnets on Brahe represent James's reactions to Brahe's sophisticated laboratory-building-observatory and the work that was going forward there under the most famous astronomer in Europe. Indeed, this admiration of Tycho Brahe may stand in instructive contrast to James's unremitting hostility to the widely admired Edmund Spenser for verses the King construed as directed against his mother, even though most English writers of the time admired Spenser as preeminent among poets (see n. 28).

James's imagination seems to have been stimulated not only by such ideas as governance and astronomical science, but also by theological distinctions.[52] Further, he was, as is well known, intrigued by what one might call, for want of appropriate early modern terms, abnormal psychology and by zoology.[53] In fact, it might be generalized that if James paid attention to high cultural product at all, it was to individual instances of such product that held immediate relevance to one or another of his own interests. James's fascination with Venice and its constitution, (adumbrated by his writing of the *Lepanto*), is an emphatic example. The ambassadorial missives of the Venetian emissaries in London consistently noted the king's curiosity about and copious knowledge of that Italian city-state. Thus it is noteworthy that one of Shakespeare's first new plays presented at the new court was the Venice-oriented *Othello,* performed during the Christmas season of 1604–5, and featuring a Venetian victory over the Turks—the subject of the *Lepanto.*

But this Christmas season at court provides even more telling evidence of James's special interests than does *Othello.* Neither this play, nor *Measure for Measure,* written, many critics suggest, to cater to James's tastes, won from him any special attention at all. Rather, it was an old play that attracted the king. Among all the dramas performed during these 1604 holiday festivities—*Othello, Merry Wives of Windsor, Measure for Measure, Comedy of Errors, Love's Labor's Lost, Henry V, Every Man Out of His Humor, Every*

Man in His Humor, and *The Merchant of Venice*—it was only *The Merchant of Venice* that James demonstrably reacted to. He specifically ordered the play repeated—and the very next time the company performed before him, two days later. Thus presumably something in that comedy—Venice? the trial scene and legal conundrums raised by Shylock and Portia?—engaged James's interest beyond the patriotic appeals of *HenryV,* the newness of *Othello* and *Measure for Measure,* or the sophistication of *Love's Labors Lost* and *Every Man Out.*[54]

If, in fact, James can be described as having any taste for dramatic literature, his reaction to *The Merchant of Venice,* taken together with his responses eleven years later, in 1615, to plays he saw when visiting Cambridge, may suggest the nature of that taste. To honor the King's visit to the university, Cambridge provided disputations in divinity, law, philosophy, and "phisicke," all of which James attended and listened to carefully. In addition, Latin plays were written and presented by the members of the various colleges. On this occasion, John Chamberlain, who was present, wrote Dudley Carleton that "the King was exceedingly pleased many times both at the plays and at the disputations, for I had the hap to be for the most time within hearing, and often at his heels he would express as much" (Chamberlain 1.587–88). Thus, on the first night the students at St. John's presented Edward Cecil's *Aemelia* (now lost); on the second night Clare Hall gave George Ruggle's longish *Ignoramus,* a play that satirized lawyers; on the third night the students at Trinity College acted Thomas Tomkis's *Albumazar;* and on the fourth evening, Samuel Brooke's Latin pastoral *Melanthe* concluded these entertainments.

Interestingly, James particularly favored two of these plays (as he had favored *Merchant of Venice*). A few days after the King had returned from Cambridge to his court, Chamberlain wrote:

> The King hath a meaning and speaks much of it to go again privately to Cambridge to see two of the plays, and hath appointed the time about the 27th of the next month: but it is not likely he will continue in that mind, for of late he hath made a motion to have the actors come hither. (*Chamberlain,* 2:591)

But, as it happened, James did choose to return to Cambridge in May "to see the play *Ignoramus*" and, I think, perhaps also *Melanthe,* if he saw, as he purposed, two plays.[55] During this return visit, he also heard Latin disputations once again (*Chamberlain,* 2.598), so it would seem that Latin disputations and Latin comedies, artistic fare perhaps more readily associated with the previous half-century, were the chief sources of the King's own pleasure on this Cambridge occasion. As for James's attraction to the genre of drama, we must deal with the fact that, as far as can be determined, Shakespeare's *Merchant of Venice* and Ruggles's *Ignoramus* share the distinction of being the only plays known to have been seen *twice* by King James—and at his command. Thus, James is clearly not to be found among those that favored the cutting edge of dramatic achievement in his time, *Merchant* having been printed five years before James's accession. Rather, in the case of *Merchant*, Venice and "law" may have been the attraction—topics that elsewhere seem to have interested the King to greater or lesser degree all his life. Similarly, questions of law and issues of disputation seem to be the link between the two Cambridge plays he most enjoyed—as is well known, *Ignoramus* was a farcical satire on lawyers.

If indeed "drama" had special meaning for the King, it did so in terms of his own agendas—though now we do not deal with stage plays. Rather, one might think of several well-known incidents offstage that seem to have engaged James closely. Take, for example, his responses to the Hampton Court Conference which he convened very early in his reign (14 January 1604) and during which he often reproved Puritan prelates for making quite radical suggestions about the administration of religion in England.[56] Writing confidentially to Henry Lord Howard after the close of the Conference, James described the experience as follows: "We have kept such a revel with the Puritans here these two days as was never heard the like, where I have peppered them as soundly as ye have the Papists there."[57] Because "revel" ordinarily described festivities and entertainments at court during the holiday season, it is significant that James playfully used the word to convey his sense of entertainment in dealing with those advocates of the Puritan religious position who were allowed to attend the second day of the Hampton Court Conference. Since the Conference was held during the winter holidays, James presumably regarded this activity as his true "revels," despite the fact that he had watched a number of plays by the London companies to which he seems to have been indifferent.[58]

In 1606, a more dramatic situation, the Gunpowder Plot, drew James to another spectacle, the one-day trial of Henry Garnet, Provincial of all Jesuits in England. John Chamberlain noted that the trial "lasted from eight in the morning till seven at night. The King was there privately and held it out all day" (1:220). Presumably James was attracted to the theoretical issues (and drama) raised by Garnet's intellectual positions. Thus when Garnet was given the opportunity to speak and he embarked on the well-known defense of the concept of equivocation that caused a sensation at the time, the Venetian ambassador claimed the speech shocked the court officials—and also the king "who is particularly versed in such matters."[59]

Perhaps, in the end, most relevant to James's own sense of "theater"—separate from his *realpolitik*—was his sense of himself, in his regal role, as a kind of Solomon. If he was at all drawn to acting, it was to the role of transcendent Judge/King, master of equity and religious and secular law. An incident in 1618 provides a cogent example of this histrionic James who was not necessarily, I think, following here his well-known observation in the *Basilikon Doron* that kings were, in some sense, like actors in a theater. Different impulses seem to have been in play in this case of the trial of Lady Roos. Daughter of James's frequent spokesman, Sir Thomas Lake, she was accused of "precontracts, adultery, incest, murder, poison" against her husband, William Cecil Lord Roos. As part of the litigation, Sir Thomas Lake and his wife put in a bill in Star Chamber against their son-in-law while, on the other side, the Earl of Exeter, who was defending Roos, put in a bill on his behalf. James himself decided to be the judge in this case, adjudicating the trial in Star Chamber beginning from 9 A.M. to noon on the first day and from 8 A.M. to 1 P.M. the next. John Chamberlain remarked during this event that James

> made a short speech the first day in which among other things he compared himself to Solomon that was to judge between two women (for so he said he would parallel them as women) and to find out the true mother of the child (that is, verity). He sits again on Monday, and then Wednesday.[60]

Such, I think, was James's notion of court recreation (perhaps unwittingly—or wittingly?—suggested much earlier, in 1604, through the Duke in *Measure for Measure*). For more leisurely moments, James evidently insisted on the vigorous activity of hunting on horseback—insisted to such an extent that he defined it (as opposed, say, to drama) as his "solace," that is, as the activity that recreated him and, it might also be speculated, was necessary to his physical and psychological well-being. At least before Cecil's death in 1612, James's sojourns in the country were clearly not viewed by him or his counselors as holiday trips. They represented a preferred locale of living and mode of governing by proxy, punctuated by necessary visits to the London area. This was a style of life obviously not conducive to ongoing involvement with artistic ambiences at court.

If we reconsider James's interest in the arts, then, we might conclude that the King's recreations and aesthetic pleasures were identifiable in the way he chose to lead his life. Certainly he was not dependent for such satisfactions on the productions of London poets and dramatists destined, ironically enough, for a greatness that would enhance James's own reputation in cultural history. Although in other spheres of activity James's intellectual legacy was considerable—including his organization of a remarkable translation of the Bible and a number of important writings on kingship and religion—he does not appear to have been a patron of poetry, painting, music or drama.[61] Put simply, James did not live an arts-centered life. For the royal patronage of the arts during the first half of James's reign we must, as I have argued elsewhere, look to his consort, Anna of Denmark.

Notes

1. See *Politics, Plague, and Shakespeare's Theater: The Stuart Years* (Ithaca, N.Y.: Cornell University Press, 1991), 32–41.

2. For representative attitudes about James I and his court in England, see D. H. Willson, *James VI and I* (London: Jonathan Cape, 1956), pp. 191ff.; David Mathew, *James I* (London: Eyre and Spottiswoode, 1967), 8.

3. Early examples of this revision are Jenny Wormald, "James VI and I: Two Kings or One?" *History* 68 (1983), 187–209, and Maurice Lee, Jr., *Great Britain's Solomon* (Urbana: University of Illinois Press, 1990). Martin Butler alludes to more recent work along this line in "The Invention of Britain and the Early Stuart Masque," in *The Stuart Courts and Europe*, ed. R. Malcolm Smuts (Cambridge: Cambridge University Press, 1996), 65–85 n. 5. Most recently Goodare and Lynch, in their introduction to *The Reign of James VI* (East Linton: The Tuckwell Press, 2000), 1–31 illustrate the current general view of the king among historians.

4. See Jennifer M. Brown, "Scottish Politics 1567–1625" in *The Reign of James VI and I*, ed. Alan G. R. Smith (London: Macmillan, 1973), 22–40 and Keith M. Brown, *Bloodfeud in Scotland 1573–1625* (Edinburgh: John Donald, 1986), 107–44.

5. See Francis Stewart, "The Fifth Earl of Bothwell and Perception Politics" in *Freedom and Authority*, ed. Jerry Brotherstone and David Ditchburn (East Linten: The Tuckwell Press, 2000), 155–65.

6. For initiatives taken by the Kirk, see, for example, *The Register of the Privy Council of Scotland,* ed. David Masson (Edinburgh: HMGRH, 1884), 6.42–42. Such matters have recently been pursued by John Morrill, "A British Patriarchy? Ecclesiastical Imperialism under the Early Stuarts," in *Religion, Culture and Society in Early Modern Britain,* ed. Anthony Fletcher and Peter Roberts (Cambridge: Cambridge University Press, 1994), 201–37.

7. R. Malcolm Smuts, for instance, contributes a fine analysis of "Early Stuart court culture" to *Court Culture and the Origins of a Royalist Tradition in Early Stuart England* (Philadelphia: University of Pennsylvania Press, 1987), but his time frame extends no farther back than 1610. In twenty-six chapters on James's English reign, Mathew has already reached the 1612 death of Robert Cecil by chapter 8.

8. See for example, G. P. V. Akrigg, *Jacobean Pageant* (Cambridge, Mass.: Harvard University Press, 1962), Chapter 14.

9. As the Venetian ambassador observed (in another context): "The Earl [of Northumberland] had been as it were banished from court because his estates on the borders of Scotland were so great, and because the Queen had some suspicions of those secret intelligences with the King of Scotland, which is now apparent" (*SPV,* 10:17). For more recent discussion of Northumberland's role and motives here, see Mark Nicholls, "The 'Wizard Earl' in Star Chamber" *The Historical Journal* 30 (1987), 173–89, esp. 174–75 and nn.

10. This was a post Cobham had vied with Essex to obtain. The Cinque Ports were situated on the southeast coast of England. The Warden had continuous jurisdiction from Seaford in Sussex to Birchington over the five ancient ports of Hastings, Sandwich, Dover, Romney, and Hithe—places which often saw Shakespeare and his fellows, or other acting companies when they were on tour, as well as over a number of other towns added to the original group. For foreign comment, and for a description of the port traffic controls themselves, see W. B. Rye, *England as Seen by Foreigners* (London: John Russell Smith, 1865), 14. Henry Cuff, secretary to the Earl of Essex, had referred to the "Cinq Portes" as "the keys of the realm" (Bruce 82). For a vignette of the passport problems encountered in 1608 by the Duke of Württemberg trying to return from England to the continent, see *Hatfield,* 20:241–42. One gathers, for example, that a shipmaster could be penalized £20 (a year's living for a grammar master) for each person carried from England without passport.

11. Sir Robert Carey, brother of the ailing 2nd Lord Hunsdon, had raced north to be the first to tell James that Queen Elizabeth was dead and that James had been declared king of England, but his authority was angrily repudiated by the Privy Council writing at 10 P.M. on 24 March. The same letter designated Percy and Somerset as the official messengers. See David Calderwood, *History of the Kirk of Scotland,* ed. Thomas Thomson (Edinburgh: Woodrow Society, 1844), 6:206–9. Carey was blundering into an otherwise systematic removal of obstacles to James's peaceful accession, a process noted in the letter of the French ambassador Marin Cavali to the Doge of Venice and to the Senate in *SPV,* 15:43. Among other activities, Robert Cecil "stayed the journey of the Captain of the Guard [Sir Walter Raleigh]" who was in process of conducting many suitors north to the King on 9 April. See *SPD,* 8:2.

12. For a closer study of Cecil's role in these matters, see Pauline Croft, "Can a Bureaucrat be a Favorite?: Robert Cecil and the Strategies of Power" in *The World of the Favorite,* ed. J. H. Elliott and L. W. B Brockliss (New Haven: Yale University

Press, 1999), 81–95. Maurice Lee, 106–7 has also commented on the smooth transition to England as an indication of James's political abilities.

13. From this and later conversations it was decided that the date of the coronation should be King James's name day (i.e., St. James Day, 25 July). Queen Anna's itinerary south was also worked out, a place being established as the rendezvous point for the new queen and the English party of ladies and lords which the Privy Council decided should journey north to meet her. These Ladies of Queen Elizabeth's Bed Chamber and Privy Chamber were released from their ceremonial attendance upon the body of Queen Elizabeth following her funeral on 28 April. See *Hatfield,* 15:49, 52–53.

14. Among his other duties, the Lord Chamberlain made the arrangements for the royal progresses—such as the one going on now from Scotland; he received ambassadors and conducted them into the Royal Presence, and he was ultimately responsible for all ceremony and entertainment, such as the performance of plays at court during the holidays. The Master of the Revels reported to the Lord Chamberlain. See references cited by E. K. Chambers, *The Elizabethan Stage* (Oxford: Clarendon Press, 1923), 1.36–42 *(ES),* and Barroll in *The Revels History of Drama in English,* ed. Clifford Leech and T. W. Craik (London: Methuen, 1975), 3:1, "Drama and the Court." For the court situation in general as it related to this office, see Wright and Cuddy in David Starkey et al., *The English Court* (London, 1987), 147–72; 173–225.

15. James's decision came sooner than indicated in the excellent minibiography of Howard of Walden in *The Dictionary of National Biography.*

16. Students of Shakespeare may wish to remind themselves that the patron of his company, the 2nd Lord Hunsdon, had been quite ill for over a year and would die shortly. Thomas Lord Howard had been assisting him in the interim and thus any presumed influence the acting company had over the Master of the Revels, a servant of the Lord Chamberlain, may well have ended a year prior to Elizabeth's death.

17. Lord Thomas had enjoyed a distinguished naval career, serving against the Spanish Armada in 1588 when he was knighted at sea by the Lord High Admiral, the future Earl of Nottingham, serving in the Azores as commander of the famous *Sir Richard Grenville,* and also serving at Cadiz.

18. See *Original Letters,* ed. Henry Ellis [First Series] (London: 1824), 3:66–67, and *Hatfield,* 15:58.

19. Northampton's influence has been extensively studied by Linda Levy Peck in *Northampton: Patronage and Politics at the Court of James I* (London: 1982) and "The Mentality of a Jacobean Grandee" in *The Mental World of the Jacobean Court* (Cambridge: Cambridge University Press, 1991), 148–68.

20. The new Lord Chamberlain seems to have been aware as early as 14 May 1603 that the attainder of his nephew's earldom would be revoked because he and his wife were then checking out exactly what lands were lost by the attainders of the Duke of Norfolk and the Earl of Arundel. See *Report on MSS in Various Collections* (London: HMSO, 1903), 2:249.

21. Suffolk and Northampton proved to be powerful political figures at the early court while the young Earl of Arundel, heir to his bachelor great-uncle Northampton's substantial fortune, would become prominent in the politics and culture of the latter part of James's reign.

22. Willson adopts this patronizing attitude: see p. 274. However, records of

James's Scottish years sufficiently attest to the real dangers he experienced: see, e.g., *SPS*, 11:96–97; 166.

23. For opposition to Ralegh in the secret correspondence see Bruce, pp. 18–19. Ralegh was summoned to the Privy Council on 8 May and relieved of his office then: see *Acts of the Privy Council of England,* ed. J. R. Dasent et al. (London: HMSO, 1890–), 32:498. But this dismissal was anticipated by 28 April, or even earlier, for Cobham had a bitter argument with Cecil about the matter. See *Hatfield,* 15:61, and John Manningham, *Diary,* ed. R. P. Sorlien (Hanover, N.H.: University of Rhode Island. 1976), 224.

24. Erskine became Viscount Fenton in March 1606 (see *Peerage,* 5.294) and a Privy Councilor on 31 January 1611; see John Stow, *Annals* (London, 1615), sig.4G6 (p. 910).

25. When James left Edinburgh for London his choice of retinue, as Meikle writes, "reflected a carefully considered balance of power between the lairds and nobility." She mentions the Duke of Lennox, the earls of Mar, Moray, and Argyll, the lords Home and Roxburgh together with the secretary James Elphinston [brother of Lord Elphinston], the comptroller (Gospertie), and the gentlemen of his Bed Chamber. See Maureen M. Meikle, "The Invisible Divide: The Greater Lairds and the Nobility of Jacobean Scotland," *Scottish Historical Review* 71 (1992), 70–87. It should be added that Elphinston and Home were the only Catholics in this group (see John Colville's "Catalogue of the Scottis Nobilitie" in John Colville, *The Original Letters of Sir John Colville,* ed. Thomas Thomson (Edinburgh: The Bannatyne Club, 1858), 350–54. For a discussion of the duties of particular Scottish nobles in England during the time of the accession, and for several additional names, see Maurice Lee, Jr., *Great Britain's Soloman* (Urbana: University of Illinois Press, 1990), 108–10.

26. *Hatfield,* 15:100–101. James had operated with the Scottish Privy Council in a similar manner in 1598 so that when he went south in 1603, that Council lost much of its impact. (See Meikle, 83).

27. The "old knave" is probably Sir Thomas Lake who often wrote letters from Royston telling Cecil how King James wished to deal with the particular problems.

28. This group also figured importantly in connection with Queen Anna: it included many of the nobles who comprised her court and who would later be instrumental in effecting the rise of Buckingham, the figure who dominated James's last years. See Barroll, *Anna of Denmark, Queen of England: A Cultural Biography* (Philadelphia: University of Pennsylvania Press, 2000), chapter 5.

29. James never met Sidney but communication probably passed between the Scottish king and Sir Philip by way of Patrick Gray, 6th Baron Gray of Scotland (known as the "Master of Gray"). Further, a report in 1599 describes King James commending Sidney as "the best and swetest wryter that ever he knewe—surely it seemeth he loved him muche." (Quoted in James I, *New Poems,* ed. Allan F. Westcott [New York: Colombia University Press, 1911], lxxix. See also 29 and 88–89 of this edition). Westcott speculates, interestingly, that James needed some poet to put up as a rival to Edmund Spenser whose *Faerie Queene* was so hostile to Mary Queen of Scots. But Sidney died in 1586 while the earliest evidence of James's displeasure with Spenser was recorded in November 1596, when the Scottish king identified "the second part of" *FQ* ("9th chapter") as offensive with respect to his mother. See *SPS,* 12:354, 359–70. Nevertheless, James's purpose in extolling Sidney may have been connected to his unsuccessful attempt to have Spenser prosecuted in England.

30. From "Polyhymnia" in *The Life and Minor Works of George Peele*, ed. David H. Horne (New Haven: Yale University Press, 1952), ll. 103–14.

31. See G. P. V. Akrigg, *Shakespeare and the Earl of Southampton* (Cambridge, Mass.: Harvard University Press, 1968), 23–31.

32. See John Chamberlain, *Letters*, ed. N. E. McClure, 2 vols. (Philadelphia: American Philosophical Society, 1939), 1:123. For the list of conspirators see *Calendar of the MSS of . . . the Marquis of Bath . . . at Longleat (Talbot, Dudley, and Devereux Papers, 1533–1639)*, ed. G. Dyfnallt Owen (London: HMSO, 1960), 5.231–82 (hereafter referred to as *Longleat MSS*).

33. See Charlotte C. Stopes, *The Life of Henry, Third Earl of Southampton* (Cambridge: Cambridge University Press, 1922), 259–60, which quotes the King's letter from Add.MS.33.051, f.53, *in extenso*.

34. See *SPD*, 9:2. See also *Chamberlain*, 1:192.

35. Mountjoy, as the head in Ireland of England's largest standing army, had to be treated with care, but he presented no problem—far from it. He had written to Sir George Carew from Ireland on 18 April: "If I shall stay here til all things be so settled that they will never break out again, God knoweth when I shall come over. . . . If I cannot get leave to come over now I shall despair for ever to be rid of this miserable country." He added: "I pray you let not the King see my last letter to our late Queen, for it is full of fustian." See *Calendar of Carew Manuscripts: 1603–74*, ed. J. S. Brewer and William Bullen (London: Master of the Rolls, 1873), 1–2. He perhaps referred to something like his letter to Queen Elizabeth (8 June 1600): "If I with all that I have may stop the gulf of these wars by throwing myself to be swallowed up therein, I shall die a happy and contented Curtius, and one gracious thought of yours thrown after me shall be more precious than all the jewels of the ladies of Rome; but while I live, O let me live in your favor" *Original Letters: 3rd Series*, ed. Ellis (London: 1846), 152–53.

36. See the essay on Mountjoy's life by Leslie Stephens in *DNB*, 2:702–5.

37. See John Nichols, *The Progresses . . . of James the First* (London: J. B. Nichols, 1828), 1.91–92 and Barroll, "The Court of the First Stuart Queen" in *The Mental World of the Jacobean Court*, ed. Linda Levy Peck (Cambridge: Cambridge University Press, 1991), 191–208.

38. Pembroke's younger brother Philip fits well what seems to have been the early prescription for a special favorite. The untitled Philip Herbert was made a member of the Bed Chamber in 1603; within two years, he was created both baron and earl.

39. See *Peerage*, 10.412. The position of the individual carrying the "great banner"—as we may gather from the funeral of Sir Philip Sidney—came just before that section of the long procession reserved for the coffin itself: first came the Great Banner, then the symbolic ornaments of the deceased (each ornament carried by one honored person), and then the coffin. See Thomas Lent, *Celebritas et Pompa Funeris* (London: 1587). For James's approach both to Queen Elizabeth's and to his mother's (re)burial, see Jennifer Woodward, *The Theatre of Death* (Woodbridge: the Boydell Press, 1997), Chapter 7. In designating Lord Howard of Effingham as Pembroke's assistant, James was presumably trying to balance the conferral of favors on two privileged groups. It was at the house of the elder Howard, the Lord Admiral, that James was proclaimed King of England by the peerage.

40. My argument here challenges the *DNB* discussion of Pembroke which follows the traditional view that King James "never loved or favored" the young earl. See 9.679.

41. He was sent to prison for a brief time by Queen Elizabeth for fathering Mary Fitton's child and then banished the court: see *DNB*, 9:679.

42. For a somewhat different approach to the question of James's favorites see Linda Levy Peck, "Monopolizing Favor: Structures of Power in the Early Seventeenth Century English Court" in *The World of the Favorite*, ed. J. H. Elliott and L. W. B. Brockliss (New Haven: Yale University Press, 1999), pp. 54–70.

43. For a recent discussion of the structure of the royal chambers beyond his earlier work, see Neill Cuddy "Reinventing a Monarchy: The Changing Structure and Political of the Stuart Court, 1603–88" in *The Stuart Courts,* ed. Eveline Cruickshanks (Sutton Publishing, 2000), 58–85.

44. Nonetheless, Southampton, over the years, did not advance at court as successfully as Pembroke. Presumably preoccupied during the first few years of James's reign with reclaiming his domain on the Isle of Wight and in reuniting himself with his wife and children, who had been housed by Penelope Rich and others during the confinement in the Tower, he continued to carry out quasi-military responsibilities including his hereditary duty of defending the Isle of Wight against foreign invaders. Although frequently found hunting with the King, he was more often at home than at court. Later, Southampton would be disappointed at lack of court advancement, especially in 1612 when Pembroke, but not he, was appointed to the Privy Council (*Chamberlain,* 1:352; 358–59).

45. For other instances of Pembroke's close relationship to James at this time, see Barroll, *Politics, Plague, and Shakespeare's Theatre* (Ithaca, N.Y.: Cornell University Press, 1991), 59–69.

46. Southampton had been nominated but not elected in 1593—see Philip Gawdy, *Letters,* ed. I. H. Jeayes (London: Roxburghe Club, 1906), p. 70. Robert Cecil, Henry Howard, and Thomas Lord Howard of Walden, members of James's influential political group, were not yet earls and thus unlikely candidates, but Cecil as Salisbury and Henry Howard as Northampton would be inducted into the Order by James at later dates.

47. See *Manuscripts of the Earl of Mar and Kellie,* ed. Henry Paton (London: HMC, 1904), 50–132. For a somewhat different recent view of the role of the hunt see Maurice Lee, 147–48; Arthur MacGregor, "The Household Out of Doors" in *The Stuart Courts,* 86–117.

48. Routine appearances were presumably the opening of Parliament on All Saints' Day, the ceremonial honoring of ambassadors extraordinary when this had a bearing on important or delicate foreign relations, and an indeterminate stay at Whitehall or Hampton Court for Christmas through Twelfth Night and then again for the beginning of Lent. Among unique circumstances were such occasions as the signing of the Spanish peace in 1604.

49. For examples of James's administration between 1604 and 1612 from such hunting locales as Royston, Newmarket, and Thetford, see *Hatfield,* 17:72, 89; 18:129; 19:360–61; 20:79; 21:142–43, 262–63; *SPV,* 12:124, 436. In 1611 James seems to have traveled less: his correspondence with Cecil is dated from London locales such as Whitehall or Hampton Court.

50. For a different view of the relation of Queen Anna's masques, especially to James's political plans, see Martin Butler, "The Invention of Britain and the Early Stuart Masque" in *The Stuart Court and Europe* ed. R. Malcolm Smuts (Cambridge: Cambridge University Press, 1996), 65–85.

51. For a somewhat different view of James's literary interests, and influence,

especially in Scotland, see Murray Pittock, "From Edinburgh to London: Scottish Court Writing and 1603" in *The Stuart Courts*, 13–28.

52. Kevin Sharpe's recent discussion of James's interests in these matters is highly relevant here. See *Remapping Early Modern England* (Cambridge: Cambridge University Press, 2000): Chapter 4: "Private Conscience and Public Duty in the Writings of James VI and I."

53. See, for example, his interest in the fortunes of a newly born lion cub in the Tower zoo—*Hatfield*, 16:207–8, as well as his treatise on witchcraft most lately contextualized by Jenny Wormald, "The Witches, the Devil, and the King," in *Freedom and Authority*, 165–80.

54. See Barroll, *Politics, Plague,* 124–25.

55. Chamberlain, whose tastes in drama seem to have accorded with those of James, himself had singled out both *Ignoramus* and also *Melanthe*. At the time of the earlier visit, he noted that *Melanthe* gave "great contentment as well to the King as to all the rest."

56. David Mathew, *James I* (London: Eyre & Spottiswoode, 1967), 124–29.

57. *Letters of James VI and I*, ed. G. P. V. Akrigg (Berkeley: University of California Pres,, 1984), 220–21.

58. See *Politics, Plague,* 26–27.

59. "A few days ago the Jesuit Provincial of England, imprisoned for complicity in the [Gunpowder] plot, was publicly tried. His Majesty was present *incognito*," the Venetian ambassador also tells us: see *SPV*, 10.337 and Winwood, 2:205.

60. See *Chamberlain*, 2:211, 214–15, 238, 246–47.

61. Especially interesting on the vexed question of James I as poetic icon is Curtis Perry, *The Making of Jacobean Court Culture* (Cambridge: Cambridge University Press, 1997), Chapter 1: "Panegyric and the Poet-King." Jenny Wormald, " 'Tis True I am a Cradle King': the View from the Throne," in *The Reign of James VI*, 241–56, argues that James's intellectual cultivation may be discovered from a reading of his poems.

REVIEWS

Words That Matter: Linguistic Perception in Renaissance English
By Judith H. Anderson
Stanford: Stanford University Press, 1996

Reviewer: Anne Lecercle

In proposing a volume devoted to the word as "thing," or the "thingness" of words, in the English Renaissance, Judith H. Anderson marshals an interesting and impressive array of texts and materials, including dictionaries and primers of grammar, to define her domain. Such a return to the letter of the text, or at least to the perception of the individual word as something of a microcosm in itself, is particularly welcome. For it is one of the greater ironies of the recent rifling of French philosophy by much of the Anglo-American academy for the humanities that this has fostered a disdain for (or at least a detour around) the practice of close reading. In fact, close reading is the bedrock on which French "critical theory" still is, and has always been, founded. Anderson's carefully researched study delineates a perspective on the word that is a much-needed counterweight to a criticism that, while insisting on historical contextualization of reference, often fails to insist equally on a concomitant historicizing of the perception of textuality itself. Such a study thus contributes to promoting a more satisfying equilibrium between endo- and exogenetic factors in the composition of a text that has, of late, been popular.

There are, however, a number of problems, some of them heralded as early as in the title. The variety of angles on the "thingness" of words is satisfying and straightforward enough as long as the book progresses by devoting a chapter to each in turn. The line of argument becomes less clear, however, in the latter half of the volume, which offers a series of very different types of textual extracts for detailed analysis. Here the "thingness" of words can jump without warning from the proverbial to the Latinate to the biblical, so that one comes to regret a certain lack of articulation of a more perceptible line of argument, and (above all) of a concluding synthesis in proportion to each analysis and to the book as a whole.

Secondly, if a word is a microcosm in itself, it is equally a microcosm *unto* itself: "thingness," in other words, has not only Heideggerian overtones, it has Heideggerian consequences. Anderson's title is *Words That Matter,* a phrase at once glossed as *Linguistic Perception in Renaissance English.* This being so, she does not, perhaps, sufficiently distinguish (although she refers to Saussure in her introductory propos) between two fundamental notions: the word and the signifier—which may, or may not, coincide. The well-known case of "dwell" in Jonson's verse, to which Anderson devotes her first in-depth analysis and the better part of a chapter, offers a suggestive instance of the limits of her conception of the materiality of the Renaissance signifier, both in context and in general. "Dwell," she writes, is a "fairly common if sonorous word, it is one [Jonson] appears to have weighed carefully, from whatever historically linguistic angle his coice is assessed" (110–11). Common it may well be; at all events this is open to a certain degree of statistical verification. But "sonorous"? Is not sonority either a subjective appreciation or context-specific? A linguist, in any case, would dispute the general validity of such a statement.

But the real point here is that if Anderson is led into making such a sweeping claim, the reason is already contained in the conditions she defines ("from whatever historically linguistic angle the choice is assessed"). The excess attaching to the word's "sonority" is the reverse face of the restriction to "historically linguistic angles" conceived of in terms of a intellectual, intentional choice on the part of the poet. Even in a writer as controlled and self-conscious as Jonson, such cannot be the sum total of "angles" from which to assess what the critic herself terms the "weight" of the word as structurally and associatively important as "dwell" in *To Penshurst.* Consequently, though Jonson is explicitly credited with employing a word "whose use he appears to have weighed carefully," the scales of critical appreciation lack the necessary wherewithal to act as effective counterweight. Were this in doubt, Anderson proceeds, in the very next sentence, to lighten even further the "pan" of appraisal, by taking out of it the little one might reasonably have expected still to find there: namely, connotation, which (thanks to a somewhat mixed metaphor) now turns up in the guise of "baggage." Surprisingly for such an intelligent critic, she thus continues: "While no word is a clean slate, *dwell* comes close to being one. It carries little connotative baggage, and Jonson can control or 'square' it." Apart from mixing her metaphors yet further, albeit this time in Jonsonian mode, the point again is that such an absolute statement about its semantics is as unwarranted as the alleged sonority of *dwell.*

Above all, however, it demonstrates that her account of "meaning" is couched overrestrictively in terms of cultural coding, of Lacan's Symbolic—in the last analysis, of the differential, and does not allow sufficiently for the upsurges or inroads stemming from the Imaginary. In doing so, rather than give an account of the term as poetry, the critic poeticizes her own criticism—hence the mixing of metaphors. The imaginary in such contexts comes into play in various ways, the point here being that, without even mentioning the "conceits" and the *copia* Bacon deplored and Jonson endeavoured to contain—*Die Sprache spricht,* as Heidegger put it: language speaks, of itself, often in spite of itself, and sometimes against itself. If the use of "dwell" resonates so powerfully as the last word celebrating the inhabitants of Penshurst and Penshurst as habitation, it is also because the signifier itself is, in its own right, inhabited—inhabited literally, by a materiality in which Renaissance poets were wont to invest exceptional "weight," namely letters. If "dwell" is one of Anderson's *Words that Matter,* it is because what matters in "dwell" is the matter of "dwell"—that is, its *letteral* rather than literal inhabitation by another signifer: by the "well" embedded within it.

The fact that this is poetry, and that this word is, in both senses of the expression, "the end of the line," has the supplementary effect of actualizing the embedded signifier: even though we are not talking about rhyming couplets, this is the sonnet-like "point" of the poem. Likewise, it is the eulogistic cast of the whole poem that creates a sympathetic context for, and lends credence to, the reactivation of "well" in "dwell" and gives it that celebrated, supplementary weight. Nor does "well" work simply: in context (i.e., as the last stone to a construction at once architectural and poetic) the raising of "well" from its embedded status signifies in so far as it functions as a conflation of both versions of that signifier—as moral concept fostered by the habitation, and as material precondition of that habitation. On the one hand, the "well-ness" of "weal," of which Jonson's "lord [who] dwells" is both the guarantor and the epitome; on the other, that without which, in the most material sense (as dramatically evidenced to this day in noble medieval piles like Penhallam or noble Elizabethan ones like Hoghton

Tower), no nobleman's house could ever be so much as envisaged, let alone a dynasty lodged within its walls. Such is the other well, the life-giving source where still waters run deep. (Elsewhere in *To Penshurst,* carps and pikes browse in hidden, slow-moving depths, bizarrely ready to rise up and nourish the household.) "Dwell" is not only weighted but fleshed out by the embedded signifier that names the alpha and omega of seigneurial existence and endeavor, an amphibological homophone that is the last signifier of the poem and *its* last word, even if it is not *the* last word. These are considerations to which a critical perspective placing itself under the sign of a Rabelais cannot forclude.

The problem is that Anderson constantly returns to one of Rabelais's paradigms of the Renaissance word (and a late one at that), the episode of the "the 'frozen words' and its radiating implications." However, what Rabelais in fact does is to create a veritable daisy chain of paradigms that reconfigure language through an array of prisms, beginning, back in the 1530s, with the mutation and transmogrification of his own name into a representation of vermin even before the sequence of four books gets under way. This is why one regrets the lack of a more comprehensive liminary overview that reserves some space for the mythic (or fantasmatic) as well as the more institutionalized prisms of language perception—something in the style of Claude-Gilbert Dubois's neat little volume on Renaissance language (*Mythe et langage au seizième siècle*). Instead, she invokes the notion of *mentalité* (in French in the text), where in France this notion has long since been laid to rest as insufficiently problematized.

The point, therefore, is that if, for the Renaissance, word was thing (*res*), it was also something of a rebus. As the Latin suggests, the frontiers between the two are (and above all were) anything but watertight, especially for a budding generation of poets—ones conscious, moreover, of the status of the English language amongst its European counterparts (Turkish was deemed more necessary in diplomatic circles.) Globalization may nowadays be reducing the role of languages other than Anglo-American, but the situation in the Renaissance was symmetrically inverse, with English having something of motley coat about it. (Terence Cave has recently returned to the question of the polyglot in Renaissance practice and perception of language.) Finally, if the Rabelais Anderson invokes was indisputably the foremost linguistic practitioner of his day across the Channel, the fact that the greatest English writer of the sixteenth century hardly gets a look-in in Anderson's book strikes one as, to say the least, bizarre.

All of which does not, however, efface the merit of the book as it stands, which is to present a number of angles on the materiality of language which gain an interest from the juxtaposition and together constitute the outline for a renewed perspective on reading what has come down to us from the period. The book is a notable contribution to recovering for the reader of the twenty first century something of both the pristine wonder and the profound whimsicality with which men and women of the Renaissance conceived and contemplated the nitty gritty of their practice or profession.

Shakespeare and the Loss of Eden: The Construction of Family Values in Early Modern Culture
By Catherine Belsey
New Brunswick: Rutgers University Press; Basingstoke: Palgrave, 2000

Reviewer: Helen Cooper

This compelling book takes as its starting point the disasters that befell the first nuclear family. Created in Paradise with the potential for an everlasting life of bliss, the first couple instead brought death into the world, as well as the pains of childbirth that were often inseparable from it. The first death, as Claudius points out, was fratricide, the offence that "hath the primal eldest curse upon it." The family structure creates the possibilities for the most intense pain of loss, and for many of the worst misdeeds: incest, parricide, the abuse of women and children, adultery. We tend to think of the literary genre most closely related to the family as being romance; in practice, it is much more likely to be tragedy.

This is the ground that Catherine Belsey explores, in the period from 1550 to 1650: a period she describes as constituting "one long moment of dissension," with its upheavals in religious and political ideology, economics, and culture. It is also the period that most comprehensively grounded its official view of the family in the Word of God, so that the disasters of that first married couple were deeply engraved in the consciousness of every one of their successors. To supplement what they had learned at the knee of their parent or minister, there were marital headboards carved with the detail of the Fall and the expulsion from Eden, so that the occupants of the bed would engage in the act of procreation beneath a reminder of the first engendering of death. The original edition of Jakob Rüff's treatise on childbirth (Frankfurt, 1580), written to educate midwives, has on the first page of its first chapter an extraordinary woodcut of Adam and Eve plucking the apple from a skeleton shaped into a tree, its legbones entwined, arms lifted and skull tilted in a curiously balletic pose, with leaves and fruit bursting forth in the place of fingers and a serpent coiled around its ribcage.

Belsey's professed aim is to "denaturalize family values" by pursuing "a distinct practice, which I shall call history at the level of the signifier"—in other words, to reconstruct cultural history through careful attention to its traces in both texts and the visual arts. The book is accordingly rich not only in quotations but in illustrations, including headboards and engravings, but most particularly tomb sculptures. It is an extension of the paradox of Eden, indeed, that funerary monuments should be substantially the most abundant form for representing the family in the early modern period. Belsey traces the changing conventions of representation, from formalized upright figures laid flat (as one can tell from looking at the way draperies fall around the feet) to the kneeling couple accompanied by an array of smaller kneeling children and a troop of the shrouded infant dead, and from there to naturalistic poses expressive of love and protection, of a mother for a swaddled newborn baby or a husband for a wife. She also makes a powerful argument for the idea that Hermione's "statue" should be represented as a tomb monument, so that the coming to life is visually represented as crossing the boundary not from art but from death itself.

The integration of Shakespeare into this matrix is both skilful and illuminating. Belsey is an excellent close reader as well as a shrewd cultural historian, and she moves between text and context with assurance—in her analysis, indeed, there is little distance to cross, for this material is precisely what Shakespeare is often writing about. The almost complete absence in his works of happy nuclear families takes on new and strong resonances against this background. His comedies may end with a couple about to be married, but his presentation of the married, on the comparatively rare occasions when both husband and wife are alive and appear on stage, is much more likely to show things going very badly wrong, whether the wrongness takes the form of a temptress Lady Macbeth or a calumniated Desdemona. Brotherhood is an equally dangerous relationship, as not just Old Hamlet and Claudius but Oliver and Orlando show (and sisters are not immune, as the murderous jealousy of Goneril and Regan proves). The child who is spoken of in the most deeply affectionate terms in all the plays, the one who carries its father's greatest emotional investment, is Mamillius, whose death is hastened by distress at his father's destruction of his mother.

A complicating factor in all this—or rather, a factor that is persistently treated now as a simplifying explanation, though Belsey is too intelligent to follow the fashion—is misogyny. This book sets out the countercurrents as well. Protestantism partly differentiated itself from Catholicism over its ideology of marriage. Not that Catholicism had been against marriage—it was, after all, Catholic doctrine that declared it to be a sacrament of the Church—but it was only the Reformation that envisaged marriage as the perfect form of living, and that could mean praise of woman to the point where her creation became the final divine act that redeemed man's only lack. Belsey quotes the polemical conclusion of such writings in the argument of Ester Sowernam ("Sourname," a name presumably invented to counter "her" opponent Joseph Swetnam, "Sweetname") that Eve was God's culminating work, "made to add perfection to the end of all creation." She was the ideal wife, and yet also, of course, the immediate cause of the Fall. Comments Belsey: "No wonder woman cannot be read: the good and the bad wife are one and the same person."

This is precisely, however, a problem of *reading,* and if there is one matter over which I would disagree with the priorities of this book, it is over the degree of emphasis given to the identity of the bad and good wife over the fact that this identity lies all too often only in the husband's interpretation. What potentially happy families there are in Shakespeare are recurrently destroyed by husbands who *believe* their good wives to be identical with a wicked counterpart: hence the destruction of Desdemona, the attempted destruction of Imogen and Hermione, the social erasure of Hero. "The plays take full account of what, in the twentieth century, Jacques Lacan calls 'the dark god in the sheep's clothing of the Good Shepherd, Eros' ": they do so indeed, but the maleness of the dark god is dealt with in a separate chapter. Marriage is "dangerous" in Shakespeare much less because the woman listens to the serpent than because the husband can't believe she has not done so. It is an extraordinary moment when Posthumus regrets the death of the wife he believes to be adulterous, but Shakespeare never takes the more momentous step of forgiveness for a wife who is in fact unfaithful. He provides very few occasions, indeed, when it could be possible at all. Married chastity is not a virtue easy for skeptical academics to extol with conviction in a postmodern age; however, the recent genetic research which has established that in the centuries since the invention of surnames, close to 99 percent of the wives of men named Sykes were faithful to their husbands, indicates that Shakespeare's good wives are more true to life than we might think.

Belsey's resistance to any simple idea of "true love" in favor of a Lacanian view that desire can never perceive itself to be adequately reciprocated is however forcefully and persuasively argued. It enables her to find ways around even such well-entrenched critical readings as Northrop Frye's mythic interpretation of act 4 of *Winter's Tale*. Belsey focuses not on Perdita/Proserpina as the embodiment of the rebirth of Spring but on the way desire creates its own lack, whether in the absence of the flowers she invokes—

> O Proserpina,
> For the flowers now . . . !;
> These I lack
> To make you garlands of . . .

—or in Florizel's unsatisfiable wish that she should dance like

> A wave o'the'sea, that you might ever do
> Nothing but that.

This kind of emphasis brings Mamillius's death into the heart of the play, and incorporates it into its spectrum of anxieties and unfulfilled desire.

Perdita rewrites the flower-strewn corpse as her orgasmic lover in her arms, inverting one of the most powerful associations of the Fall, that of sex and death: the equation carved into those headboards. Belsey adds another representation, Niklaus Manuel Deutsch's grim picture of a decaying corpse groping a sexually welcoming young woman. *Hamlet* in particular, as Roland Mushat Frye and Michael Neill have shown, is a dramatic variant on the dance of death, the iconographic representation of the universality of death to all the sons of Adam and the daughters of Eve. Belsey reads the graveyard scene as one in which Hamlet himself plays the part of Death, performing his own *danse macabre* with "the politician, the courtier, the lawyer, the lady, the emperor and the fool." This in turn opens out into a strenuous attack on the Aristotelean idea of tragedy as giving pleasure, to relocate its appeal beyond the Freudian pleasure principle into the realm of death itself. The rise of scientific psychology may have dismantled much of Freud's work, but some of his ideas remain gripping at a level that rationality cannot explain. This book appropriates some of that power, in its arresting synthesis of sex, death, biblical myth, Shakespeare, and tragedy itself.

King James and Letters of Homoerotic Desire
By David M. Bergeron
Iowa City: University of Iowa Press, 1999

Reviewer: *Nicholas F. Radel*

There is perhaps no better evidence than the life and loves of King James I of England that (as Jonathan Goldberg convincingly insists) homoeroticism in the early modern period was not positioned on the margins of culture and the social life (as it apparently is today) but at its center. James's relationships with his favorites has been and continues to be a central theme of historical analysis of the first Stuart monarch in England, and perhaps a good case can be made that the tendency to view James's preference for his favorites either favorably or un- is at least partially bound to individual historians' attitudes toward homosexuality and homoerotic desire—or, to put it less kindly, to their investment in homophobic thinking. That there was something between James and men like Esmé Stuart, Robert Carr, and George Villiers that differs from the seemingly chaste homosociality of twentieth-century male-male friendships and alliances cannot be denied. That this something had a significant impact on the court and culture of England in the early seventeenth century is manifest. But as central as the homoeroticism of

James's relationships may be to the early modern social imaginary, its exact nature is open to varied interpretation; and just as earlier historians could see it or not depending on their own homophobia, recent analysis of James and his favorites from a nonhomophobic vantage is also colored by one's take on the place and significance of modern homosexuality. If ever an example were needed to illustrate Hayden White's argument that history is always written from a presentist bias, it could certainly be the case of James and his favorites—a point born out by the study at hand, David Bergeron's latest book, *King James and Letters of Homoerotic Desire*.

As anyone with a minimal knowledge of the period might guess, James and each of his favorites, and the detailed and evocative letters that passed between them, have become central examples in the relatively new field of inquiry into the history of sex and sexuality in early modern England. Because this is so, Bergeron's book covers ground already well-tilled by critics—most notably Bergeron himself, in his earlier work, *Royal Family, Royal Lovers: King James of England and Scotland*.[1] The new work, however, performs a valuable service on two counts: first, by providing a generous sampling of the letters (with their spelling modernized and arcane references annotated) and, second, by contextualizing them through brief, highly readable biographical accounts of James's involvements with all three of his most important favorites. These virtues, along with Bergeron's reprinting and interpreting a poem that he believes James wrote about his love for Esmé Stuart, "Ane Metaphoricall Invention of a Tragedie Called Phoenix," and a brief introductory outline of early modern and contemporary ideas about the intimate nature of letters, make *King James and Letters of Homoerotic Desire* a highly useful compendium of empirical knowledge about James's homoerotic involvements.

King James and Letters of Homoerotic Desire provides detailed accountings of people and events that can seem shocking and provocative, as when it argues that the thirteen-year-old James's infatuation with the thirty-seven-year-old Esmé Stuart bears a striking resemblance to his later relationships with men considerably younger than he. Rather than shying away from the embarrassments of the age-related issues, Bergeron suggests that the erotics of James's attachment to his cousin Stuart and his later infatuations with Carr and Villiers seem to reflect the King's need for a family that his own childhood failed to provide. If the implications of Bergeron's analysis veer toward a type of pseudo-psychology that sees homosexuality as an inherently flawed family drama, they nevertheless mark a significant overlap between early modern discourses of familial desire and the language of same-sex eroticism that would seem to demand more sustained analysis in future inquiries. As Bergeron points out, it is not simply that the eroticized language of James's letters to (especially) Villiers often overlaps with the discourse of heterosexual marriage ("And so God bless you, my sweet child and wife, and grant that ye may ever be a comfort to your dear dad and husband," James writes in a by-now well-known letter to Buckingham [175]). It is that the eroticism of these letters is often conterminus with the language of familial (as opposed to marital) blood relationships. As Bergeron notes, "in [James's] lexicon 'child' comprises the terms of love" (136).

More important—and here the value of Bergeron's book is as absolute as when it collects the known data about James and his favorites in one convenient place—Bergeron provides detailed close readings of the letters, drawing the reader unerringly in the direction of what needs to be seen—and seen clearly—in James's poem and in both his and Villiers's letters if we are to begin to understand the homoeroticism in their lives, in their writings, and, indeed, in the period in which they lived. Bergeron devotes a significant portion of his contextualizing, biographical chapters to close readings of the letters—and he again does not flinch at revealing what may be specifically sexual and potentially unsettling. So, for instance, he provides the necessary sexual gloss to a puzzling reference in an undated letter from Villiers to James:

> For my reception yesterday when I came, my entertainment being there, and my leave-taking was such, nay I say such, Sir, that all the way hither I entertained myself your unworthy servant with this dispute, whether you loved me now (my ever dear master, here give me leave to say, a full heart must either vent itself or break, and that oftentimes the senses are better expressed in absence and by letter than otherwise: you know full thoughts cause long parentheses) better than at the time which I shall never forget at Farnham, where the bed's head could not be found between the master and his dog. Sir, if you mark not well the parenthesis, it does break the sense that was my desire, and if therein I did deceive, it was with my goodwill. (179)

Bergeron comments: "However we choose to construe this letter, we cannot overlook its sexual implications: desire, if not also behavior. . . . A probable first sexual encounter at Farnham should strain no one's credulity" (111).

In these examples Bergeron's primary purposes in writing this book become clear: to counter the prevailing tendency of history and criticism to cover up, to gloss over, to dismiss the evident presence of homoerotic sentiment, feeling, and discourse in the life and writing of James and his favorites—and to do so by culling evidence in such a way that the reader can judge the nature of this sentiment or discourse. (As Bergeron puts it, "the letters appear together for the first time in the context of [James's and Villiers's] shared love. Readers may judge for themselves the nature of this love and desire" [147].) If Bergeron's readings sometimes seem like special pleading, that is because they must counter the still-prevalent objections of society at large and many members of the academy that what looks like a fish and smells like a fish is somehow a fowl. In this, Bergeron's book is useful if not entirely original. That it is carefully documented and that it takes pains to check various printed versions of the letters against the originals—with often useful results—will make it in some ways indispensable. That it is a good read (as I've already suggested) may mean that it will be widely used, even by those without a scholar's interest in the period.

And yet many will remain skeptical of the theoretical and historical paradigms in which Bergeron contextualizes the letters. Bergeron understands well that, as Bruce Smith, says, "homo*sexuality* [as opposed to homosexual behavior] is specific to our own culture and to our own moment in history,"[2] and that it is, thus, not an appropriate concept for describing erotic activity in the early modern period. But he does not seem to agree with what has come to be a widely accepted view of homosexual behavior and homoerotic desire in the Renaissance: the idea that it is always elsewhere, displaced into institutions and discourses that are not wholly sexual and not primarily erotic. For Bergeron, the homoeroticism that he reveals, the homoeroticism that has traditionally been hidden and obscured in commentary on these texts, tends to move perceptibly toward sexual love knowable as such—with the result that the rhetoric of analysis in *King James and Letters of Homoerotic Desire* can seem to visualize homoerotic desire in the Renaissance as being in some ways similar to versions of homosexual desire in the present.

For instance, Bergeron emphasizes the ability of letters to create a metaphorical space of intimate knowledge, withdrawn from public awareness and censure. He quotes the introductory poem of James Howell's seventeenth-century compilation of letters, *Epistolae Ho-Elianae* (1645), to the effect that the sovereign's most private thoughts can be penetrated through letters: Letters, Howell writes, "can the Cabinets of Kings unscrue, / And hardest Intricacies of *State* unclue" (qtd. Bergeron 8). For Bergeron, the lines mean that letters have "the ability to penetrate the most private space of the sovereign" (8). Clearly trading in witty puns meant to evoke a smile, Bergeron's sentence nevertheless implies what a few words later he specifies: "I suggest that King James's letters indeed unbolt his interior space; they open closets (8). As Alan Stewart has argued, however, it is not clear that the closet is an apposite image for discussing homoeroticism in the early seventeenth century,[3] and many scholars would contest Bergeron's implication that it is. Perhaps the erotic frisson that derives from penetrating the sovereign's most private spaces proceeds not from the body of the king per se nor from the privileged access to his most intimate self. It may proceed, rather, from the nearness to political secrets and power such ingress provides. There are sexual possibilities here, to be sure, but they may not be organized in binary distinctions around the public and private, the personal and the political, as, I think, Bergeron's reading suggests.

King James and Letters of Homoerotic Desire also depends on a liberal or idealized rhetoric of love that is taken to justify and validate the homoerotic desire between James and his favorites. It is a sentimental gesture that erases the interesting interplay between sex and power that may have predominated in the homoeroticism of the period more fully than love. So, for example, Bergeron writes away the implications of Villiers's calling himself a dog in the letter about his encounter with James at Farnham: "Buckingham regularly referred to himself as 'dog,' an affectionate term with which he signed his letters to James" (111). But it might be argued that Buckingham's metaphor of the master and his dog reverberates in the letters with hierarchical and other discourses that regularly define and normalize erotic relations between men throughout the period, discourses not implied by the word "affectionate." It is no doubt the case that James and Buckingham were in some sense of the word in "love"—the evidence educed by Bergeron makes this fact seemingly indisputable. But that love may have been the entirely orderly and usual erotics of master and servant relationships—sexually legitimized within that explicitly hierarchical relation. As Bruce Smith and Mario DiGangi, among others, have shown, master-servant relations (as expressed through the discourses of master and servants) seem to have been genuine sites of homoerotic desire.[4]

In another instance, Bergeron (usefully, and with a keen eye to the importance of the texts themselves) points to a manuscript correction in one of the letters to Buckingham. A photograph reveals that James crossed out the word "master" and substituted "husband" for it. Bergeron points to this change as evidence of the love the King feels for his favorite, implying that "master" and "slave" or "servant" betokens an inferior relationship to "husband" and "wife" and that James's shift to a metaphor of heterosexual alliance reveals the authenticity of his homoerotic desire for Villiers. In reading the letter Bergeron admits and then dismisses the possibility that James may simply have settled on this new word because he had earlier imagined himself in separation from Buckingham as a widow—thus completing the metaphor he had begun. But why not read this change as a gesture of rhetorical consistency? Why not find the master in the husband, or the opposite? And why privilege marriage in this way? While the word "husband" denotes a relationship that certainly may have signified the sexual, it may also have signaled nothing more nor less than an affectional (or even political) alliance. In fact, given the book's evidence about the nature of James's own marriage to Anne of Denmark, and about his contrivances to bring the duke of Buckingham speeding hastily from his marriage bed to the King's bedchamber, one wonders if marriage is an apt metaphor for sexual desire, sexual love, and genuine affection?

If *King James and Letters of Homoerotic Desire* usefully counters the neglect of homoeroticism in the critical and historical writings of the past, the book seems to substitute for it a vision of homoerotic desire in a modern idiom: secret or private and intimate, knowable as a deviation or variation in desire, and, when known, deserving of liberal tolerance. Such a reading bears the marks of a particular presentist bias that many scholars of early modern sex and eroticism will find problematic. I am not necessarily arguing that *King James and Letters of Homoerotic Desire* is anachronistic in its recovery of a neglected history. Bergeron provides clear evidence of historical documents in a particular case and he reads these documents in a reasonable and precise way. But the closest he comes to a theoretical engagement with the issue of just how much one's erotic desire in the early modern period expresses or reveals one's intimate (as opposed to one's public or social) self is in his introductory discussion of early modern letters, a literary form that, he rightly points out, was emerging in the period from the quasi-public mode of classical letters toward what Nancy Struever calls the "intimacy, spontaneity, and self-revelation" of modern examples.[5] *King James and Letters of Homoerotic Desire* would have been more powerful if, in fact, it had presented its interpretation of history as a sustained counter to those strongly constructionist formulations of early modern sexuality that now seem to dominate so much thinking in the field. As is, the book merely stands in contrast to those accounts.

Still, it is fair to say that Bergeron's book makes an important critical intervention into the biography of James and his favorites, one that places male-male affectional desire front and center at the English court and, in doing so, challenges the veracity and intentions of future critics who fail to take this affection into account. In this sense, *King James and Letters of Homoerotic Desire* takes its place among those recent efforts to "queer" the Renaissance by revealing just how much Buckingham's very real power at court was based in an affectional alliance with the King that is clearly homoerotic. That alone justifies its importance.

Notes

1. David M. Bergeron, *Royal Family, Royal Lovers: King James of England and Scotland* (Columbia: University of Missouri Press, 1991).

2. Bruce Smith, *Homosexual Desire in Shakespeare's England: A Cultural Poetics* (Chicago: University of Chicago Press, 1991), 12.

3. Alan Stewart, "Epistemologies of the Early Modern Closet," in *Close Readers: Humanism and Sodomy in Early Modern England* (Princeton: Princeton University Press, 1997), 161–87.

4. Mario DiGangi, *The Homoerotics of Early Modern Dramas* (Cambridge: Cambridge University Press, 1997).

5. Nancy Struever, *Theory as Practice: Ethical Inquiry in the Renaissance* (Chicago: University of Chicago Press, 1992), 8.

Shakespeare's Feminine Endings: Disfiguring Death in the Tragedies
By Philippa Berry.
London and New York: Routledge, 1999

Reviewer: Cynthia Marshall

Unlike the two previous volumes in Routledge's series of Feminist Readings of Shakespeare (Jean Howard and Phyllis Rackin's *Engendering a Nation* and Coppélia Kahn's *Roman Shakespeare*), both of which primarily employ a liberal feminism that is easily congenial to student audiences, Philippa Berry's new book advances a deconstructive feminism focused on the texture of language rather than on character. In one of his earliest definitions of deconstruction, Jacques Derrida called it a matter of "being alert to the implications, to the historical sedimentation of the language we use,"[1] but that linguistic emphasis has often been forgotten, at least in American deployments of deconstructive theory as the manipulation of reified terms. The significant critical achievement of *Shakespeare's Feminine Endings* is to track down from a feminist perspective the implications and weblike linkages of interlingual puns and wordplay in Shakespeare's tragedies. The result is to explode the humanist reading of the tragedies as affirmations of heroic male identity and to reveal a richly gendered poetic subtext in the plays. The wide learning and verbal sensitivity that are everywhere on display make this an invigorating work to read and learn from. *Shakespeare's Feminine Endings* provocatively "challenges dominant cultural notions of what is 'fundamental' and 'final' both to tragedy and to human identity" (3).

Readers of Freud's "Theme of the Three Caskets" will recall that essay's curiously branching structure, whereby an initial discussion of the suitors' choice of caskets in *The Merchant of Venice* mutates under Freud's analysis into an account of King Lear's division of his kingdom and his disowning of Cordelia, an action that is taken to mask the King's own refusal to "choose" his imminent death. Freud proposes that Lear confronts, in the guise of his daughters, the three Fates or woman in her three relations to man: as mother, as mate, and as Mother Earth or death. Thus, through a series of partially occluded associations, Freud links male erotic choice with death by way of a maternal figure, a linkage demonstrating how the romantic or heroic *agon* is undercut by a man's reliance on and ultimate submission to an encompassing nature (troped as feminine) that swallows up individual identity.

Berry's style of argument built on associative logic, as well as her basic thesis regarding women, nature, and tragic ending, strongly resemble Freud's essay (which she does not cite). But where Freud attributes the perception of mythic femininity to the tragic king, thereby shoring up his role as suffering consciousness, Berry's insistent focus on linguistic texture has the effect of further deflating a sense of characterological presence and of masculine identity as its central avatar. Berry's psychoanalytic points are absorbed through Julia Kristeva and Luce Irigaray, feminist revisionists of Freud who have pushed his ideas in a poststructuralist direction. Built on such a provocative foundation, the book's readings are always inventive and frequently breathtaking in their originality and their rapid traversal of material. Chapters are devoted to each of the four major tragedies and to *Romeo and Juliet,* although Berry's discussions range widely through the Shakespearean canon and include attention to all the tragedies except *Timon of Athens.*

In an introductory chapter, Berry elucidates what she means by "feminine endings." Whereas a traditional emphasis on the teleological structure of tragedy (recently restated by Michael Neill in *Issues of Death: Mortality and Identity in English Renaissance Tragedy*) finds masculine heroic identity confirmed in the plays' narrative design, Berry finds in the linguistic texture of the plays a "pattern of feminine or feminized tropes" that "unravel[s]" (3) a concept of singular identity and the linear notion of time on which it is based. Acknowledging a debt to Patricia Parker, Berry compares the "surfeit of signification" (4) revealed by such an analysis to the metrical supplements, or feminine endings, common to Shakespearean blank verse. This linguistic excess associates death with nature; the often grotesque fecundity that Shakespeare locates in organic cycles challenges the orderliness and the dignity of established identity. Berry locates an "animist or vitalist materialism" (12) in tragic wordplay, and traces it to the influence of Lucretius, Giordano Bruno, and other classical thinkers, both Stoic and Epicurean.

In her chapter on *Romeo and Juliet,* Berry explores what she calls "double dying," a motif with proliferating meanings derived from the association of death and sexuality. The sexualized female body is seen as "a portal of both life and death" (21); women, subject to both genital and anal penetration, feature a "double bodily 'end' " (22); poetic privileging of women's sexual "dying" can seem to defer or overcome bodily extinction; and residual traces of "the ecstatic deaths of Catholic saints" (23) extend and complicate the tragic conception of death's finality. Berry's interesting discussion locates a "residual catholic 'idolatry' " (37) in *Romeo and Juliet,* which together with references to astrology and to a pagan, seasonal calendar render the deaths of the protagonists open rather than closed in their resonance and implication.

Chapter 3 concentrates on sound, specifically "echoic language." Berry employs Kristeva's concept of semiotic *chora* to focus on "the hidden materiality of language" revealed when "sound takes precedence over sense" (45), establishing the link with Renaissance verse through the classical mythology of the nymph Echo. After pointing out how women are associated with an echoic rhetoric of insincerity (Goneril and Regan, Tamora) and a reverberant emptying of language (Desdemona's "willow" song, Cordelia's "nothing"), Berry concentrates on Hamlet's "choric activity" (57) of punning. By multiplying verbal meanings and particularly by "reintroduc[ing] nature, the body and death into the sphere of courtly discourse," Hamlet "reassimilat[es] culture into nature" (59). Some feminists may object to this focus on Hamlet rather than on Ophelia, to whom Berry devotes only a few pages, reiterating the (in)significance of her mad words and songs, and attending briefly to her association with fecundity through flowers and watery death. But Hamlet has always been viewed as the most feminine of the major tragic heroes, and as Berry points out, Polonius's reference to his speech as "pregnant" seems to attribute "a feminine or fecund character" (64) to his punning language. Her aim is thus to show tragic male identity dissolved, as it were, from within, by language.

Chapter 4, the best in the book, is concerned broadly with sight, and more specifically with what Berry calls "the feminine eye of death." Here she is indebted to Irigaray's *Speculum: Of the Other Woman,* which challenges the masculine, disembodied gaze of traditional Western knowledge by articulating an alternative mode of "dilated and inturned vision . . . entwined with the darkness within matter, as well as within the 'empty' female body" (76). Berry shows a repeated pattern in the tragedies of characters confronting darkness (again troped as feminine) within the state, family, body, or self, as for instance when the surveillance activity of the "watch" in the opening scene of *Hamlet* is disruptively turned inward toward the ghost, and the action of the play turned toward a feminized domestic center. Such turning inward occasions a disruptive doubling, a sense of being mirrored and looked at, as when the murdered Duncan is imaged as a Gorgon whose look might turn the beholder to stone, or when Banquo's ghost confronts its murderer, or when Macbeth is shown the line of Banquo's heirs, the last holding a looking glass. "Like Irigaray's dilated eye, which mirrors only the fissures in identity, the glass gives literal shape to the effect of being looked at from beyond the grave by a fertility that transcends death" (85). Parker has previously applied the idea of dilation to *Othello*, the main subject of this chapter. Berry positions her argument as an extension of Parker's (and that of an important article by Neill) by emphasizing the play's concern with the darkness of "what *cannot* be seen" (89, Berry's emphasis) and by finding recurrent reference to "a nocturnal mode of bodily seeing that is intimately allied to love" (91). Othello's demand for an "ocular proof" that significantly devolves onto a handkerchief described as "a love gift . . . which symbolizes, not the revelation, but the covering and concealment of woman's body" (94–95) supports this reading.

The relatively primal emphases on sound and sight of chapters 3 and 4 are complicated and extended outward in the two final chapters, which address concepts of time (in *Macbeth*) and space or geography (in *King Lear*). Historical context figures more prominently in these chapters. Chapter 5 shows how the prevalence of notions of cyclical time in *Macbeth* undercuts the protagonist's own linear, teleological temporal assumptions. The fact of King James's "political *renovatio* and genealogical inheritance" (127) underscores an aspect of recurrence in his own relation to the play. Berry stunningly follows a series of bawdy puns in which she claims are "oblique allusions to King James' presumed sexual preferences" implying "a certain backwardness or 'posteriority' " (127) characterizing Stuart kingship.

Chapter 6 similarly finds a bodily image furnishing a political emblem. Here, "the rejected territorial middle which was seemingly to have been Cordelia's jointure is figuratively 'digested' and, it is implied, excreted by her brothers-in-law" (136). Berry reads the play's "catastrophic partition or 'breaching' of British national identity" (152) as a comment on James's appeal for a unified Britannia, with Cordelia as the uncanny, riddling figure of a union that occasions both death and birth. In the play's middle sections, Lear suffers from his exposure to the "nature" of England's midsection, but the King is refigured through association with flowers, weeds, natural growth, rebirth, and mystery. Even the apocalyptic rhetoric of the final scene is "disfigured" by doubling (the looking glass held to Cordelia's lips) and riddling (the mystery of Cordelia's life-in-death), rendering the play (as has been argued before in other ways) incompletely closed.

If Berry's readings occasionally stretch the limits of readerly credulity, that is probably inevitable with a work of such sustained originality. *Shakespeare's Feminine Endings* delivers an exciting revision of Shakespearean tragedy, rendering the plays stranger, and richer.

Note

1. Jacques Derrida, "Structure, Sign, and Play in the Discourse of the Human Sciences," *The Languages of Criticism and the Sciences of Man: The Structuralist Controversy,* ed. Richard Macksey and Eugenio Donato (Baltimore: Johns Hopkins University Press, 1970), 271.

Shakespeare and the Japanese Stage
Edited by Takashi Sasayama, J. R. Mulryne, and Margaret Shewring
Cambridge: Cambridge University Press, 1998

New Sites for Shakespeare: Theatre, the Audience, and Asia.
By John Russell Brown
London and New York: Routledge, 1999

Reviewer: Lois Potter

In 1991 the International Shakespeare Conference met in Tokyo, and this contact between two major theatrical cultures produced a Big Bang in Shakespeare studies. Coming as it did at a time when scholars were becoming aware of the dangers of appropriation and Orientalism, the conference inspired not only an interest in comparative studies but also a questioning of what these studies entail and whether they can be justified in the first place. The two books reviewed here are among the results of such questioning.

Shakespeare and the Japanese Stage, a multi-authored volume with three editors, is complex but well-organized, giving both an historical and a theoretical dimension to the discussion of Japanese and Western theatrical traditions. It begins with Akihiko Senda's survey of the last thirty years of Shakespeare productions in Japan, and pays tribute to a number of Japanese directors and adapters of Shakespeare: the pioneering Shakespeare scholar/director Shoyo Tsubouchi, whose 1911 *Hamlet* is described by Brian Powell; the Marxist Koreya Senda; and the free adaptations and productions of Hideki Noda, Tadashi Suzuki, and Tetsuo Anzai (who describes, in fascinating detail, the problems of translating and directing *King Lear* in Japanese). The essays that follow skillfully combine a history of each traditional Japanese dramatic genre—No, Bunraku, Kabuki, and Kyogen—with a discussion of its theoretical or practical relation to Shakespeare. Gerry Yokota-Murakami and Izumi Momose compare No with Shakespearean drama. Minoru Fujita describes the creation of a Bunraku version of *The Tempest.* Two items in the collection derive directly from the 1991 conference, and are in fact expanded from versions already published in the volume of conference proceedings, *Shakespeare and Cultural Traditions.* One is Takashi Sasayama's brilliant comparison of Shakespeare and the Bunraku author Chikamatsu in terms of their control of audience response. Yasunari Takahashi's Kyogen adaptation of *The Merry Wives of Windsor* as *The Braggart Samurai,* prefaced by his witty account of the problems of transforming Shakespeare into Kyogen, will also be a welcome feature of the volume.

The comprehensive nature of this book (which even includes an apparently exhaustive list of Shakespeare productions in Japan up to 1994) would make it the ideal text for a course on intercultural Shakespeare. Many of the essays also have implications for other areas of study. Drawing attention to non-Western theatrical traditions can be pedagogically useful as a way of questioning common Western assumptions about the nature of theatrical performance. The essays by Kishi and Sasayama draw attention to many points of similarity often overlooked in the kind of Shakespeare scholarship that focuses on words and concepts: the connection of pathos, music, and the female character (Sasayama), or the use of speech for choric functions (Kishi). As Roland Barthes points out in his brief essay on "The Three Writings" of Bunraku, Japanese theater literally deconstructs the Western concept of dramatic character by dividing its functions between "the puppet, the manipulator and the vociferant."[1] Fujita's account of the Bunraku adaptation of *The Tempest* adds another layer to this complex construction: instead of having a new head made for the Prospero puppet, the puppeteers decided to use one that traditionally represented two legendary tragic heroes of Bunraku plays, the exiled aristocrat Kan Shojo in *Sugawara* and the banished Shunkan, title character of a play that also exists in Kabuki and No versions. For the experienced member of a Bunraku audience who recognized the puppet head, the effect would be to insert Prospero into an ancient Japanese tradition.

Two other essays of particular interest emphasize the political aspect of Japanese theatre. Writing on the Marxist Koreya Senda, Dennis Kennedy and J. Thomas Rimer suggest that political coding in the Japan of the 1930s worked in much the same way as in Cold War–era Soviet bloc countries. As one director put it, "the audience always applauded because they understood what we were trying to say" (59). It is more surprising to find Gerry Yokota-Murakami applying a political approach to the fourteenth-century No dramatist Zeami, whose most highly regarded plays came to be those that served the purposes of the ruling Shogunate—those, that is, that encouraged submission to authority and subordinated female to male deities. If we think of his works as expressing "universals," this author argues, it is because we fail to understand the extent to which these universals (and, by analogy, Shakespeare's) are "projections of individual or nationalist values."

Cross-gender casting is, of course, the aspect of Japanese theatre most often compared to Elizabethan practice. Yoko Takakuwa develops the comparison in a more interesting direction when she notes that both the male actor playing Cleopatra and the *onnagata* playing a *keisei* (the most refined of courtesans) are impersonating a woman who is herself an impersonation. Margaret Shewring's essay on Hideki Noda mentions a *Twelfth Night* in which Viola was played by a famous Takazakura actress who habitually played male characters. This incidental comment points to a fascinating area for further study. Takazakura is an all-female musical theater in which the star performers are those who play male roles. Their fans consist almost entirely of women who see in them the ideal, understanding, un-macho man; one might compare Stephen Orgel's evidence, in *Impersonations,* about the special popularity of boy actors among the women in their audience. In my own Kabuki-watching experience, I discovered another possibly relevant practice not mentioned by any of the writers here: sometimes productions will cast in the role of a young lover an actor who normally plays female parts, while the role of a wicked woman will be given to an actor who normally plays male roles.

John Russell Brown's *New Sites for Shakespeare* is the result of a personal quest, among the popular theatres of Asia, for alternatives to current styles of Shakespeare production in the West. At present, he feels, the latter divide into two unacceptable extremes: the one overly rehearsed, concept-driven, and emotionally dead, the other spontaneous and creative but technically weak and lacking resources. While he favors an "actors' theatre," as free as possible from middlemen like directors, producers, and designers, he is aware that virtually every company that has attempted such an "alternative" project has ended, usually for economic reasons, by becoming indistinguishable from its rivals. Beginning with a description of what it feels like to attend Jatra drama in India, he then analyzes other experiences from which he feels he learned something about the actor-audience relationship: a funeral on Bali, a Kutiyattam performer in rehearsal, the experience of directing *King Lear* in India. These accounts are fascinating, and will certainly stimulate thought in readers as much as the original experience clearly did in Brown himself. He does not overdo the analogies between this drama and Shakespeare's; what interests him far more is the large role given to the audience in successful popular drama, sometimes through actual participation and sometimes by the demands that are made on its imagination. For him, the most valuable lesson of Asian theater is that it can be technically highly skilled while at the same time leaving room for improvisation and openness to audience response. For modern directors who seek to recreate these qualities in productions of Shakespeare, he suggests specific measures: shorter rehearsal periods, a frequently changing repertory system, more willingness to tolerate contingent, uncontrollable elements (one example is the large number of supernumeraries in the cast who are only minimally better informed than the audience), more choric and musical effects, more direct address to the audience, and—perhaps most interesting—more awareness of the possibilities for creating ceremony out of everyday life.

Most people will agree that all these ideas would be likely to result in a livelier theater. The question is how far such a theater would necessarily relate to the culture of a popular audience in Britain and the other countries that Brown seems to be targeting. As he himself notes, the productions he saw were aimed at a clearly defined local audience of native speakers, which meant that not only the performance but also the performance text could be adapted to the specific audience that was watching it. In fact, the Kutiyattam drama of south India also allows the performer to improvise on the basis of a set text (usefully, Brown prints both the original text and a translation of what was actually said by the performer he witnessed). Renaissance English drama differs completely from Asian drama in the sheer number of words the actors are expected to learn and in the importance attached to accurate delivery of those words. (In Bunraku, as Fujita explains [194], the script in front of the narrator, though impressively bound and presented, is only the scenario on the basis of which he is expected to improvise. Respect for the play is not respect for its exact words.) Moreover, it is hard to see how any Shakespeare production apart from one given at a school could ever be completely local.

In many ways, it seemed to me that the audience Brown most wants to recreate is not the one that watched Shakespeare's plays when they were first performed but the one that, two hundred years later, cheered and booed at melodrama and at heavily cut, stardominated Shakespeare played in melodrama style; most classic Kabuki drama in fact is contemporary with English sentimental comedy and melodrama. While much of this audience has gone over to sports, which offer the most genuinely participatory role for spectators, some of its members occasionally turn up at Shakespeare's Globe, which Brown compares to "an Elizabethan theme park" (190), and enjoy the experience in much the same way that Brown approves of when it is happening in India. It's important that the Globe groundlings pay very little and can walk out on the show whenever they want, so that the actors have to work to keep them there. It is of course true that "to stage Shakespeare's plays authentically at the new Globe, a culture that has almost entirely disappeared would have to be reconstructed along with it" (191). But this doesn't mean that Globe spectators are only playing the role of an inauthentic hypothetical Elizabethan audience; all audiences play the part of an audience and each performance creates its audience as well as being created by it. Those who get most out of the experience do so because they find a role that they like to play. Incidentally, it strikes me that one common factor between popular sporting events and the traditional popular theatres that Brown describes is their domination by male spectators. Can it be that the main requirement for popular culture is the exclusion of women, or at least of those elements of "culture" that are defined as female? Still, no one can deny that what Brown found in popular theater at its best is what everyone enjoys most on the rare occasion when it happens.

Both books left me with a lot of useful and interesting information but a sense of unease about how to use it. There was a time when the comparative approach to theater needed no justification. Now, however, the problem is simply the diversity of audiences. For a spectator who knows nothing about Asian theatre, hybrid productions like those of Yukio Ninagawa and, at the Royal Shakespeare Company, Barry Kyle's *Two Noble Kinsmen* (1986) and Adrian Noble's *Cymbeline* (1997) may have a valuable effect in showing that the play, however familiar some of its language and situations may appear to be, is really the product of a very different world. On the other hand, those who know most about Japanese drama tend to be most hostile to such productions. Brown dislikes them because they are deliberately archaic and removed from the real lives of their audiences. In *Shakespeare and the Japanese Stage,* Tetsuo Kishi points out that the enthusiasm of Western reviewers for Ninagawa and other exported "Japanese Shakespeares" is often the result of ignorance; Robert Hapgood realizes that two years' intensive theater-going in Japan made him "the worst possible spectator" for the Ninagawa *Tempest* (251). The most thorough analysis of the problems of interculturalism, J. R. Mulryne's thoughtful essay on the work of Tadashi Suzuki, uses the phrase "cultural tourism" (76), though at the same time Mulryne recognizes the impossibility of being anything other than a tourist with regard to most cultures. It is good that scholars and theater practitioners are aware of the dangers involved in their own projects. At the same time, I wonder whether there is any real alternative. In an age that both embraces and dreads globalization does the price of authenticity have to be isolation? Surely even "appropriation"—that is, admiration based on imperfect knowledge or imperfect analogies with elements of one's own culture—is better than hostility and rejection.

Note

1. Roland Barthes, *Empire of Signs,* translated by Richard Howard (New York: Hill and Wang, 1982), 49.

Shakespeare Without Women: Representing Gender and Race on the Renaissance Stage
By Dympna Callaghan
London and New York: Routledge, 2000

Reviewer: Nora Johnson

In Nathan Field's play *Amends for Ladies* (published in 1618), the much-wronged Lady Perfect cries out against her own position as a female character in a play produced by men:

> Oh men! what are you? why is our poore sexe
> Still made the disgrac't subjects, in these plaies?
> For vices, follie, and inconstancie?[1]

Nevertheless, by the last act Lady Perfect professes to be happy with the brutal treatment she has received. Somewhere, one imagines, between her defiant resistance and her passive acquiescence, lies the elusive female spectator of early modern drama, the theatergoing woman whose pleasures and opinions may or may not have been taken into consideration by those who crafted and presented plays. Knowing that women made up more than half of the population of London and that they were present in theatrical audiences, scholars have in recent years begun to suggest that consumption equals complicity, that the presence of women in the theaters implies some ratification of the plays' ideological content, or at least some measure of agency in the representational economy of the early modern stage. The consequences of such speculation are mixed. It is clearly important not to overlook the agency of women, silent or otherwise, in the rush to identify patriarchal hegemony. On the other hand, there is a real temptation in this line of thought to underestimate the patriarchal bias of the playing companies, or to claim that women desired their own subordination. Nor is this a conflict without consequences; the way we read and teach these plays has a great deal to do with the way that our students learn to identify with or talk back to the Shakespearean canon.

Long a cautionary voice where the question of female agency is concerned, Dympna Callaghan argues in *Shakespeare Without Women* that we must respect the lack of evidence about women's responses to plays, turning away from speculation about what women might have thought to consider instead the ideological effects of their exclusion from theatrical representation. Doing so allows Callaghan to think in subtler ways about how their presence was managed by the playing companies. Fascinatingly, she demonstrates that early modern female spectators, when they were discussed at all by their contemporaries, tended to be represented as hyper-receptive to male playing, all too apt to lose their wits or their morals as a result of the compelling male performances they witnessed. By contrast, plebeian men were most frequently depicted as insensitive brutes, unable to take in the spectacle before them. What begins to emerge in her account is a pattern of motivated representation, a tendency to talk about women or the lower classes as a way of making a statement about something else, perhaps in this case the theatrical correctness of aristocratic men. Thus, as Callaghan points out, to attribute responses to female audiences is to perpetuate a habit begun by Shakespeare's contemporaries, a habit of speaking for and about a section of that culture that has left no clear information about its preferences. It is a real strength of her work that Callaghan refuses that habit. Instead, *Shakespeare Without Women* has at its center a meditation upon the fact of female exclusion from the playing companies, understood as an absence that allows the theater of this period to address and contain a host of cultural anxieties, gendered and otherwise.

Shakespeare Without Women considers the absence of biological females on stage, in other words, but its argument encompasses more than gender. In fact, the title of this book is at least partially metaphorical. The exclusion of women from the Shakespearean stage constitutes a central focus in Callaghan's work, but it also stands in as a sign of the institution's more general habit of representing what it nevertheles cannot allow physically upon the stage. There are no actual women in Shakespeare's plays, but also no Africans, no Turks, and no Irish, however central representations of the exoticized other might have been to the theater's appeal in this period. Thus, individual chapters consider the missing persons of Shakespearean theater: women, the indigenous Irish, Moors and Turks, even the castrati who were so popular elsewhere. In some ways Callaghan's decision to connect chapters by way of absence and exclusion presents a challenge; this is not a big-thesis book, a sustained argument for a single way of reimagining early modern theater. One would be hard-pressed to name the central insight about exclusion that grows out of a project like this. On the other hand, Callaghan has the opportunity here—and this is surely the point—to examine disparate logics of exclusion, to ask why the representation of women by an all-male theater company is or is not like the representation of Moors by an all-white company in early modern England. This is important work that implicitly complicates some of the more euphoric accounts of performance we've become familiar with in recent years. Many of us are accustomed to the argument, for instance, that transvestite performance wages an implicit attack on the notion of gender difference, but it is much less clear that blackface can be recuperated as a deconstruction of racial difference. In that sense, Callaghan's habit of presenting numerous provocative formulations instead of one definitive thesis becomes one of the book's great strengths, allowing her to draw surprising connections and to open up radically new ways of approaching familiar plays.

Nowhere is that strength more apparent than in the haunting chapter in which Callaghan argues that Irish colonial politics form a kind of occluded center in *The Tempest.* For a generation of critics used to reading the play in terms of New World expansion, the Irish context is a surprising—and surprisingly powerful—way into some of the play's central debates. Indeed, in Callaghan's reading, the very presence of debate about Prospero's control of the island points toward the pervasive influence of the Irish question in English culture. As she points out, the Irish were undeniably literate at the beginning of the seventeenth century, with historians, poets, and genealogists all dedicated to preserving Irish memory and resisting English attempts at cultural annihilation. The Irish habit of talking back to English domination would thus seem to provide a new way for us to understand Caliban's relative freedom to curse. While some have read the play's ambiguities as typifying a historical moment prior to slave trading and colonial conquest on a massive scale, and while others have been willing simply to credit Shakespeare with an expansive sense of human sympathy, Callaghan suggests that the sustained English attempt to master the Irish had left a deep impression on the colonial imagination. Thus, *The Tempest* in her reading registers anxieties about Anglo-Irish miscegenation and about Irish intractability. Its songs echo Irish tunes, and its vocabulary, including works like "scamel" and "gabble," can be traced to the Irish vernacular. It would be useful to hear in more detail about what Shakespeare's audiences could have known regarding the Irish; many of Callaghan's sources seem as if they might have been available only to the Irish themselves or to relatively aristocratic English readers. But the chapter opens up such rich possibilities for rereading the play's colonial contexts that its central point—that the play taps into "a cultural unconscious" the English could not wholly have ignored—is readily acceptable (11). This is the kind of work that seems destined to attract further investigation by other scholars, profitably revisiting a set of questions about the colonial imaginary from what is unarguably an important perspective.

Other forms of absence explored in this book require greater imaginative leaps. Callaghan argues, for instance, that "the castrato hangs over the English stage as an (in)credible threat" (52). Initially this seems a doubtful premise, since English boy players, however exploited, appear very securely to have been spared the fate of Italian castrati. The chapter ultimately makes a compelling case, however, for the prevalence of castration as a medical solution of last resort for victims of venereal disease. Though it is difficult to accept Callaghan's conjecture that early modern English men may have been about as likely to face castration as contemporary women are to undergo mastectomies, her argument does go a long way toward establishing castration as more than a symbolic threat.

Once castration becomes a physical possibility rather than merely a psychological fixation, moreover, new questions about transvestite theater emerge. In Callaghan's reading, when castration is relatively prevalent in the larger culture, the absence of castration in English theater companies becomes a fact worth investigating. She speculates that not displaying castrati onstage was a strategy for managing anxiety about male vulnerability. But the absence of castration also seems to have served a function for women in the audience, shielding them from the violent patriarchal equation of the female with the castrated male. In this sense, early modern theater proceeds in a more honest way than contemporary film, to which Callaghan turns briefly. Where film appears to include "real" women as subjects of representation, it has often been argued, the logic of cinematic representation actually confines its female figures to the realm of the missing phallus. If women on screen are castrated, the argument goes, male spectators are not. Surprisingly, Callaghan identifies in early modern drama an opposite logic: here it is the female spectator who is reassured, safely distanced from the possibility that the female body is merely a monstrous version of the male. "Don't worry," the transvestite theater seems to say, "we all know this is by and about men."

As intriguing as this reversal may be, crucial questions remain. Surely the content of much early modern drama works against whatever reassurance its modes of performance can offer. If the plays themselves equate women with castration thematically, there is more going on in the theaters than can be accounted for by the absence of castrati. True, the failure to practice castration means, as Callaghan points out, that boy actors will routinely remind their audiences that they are boys rather than women; the ubiquitous threat of the breaking voice may well shield female audiences from naive identification with the women they see represented on stage. But a whole host of theatrical strategies work to reinforce the connections between actual women and staged representations, and from this perspective the absence of castration seems a relatively small consolation. More fundamentally, this chapter points toward the need for a more wholesale re-evaluation of the metatheatrical and phenomenological as they relate to the ideological. Even Lady Perfect's lines quoted above, for instance, raise important questions about dramatic ontology. If she can call attention to the constructedness of the play she's in, Lady Perfect is positioned both to question and to reinforce the plot's misogynistic logic. She steps out of the play to remind us that only men think of women as "disgrac't subjects," but in doing so she assumes quasi-reality, and her subjection becomes something more than artifice. Perhaps if her voice squeaks like an adolescent boy's during the process the women in the audience will be spared identification with her, but the possibilities here seem too multiple to be categorized neatly.

Callaghan's chapter on *Othello* begins with the recognition that Africans were present in England in sufficiently large numbers that their absence from the acting companies should be examined. Identifying the performance of blackness as the "production of a difference that could not possess itself" (94)—in part because the representation of blackness in England is ineluctably by and for white men—Callaghan draws a compelling set of associations between the construction of the exotic and the "representational systems required by emergent capitalism" (76). In other words, capitalist exploitation of the world's resources—especially including the trade in foreign goods and the slave trade in foreign people—requires that the English imagine the racialized other as always already appropriated by others, never self-possessed. Interestingly, there are important connections between a racialized failure of self-possession and a gendered one. The similarities and differences between the stage's representation of white femininity and black masculinity are in this reading due at least in part to the different forms of exploitation to which African men and English women were subjected, and it is a strength of the argument that Callaghan reads them together.

The appropriation of the female body is similarly the focus of a chapter on *Twelfth Night.* Here the literal absence of women on the early modern stage becomes the occasion for a spectacular, if metaphorical, display of Olivia's genitals as Malvolio reads her forged C's, U's, and T's. It isn't quite true, as it turns out, to say that the female body can be displayed ostentatiously as an abstraction. These observations bolster Callaghan's very welcome reflections upon the limited power of "the material"—understood as bodies, as matter, as the material sign—versus actual materialism, with its far-reaching critique of the social and the economic. The reading of *Twelfth Night* also gives her a way of questioning the prevalent feminist belief that the female body is disruptive to patriarchy. Though readings of plays are not the central purpose of this work, however, certain aspects of both *Twelfth Night* and *Othello* deserve more exploration. Why, for instance, is white femininity so relentlessly imperiled by black masculinity in a play like *Othello?* Why jealousy? Why in *Twelfth Night* is Maria, as author of Malvolio's letter, given so much responsibility for the exploitation of Olivia's body? Both chapters make useful statements about the exclusionary practices of Shakespearean playing, but one might go further to explain contradictions within the plays themselves as they relate to those practices.

All in all, this is a provocative attempt to render visible what Shakespearean drama occluded. Callaghan leaves us a great deal to debate: the exact prominence of Irish colonial policies in the minds of Shakespeare's audiences, the possible relations between the threat of male castration and the pleasures of the female spectator, sometimes even the finer points of the plays themselves as ideological structures. Moreover, in spite of Callaghan's efforts to survey a wider range of practices than those of the King's Men alone, this is an argument that wants to be expanded to include more dialogue between competing playwrights and playing companies. Nevertheless, by looking hard at what isn't there in the plays she considers, Callaghan goes a long way toward forwarding the goals of the Accents on Shakespeare series, of which this book constitutes the second volume. Shakespeare is assumed to be almost home territory for most readers, and to think about the constitutive exclusions that go into building that home is to estrange us from it. Ultimately Callaghan effects a productive estrangement.

Notes

1. *The Plays of Nathan Field,* ed. William Peery (Austin: University of Texas Press, 1950) 2.2.106–8.

A Dictionary of Stage Directions in English Drama, 1580–1642
by Alan C. Dessen and Leslie Thomson
Cambridge and New York: Cambridge University Press, 1999

Reviewer: Barry Gaines

For a generation, Alan C. Dessen has been our Renaissance theatrical guide. His numerous insightful reviews of modern productions of Shakespeare and his contemporaries have preserved those events for present and future study. More importantly, his articles and books about early modern theatrical practice have helped us see how plays were enacted and perceived in Tudor and Stuart England. In the course of writing *Elizabethan Drama and the Viewer's Eye* (1977), *Elizabethan Stage Conventions and Modern Interpreters* (1984), and *Recovering Shakespeare's Theatrical Vocabulary* (1995), Dessen amassed a vast database of stage directions in Renaissance drama. Now, with collaborator Leslie Thomson, who has also published a series of articles on Renaissance staging, Dessen has published this treasure trove in *A Dictionary of Stage Directions in English Drama, 1580–1642*.

The compilers provide this description in the introduction:

> The purpose of this volume is to define and provide examples of terms found in the stage directions of English professional plays that date from the 1580s to the early 1640s. By providing such definitions we hope to make readily available information about English Renaissance theatrical terminology already known to specialists but not to other readers of Shakespeare and his contemporaries, and to present informa-

tion and documentation unfamiliar even to theatre historians and editors. (vii)

The *Dictionary* is compiled from a database of more than 22,000 stage directions from over five hundred plays, some plays considered in multiple versions. The "focus is on the terms—what we conceive of as the *theatrical vocabulary*—actually used by the playwrights, bookkeepers, and scribes of the period" (vii). The term "theatrical vocabulary" was, of course, used by Dessen in the title of his 1995 book. In a chapter of that book, providently entitled "Interpreting without a Dictionary," he noted that "most readers of this book (understandably) would prefer more space devoted to illumination and less to problems, pitfalls, and anomalies. Indeed, most attractive to such readers would be a dictionary or a handbook comparable to the *OED* that would define both stock terms and less familiar usages so as to facilitate interpretation."[1] He tries his hand at a few such dictionary entries, but he concludes, "if the evidence were more plentiful and the problems fewer, a series of dictionary entries *would* be an excellent way to set forth the theatrical vocabulary of Shakespeare and his contemporaries. Such, however, is not the case."[2]

Fortunately, Dessen and Thomson overcame their reservations and produced the *Dictionary* despite the challenges. They are still uncomfortable with the distinction between "fictional" and "theatrical" stage directions (terms suggested earlier by Richard Hosley), and they include a thoughtful entry for "fictional stage directions." The page-long definition given "aside" suggests that even familiar terms may be more complex in their application to the Renaissance theater than we imagine. But the enterprise is a rousing success.

The coverage is comprehensive. Unique terms (such as "astringer") are included as are extremely common terms. While the six hundred appearances of "door" are not individually enumerated, generous selections of and references to examples are included in all of the listings. References to editions cited are, of necessity, awkward. The examples were originally extracted from the quartos and folios, octavos and manuscripts in which the plays first appeared. Citation of those sources would have limited the utility of the work, so references have been made instead to modern reprints or editions. Peter W. M. Blayney has compiled the extensive "Plays and Editions Cited" at the end of the book.

A few examples will illustrate the scope of the *Dictionary*. We all have our favorite stage directions. Mine include (1) *"Exit, pursued* by a bear" (Folio *Winter's Tale*), (2) *"Enter the ghost in his night gown"* (Q1 *Hamlet*), (3) *"Enter Clifford wounded, with an arrow in his neck"* (Octavo *3 Henry VI*), (4) *"Enter Jasper, his face mealed"* (Beaumont, *Knight of the Burning Pestle*), and (5) *"Ithocles sits down, and is catcht in the engine"* (Ford, *Broken Heart*). Checking keywords in the *Dictionary,* an interested reader can find useful information about each: (1) Bears also pursue characters in Henry Killigrew's *The Conspiracy* (1635) and the popular *Mucedorus* (1590). Dessen and Thomson provide those references, but they do not consider questions such as whether real bears were employed in the theaters. (2) We are told that there are roughly forty examples of "nightgown" in stage directions signaling "the time as night or early morning," "the place as a bedroom or other domestic space" or "more generally unreadiness, a troubled conscience, or sleeplessness" (150). No comment is made on this particular example or on the texts of *Hamlet.* (3) Another half-dozen characters who enter with arrows in various parts of their anatomy are listed, but the authors do not point out that the Folio direction stops at "wounded" without adding the detail that is present in Holinshed. (4) The *Dictionary* furnishes other examples of characters entering as ghosts, but it quite appropriately avoids questions of responses to ghosts by either contemporary or modern audiences. (5) The *Dictionary* tells us that the other similar usage, *"an Engine fastened to a Post"* in Brome's *The Queen's Exchange* (1631) refers to "a mechanism to lower figures through the trapdoor" (83). We are not provided with any conjecture about the nature of the trick chair that subdued Ithocles.

While this reference book is not designed to be read cover to cover, there is fascinating material on almost every page. The range of plays treated is amazing. The compilers do not claim infallibility (the "eye may have skipped over a stage direction or two, or even an entire page" [xiv]), and I was able to find a "glove" in the opening group entry of Dekker's *Blurt, Master Constable,* and a "couch" from Fletcher's *A Wife for a Month* not included (the latter probably because F1 reads "coach"). But these are insignificant.

Dessen and Thomson have not only made their database of stage directions available to other scholars; they have provided a theatrical reference book that will be consulted and mined by generations of generalists and specialists alike. Let us hope that Cambridge University Press issues a less expensive paperback edition so that individuals can add this valuable resource to their personal libraries.

In the interest of full disclosure, I should acknowledge that Alan

Dessen was my teacher at the University of Wisconsin some thirty-five years ago. I have been learning from him ever since.

Notes

1. Alan C. Dessen, *Recovering Shakespeare's Theatrical Vocabulary* (Cambridge: Cambridge University Press, 1995), 42.
2. Dessen, *Recovering Shakespeare's Theatrical Vocabulary*, 63.

Shakespeare and Domestic Loss: Forms of Deprivation, Mourning, and Recuperation
By Heather Dubrow
Cambridge University Press, 1999

Reviewer: Gordon Teskey

The title of Heather Dubrow's first book, *Captive Victors* (1987), is taken from the splendid epithet of Tarquin in *The Rape of Lucrece:* "A captive victor that hath lost his gain" (729–30). In that book, Dubrow traced in Shakespeare's narrative poems and sonnets a proclivity for representing the dynamism of human experience in terms of fluctuations of profit and loss, getting and spending. It was Shakespeare's ability to capture this dynamic oscillation in the movement of his rhetoric, and to show it in moments of severely defining arrest (as in the phrase "captive victor"), that chiefly interested Dubrow. In her fourth book, Dubrow returns to this subject, or to a narrower version of it, in discussing the theme of loss in Shakespeare, particularly as it relates to the home. I say "narrower" because, although the word "recuperation" appears in the title, and although the introduction is called "the circular staircase," Dubrow focuses almost exclusively on loss. The circular staircase leads downwards. The three main chapters, which contain a great deal of social history, treat the themes of burglary, loss of one's dwelling, and the early death of parents. Essentially thematic, these chapters argue, as Dubrow says in her final sentence, that "throughout his poems and plays Shakespeare writes out of, writes about, and writes against the domestic losses of early modern England" (201).

The conclusion, which focuses on Elizabeth's Bishop's "One Art," that masterly squib of gallows humor ("The art of losing isn't hard to master"), shows an interest in recuperating the book's social-historical emphasis on domestic loss to an aesthetic register that would allow for a fuller engagement with Shakespeare's art. But is a fuller engagement with art possible through loss alone? And if it is, does Bishop's poem authorize it? Although Dubrow refers to Bishop's "urbane ironies," she appears to miss the simplest irony of all: that whatever losing is, it isn't art. The speaker of Bishop's poem repeatedly asserts that it is, but the assertion does not become any truer for that: on the contrary, it is that form of irony called antiphrasis, opposite speaking. It is saying that loss isn't an art and loss is never mastered. The repetition, nicely exploiting the obsessiveness of the villanelle, is merely a way of putting off the truth until the speaker says, "the art of losing's not too hard to master / though it may look like (*write* it!) like disaster." One feels reading this book, with its relentless catalogue of domestic calamities juxtaposed to selected readings of Shakespeare, that for Dubrow loss can be art, if only as part of "the text that is Renaissance culture" (149), a phrase to which I shall return.

Occasionally Dubrow strives against the downward spiral: "Sometimes, to be sure, apparent healing merely conceals further disease, further loss. Thus, the processes of loss, which are implicated in figuration in so many ways, can themselves be aptly figured through the trope . . . syneciosis ["holding together" of opposites, as in "captive victor"]: apparent victories could be described as 'lossless losses,' with all the instability that mischievous phrase involves. . . . Yet elsewhere Shakespeare's texts celebrate significant types of recovery from the domestic losses chronicled in this study" (14). An example of such recovery is the corselet (inherited from his father) that Pericles lost and recovered from the sea, as he would do his wife: "My shipwreck now's no ill, / Since I have here my father gave in his will" (*Pericles* 2.2.134; "in his" must be elided as "in's"). Dubrow gives an interesting reading of this passage. But even when speaking of the romances she is interested less in recovery, or partial recovery, that in the ways in which loss itself, rather than a strengthened sense of personal identity, is conferred by what a parent has left. Loss becomes a presence that continually returns: "in the romances the effects of parental death, one of the most persistent of Shakespeare's revenants, return yet again from their earlier incarnations in *A Midsummer Night's Dream* and so many other texts in the canon" (193).

In her reading of the conflict between Oberon and Titania over the Indian boy, or changeling, of *A Midsummer Night's Dream*, Dubrow mentions that

> any Hollywood agent worth his swimming pool would have insisted that the playwright . . . realize the changeling in a dramatic character. He does not. And when Titania abandons that child, the play in effect abandons him rhetorically and narratively as well: not only do we not witness the episode in question, but it is further distanced by Oberon's brevity:
>
>> I then did ask of her her changeling child;
>> Which straight she gave me, and her fairy sent
>> To bear him to my bower in fairly land.
>> (IV.i.59–61)

"Thus," Dubrow writes, "he effects the sinking of the Titania" because he has caused her to "abandon" the child. Dubrow excuses Titania of the moral crime of "abandonment" because Titania is under the influence, at Oberon's instigation, of the magical juice of the flower, "love in idleness" (2.1.168). It is thus Oberon's fault that the child is abandoned and Oberon's fault, too, that Titania is morally at fault for having abandoned the child. There is some loading of the charges here: if Oberon is at fault for the child's abandonment, then it seems unreasonable to fault him for causing Titania to be at fault for the same crime. Perhaps Dubrow means Oberon is responsible for Titania's *feeling* at fault. But this can't be so: Titania feels nothing of the kind. The entire line of thought follows from an error, for no crime against the child, no "abandonment," has occurred. Despite the emotional power of the speech in which Titania initially refuses to give up the boy, it is, as she emphatically states, for the sake of the boy's dead *mother* that she will not give him up. What about the boy? Surely we are meant to consider that the boy is growing up and that it will be better for him now to be Oberon's "henchman" instead of Titania's brat. Sending the boy to Oberon is one of several positive things that comes from Titania's being in love, even (especially?) with an ass: a loss of selfish, nostalgic possessiveness, and with that the recognition that what is now best for the boy for whom she has so loyally cared is to take his place in Oberon's train.

Dubrow occasionally strains against the loss she promotes, as she does, less frequently, against the exhausted formulae of new historicism and postmodernism, for which she retains a striking loyalty. Perhaps, Dubrow concedes, Titania's speech on how she and the pregnant "vot'ress of my order" used to sit, "on Neptune's yellow sands, / Marking th'embarked traders on the flood" (2.1.126–27) is not *entirely* devoted to exploring "the financial and other material implications of paternal death, which . . . surely activated the mercenary implications of this speech" (149). Dubrow continues:

> the winds of the contemporary critical climate may and should direct our own sails in directions like these; yet refreshing breezes can turn into gales that force the unwary or unskillful way off course. The text is indubitably concerned with guardianship and its self-serving rewards, but it raises these questions within a scene whose language primarily and predominantly celebrates the relationship between Titania and her votress in very different terms. Surely merchant ships would have connoted excitement and adventure as well as material rewards to an Elizabethan audience. (149)

It is by no means indubitable that the text is concerned with guardianship and its self-serving rewards. The sometimes profitable institution of guardianship in Elizabethan England is totally irrelevant to a reading of the conflict between Oberon and Titania over the custody of the Indian boy. There's no money at stake. Although I am no Elizabethan, I confess to being excited by the image of merchant ships with sails billowing on the Indian ocean. Despite the antiseptic phrase, "to an Elizabethan audience," I'd bet the ships excite Heather Dubrow too.

We see what is at issue here later on in the same paragraph: a new historicist dislike of art, of its pleasures and excitements, of its ("*write* it!") hallucinogenic power. Dubrow strives against this dislike, but her commitment to new historicism makes it impossible to deal with art except in indirect ways: "In the texts of Renaissance culture, and in the text that is Renaissance culture, fears of parental loss and of the financial conflicts and familial disruptions and reorganizations that could ensue are sometimes precisely this: an undertone and an undertow in a scene of a very different tonality." By a "different tonality" Dubrow really does mean the beauty and sweetness of Titania's account of how her pregnant companion, her robes billowing like the sails of a ship, would sail upon the land. But one wonders about the elaborate defense-work that is built up before the reticent formulation, "a very different tonality." Consider the phrase, "in the texts of Renaissance culture, and in the text that is Renaissance culture." New historicism and postmodernism are intellectually exhausted precisely because they affirm a specious reciprocity between such things as "the texts of Renaissance culture" and "the text that is Renaissance culture," between monuments and documents. If you believe in that reciprocity you will believe anything and be excited by nothing.

Charismatic Authority in Early Modern English Tragedy
By Raphael Falco
Baltimore and London: The Johns Hopkins University Press, 2000

Reviewer: Michael D. Bristol

Charisma is easy to recognize but hard to explain. Some people just have it—the rest don't. Raphael Falco's *Charismatic Authority in Early Modern English Tragedy* is an ambitious attempt to understand the essentially tragic character of this compelling but finally elusive personality trait. The central argument of this book is that charisma only really exists in the emotionally charged social relations that come to exist between certain exceptional leaders and their followers. Falco's discussion begins with St. Paul's discussion of the gifts of grace, or *charismata* in 1 Corinthians 12. The Pauline treatment of charismatic leadership reinterprets the various prophetic "gifts"—wisdom, knowledge, great works—as the expression of "one and the selfe same Spirit, distributing to every man severally as he will (1 Cor. 12:7–11)." According to Falco, Paul understands the charismata not as individual traits of personality but rather as a property of the mystical body of the early church. Put more simply, "charisma is . . . a shared experience" (2). On this account, then, the charisma of individual leaders can only be grasped in terms of the larger concept, first articulated by Max Weber, of charismatic authority.

Weber's notion of charismatic authority is part of a larger theory that attempts to identify and classify the major sources of social cohesion. According to Weber, political order and stability may be anchored in a shared tradition of social life, or in a formally codified system of laws and regulations, or in the personality of an extraordinary leader whose task is to embody and to express the collective will. Interestingly, Weber's account of authority would have seemed absolutely clear and right to almost every citizen of early modern England. The issue of legitimate authority was energetically contested both in formal political debates and in extensive private litigation. These controversies were, more often than not, three-sided. Should England be governed in the light of established local customs and traditional ways of doing things, or should it follow a more rational program based on the institutions of Parliament, common law, and the judicial system? Both of these notions were in conflict with the basic idea of the royal decree as the ultimate source of social authority for the whole society. The entire Weberian scheme of tradition, bureaucracy, and charismatic leadership was powerfully manifested in the political life of early modern England. But, as Weber clearly understood, charismatic authority is a wild card, based on a fundamentally irrational bond between individual leaders and their followers.

It's unfortunate, in my view, that *Charismatic Authority in Early Modern English Tragedy* makes no attempt to explore or even to identify the historical context I've just sketched out. Falco's otherwise perfectly cogent arguments would have been much more persuasive if he had been able to reference the compelling interest ideas of charismatic authority would have had for the original audiences of plays like *Richard II* and *Hamlet*. In a more general way, my principal criticism of Falco's book has to do with other sins of omission in the management of the exposition. It would have been helpful to have at least brief discussion of the various qualities that groups typically recognize in their charismatic leaders. Who are the typical examples of charismatic authority—Alexander the Great? Napoleon? Marilyn Monroe? And it would have been extremely interesting to establish a contemporary topical context for the discussion of charisma as the basis for the modern forms of authoritarian populism represented by such diverse figures as Adolf Hitler, Gandhi, and Ayatollah Khomeini. These omissions do not compromise Falco's argument, but in my view they seriously limit his potential readership. Readers who are fully au courant with the extensive recent developments in early modern literary scholarship, ranging from Linda Charnes *Notorious Identity* to Constance Jordan's

Shakespeare's Monarchies: Ruler and Subject in the Romances, may profit considerably from a careful study of Falco's book. But for others it may prove to be something of a struggle.

In a way it's unfair of me to criticize Raphael Falco for not doing things he clearly never intended to do. And so to provide a better sense of his contribution to the scholarship on early modern tragedy, I want to look at least briefly at his very detailed readings of specific plays. The first example taken up is Christopher Marlowe's *Tamburlaine.* Falco reads this text as the manifestation of a pure revolutionary charisma. This turns out to be a form of compulsive transgression against any and all forms of hitherto existing authority. Whatever it is charismatic leaders set out to do, they can't stop doing it. And in fact the compulsion to repeat entails an escalating spiral of grotesque and gratuitous violence. The monotonous and emotionally flat quality of the play flows from this increasingly strained attempt at ever greater histrionic excess. Falco's account of *Tamburlaine* as pure charisma also reveals a disquieting aspect of the real truth about monarchy. As Constance Jordan has shown, the early modern idea of royal absolutism implies that monarchy is fundamentally abusive, since the monarch is perfectly free to act against the interests of his subjects if that's what he wishes to do.

The complexity of charismatic authority is much more fully elaborated in Shakespeare's *Richard II.* As Falco shows, Richard's charisma is something larger than any exceptional qualities of his personality or "body natural." He is endowed both with lineage charisma as the rightful heir of the Plantagenet dynasty and with office charisma as the anointed king. These aspects of charisma are to a significant degree impersonal, expressions of the corporate body the king represents. Richard's personal charisma is perhaps easier to grasp in performance. In the recent production of *Richard II* at the Stratford Festival in Canada the role of the king was performed by Geordie Johnson, a beautiful and physically compelling actor who literally towered over all the other figures in the play. Johnson's Richard possessed a grace and a depth of intelligence completely lacking in his enemies, who were moved only by rancour and shabby opportunism. In this staging, the play no longer seems to be the story of a weak and guilty king providentially overthrown by a more skilful politician. Instead it recalls Nietzsche's account of tragedy as a drama of ritual dismemberment: "symbolic dismemberment—what Nietzsche calls the 'spell of individuation'—invariably precipitates the catastrophes in tragedies centring on charismatic authority and charismatic group function" (21–22).

Falco's account of *Richard II* complicates the *roi fainéant* interpretation of the play in a different way, by exploring the "charismatic capital" that accrues to Bolingbroke, especially in his ability to appeal to the popular element. But his "courtship to the common people" is not incompatible with the strong attraction he has for his fellow aristocrats. "In the best Pauline sense the duke is 'all things to all men.' " The rebellion against Richard, then, represents a successful instance of charismatic group function. This certainly helps to explain exactly how Bolingbroke gets away with the various crimes he commits in the name of restoring "good government." What remains uncertain here is whether England is really better off with Bolingbroke than they were with Richard. As Falco shows, the charismatic group function established between Bolingbroke and his followers is just as irrational as the one that existed under Richard. There can be no rationalization or routinization of charismatic authority under Henry IV because Bolingbroke has absolutely no conception of "good government" that he intends to implement other than a more skilful management of charismatic capital. But as Falco's analysis suggests, the notion of skilfully managing charisma is in the end a contradiction in terms.

Charismatic Authority in Early Modern English Tragedy explores the subtle ramifications of charismatic group function in detailed readings of *Hamlet, Othello,* and *Samson Agonistes.* Falco then proceeds to a provocative discussion of erotic charisma in the tragedies of Cleopatra. The notion of erotic charisma is to some extent unexplored territory, though it becomes increasingly clear in this final chapter of Falco's book that charismatic group function is a powerfully libidinized relationship. I cannot hope to do justice to the arguments presented in these chapters within the scope of a brief review. But I can perhaps give some idea of Falco's achievement by looking at a brief epilogue on Shakespeare's *Coriolanus.* Falco suggests that the figure of Coriolanus manifests "what might be called *anticharisma*" (201). The Roman citizens absolutely hate him but at the same time they are fascinated with what he does—they just can't get enough of him. Paradoxically, when Coriolanus is killed by his own Volscian followers, the resistance of the Plebeians almost immediately fades away. This all-too-brief discussion suggests just how fruitful the ideas explored in this book can be for future research and criticism. And indeed this is exactly the hope expressed by Falco in his own summation of his achievement. "Let me conclude, therefore, with the dual hope that this book will serve as a catalyst for the further study of charisma and tragedy and that it will soon be superseded" (206). This is, in my view, a graceful way to wind things up. Raphael Falco does not make things easy for his readers. His work demands much in the way of intellectual preparation. But I have found it provocative and challenging. It is a book that will reward anyone who is willing to engage with its often-difficult arguments.

Maids and Mistresses, Cousins and Queens: Women's Alliances in Early Modern England
Edited by Susan Frye and Karen Robertson
Oxford: Oxford University Press, 1999

Reviewer: Lisa Hopkins

Maids and Mistresses, Cousins and Queens is a sustained attempt to recover from texts of the early modern period, both literary and nonliterary, histories of women functioning not only as isolated, unusual individuals but also as members of female networks and alliances. Some of them examine representations of female bonding in dramas by Shakespeare, Jonson, Dekker and Webster, and the anonymous author of *Swetnam the Woman-hater;* some of them examine groupings of actual women such as London maidservants, the kinship circle of Elizabeth Ralegh, named and unnamed needlewomen, and the members of the religious community founded by Mary Ward; and some of them look at female authors such as Aphra Behn, Aemilia Lanyer, Diana Primrose, and Bathsua Makin. Inevitably, this is an enterprise fraught with difficulties, since records of such groupings (which might in any case have been too informal to be recorded in the first place) are so much less likely to survive than accounts of the doings of the isolated, notable individual. The essays in this collection can be roughly divided into those that thrive on this difficulty and those that are bedevilled by it.

The one that addresses it most centrally, and is thus arguably the most interesting essay in the collection, is Jodi Mikalacki's "Women's Networks and the Female Vagrant: A Hard Case," which examines the ways in which the written account of the experiences of one particular female vagrant may encode fictionalized versions of the experiences of others. Jean Howard, in her afterword to the volume, first deplores the fact that the traffic between literature and history continues to be largely one way; she then suggests that Mikalachki's essay at least could and should be profitably read by historians. I suspect that they would in fact be struck by the weakness of her evidence rather than its strengths, but this in turn is Mikalachki's own strength, for she is absolutely clear about the nature and limitations of her project and of what exactly such testimony as she is able to recover might be used to establish. Her essay thus represents an advance not only in the knowledge-base for such projects but in the theorization of them.

Some of the work in the collection is by historians: Kathleen M. Brown's " 'A P[ar]cell of Murdereing Bitches': Female Relationships in an Eighteenth-Century Slaveholding Household" offers a tantalizing glimpse into the class, race, and gender hierarchies of an American plantation. Along rather similar lines, albeit on a very different subject, is Mary Wack's "Women, Work, and Plays in an English Medieval Town," which offers a beautifully neat reading of two apparently late interpolations into the Chester mystery cycle by historicizing the moment of their production. Also worthy of mention is Valerie Wayne's sophisticated analysis of *Swetnam the Woman-hater,* which not only negotiates but makes a strength of the anonymity of the text it analyzes.

In stark contrast, I found Margo Hendricks's essay "Alliance and Exile: Aphra Behn's Racial Identity" positively frightening, and I think that if historians are indeed to attend to what literary critics have to say, they had better not be asked to read Hendricks's essay. Building on a chance question that she was once asked, Hendricks departs entirely from the realms of verifiability to enter into an extended speculation on the possibility that Aphra Behn might have had black ancestry. So she might; biographical knowledge about Behn is certainly slender and contradictory enough, but for that very reason we cannot know so. In under a page, however, Hendricks's initial assurance that we have enough evidence to know this not to have been so has turned into cavalier disregard of evidence and guesswork about how it could have happened: "If Behn was a passer, from which parent did she inherit her black African ancestry? How did that ancestor end up in Canterbury, if the parish records cited by Behn's biographers are accurate?" (267). How indeed? After all, why on earth should be suppose that parish records examined by presumably competent scholars should be any more reliable than a piece of speculation? Hendricks does concede that she will not "attempt to prove definitively that Behn may have had a black African ancestor," but she assures us instead that "there is another way of 'knowing' the pass, of establishing one's status as a member of the 'in-group'—intuition" (267). In that case, there would really be no point in bothering with scholarship at all, and that would be a pity, because it would totally disable the point and achievement of the many other essays in this volume, which do take the pains to build a careful case on available evidence, and, in doing so, offer fresh understandings of modes of female networking in the early modern period.

Literature, Travel, and Colonial Writing in the English Renaissance, 1545–1625
By Andrew Hadfield
Oxford: Clarendon Press, 1998

Colonial Writing and the New World 1583–1671: Allegories of Desire
By Thomas J. Scanlon
Cambridge: Cambridge University Press, 1999

Reviewer: Ania Loomba

In the past few decades, the work of Michel Foucault and Edward Said has been a major influence on the study of early modern colonialism, travel, and cross-cultural encounters. Even though Foucault himself did not address the colonial sphere, his suggestion that there is a sort of symbiosis, however asymmetrical, between those who possess social and cultural power and those who don't— that the former need to describe and define the latter not simply in order to control them, but also in order to define their own selves— has been, especially since Said's use of it in *Orientalism,* widely used to think about the dynamics of colonial encounters. The idea that the European "Self" defined itself against various "Others" who were encountered both far away in America, Africa, and parts of Asia, or nearer home in Ireland and Wales, has shaped a wide variety of critical and historical writings that do not necessarily share other methodological and political emphases. In Renaissance studies, the writings of Stephen Greenblatt and Kim Hall (to take just two influential examples that are quite different from one another) develop the idea of such mirroring—Greenblatt suggests that encounters with non-Europeans were central to upper-class ideologies of self-fashioning, and Hall shows how English ideals of femininity, race, and beauty developed against the foil of images of blackness. Recent work has also detailed, with increasing sophistication, the place of gender and sexuality in colonial encounters and discourses of the period.

But, despite the influence of a Self/Other symbiosis model, English nationalism and colonialism are still often analyzed in isolation from one another. Thomas J. Scanlon's *Colonial Writing and the New World 1583–1671: Allegories of Desire* opens by suggesting that scholars of early America have insufficiently considered the European origins or roots of colonialism and of American Protestant identity; on the other hand, scholars of the English Renaissance "construct the colonial phenomenon as something that was exported intact from Europe" (2). Scanlon himself hopes to start a dialogue between the two tendencies, suggesting that "the colonial project became one of the primary ways that the English used to articulate and define their own emerging sense of nationhood" (3). Andrew Hadfield's *Literature, Travel, and Colonial Writing in the English Renaissance* also wants to demonstrate that "colonial and national histories did not occur, and were not regarded in isolation" (3), a point that it makes by exploring the interrelation between the domestic and the foreign in travel writings of the second half of the sixteenth and first quarter of the seventeenth centuries. Both books are interested in the development of a specifically Protestant colonial/national ideology in England; therefore, it is not surprising that they cover overlapping terrain, such the circulation of anti-Spanish Black Legend in England (including specific events such as the St. Bartholomew's Day Massacres in 1572) and texts like English translations of Las Casas's *Brevíssima relación* and Théodore de Bry's *Great Voyages,* especially Thomas Harriot's *Briefe and True Report* with John White's watercolor drawings (they even reproduce and discuss some of the same pictures). Both books complicate our understanding of the interrelation between colonialism and English nationhood, although both of them almost entirely ignore the way in which gender might have shaped colonial or domestic politics.

Andrew Hadfield's aim is to see how texts that are set in foreign bodies "reflected on contemporary problems within the English—sometimes British—body politic" (1). He rightly points out that during this period, generic distinctions that we take for granted today were unclear: therefore, he expands the category of "travel writing" to include not only travelogues or accounts of voyages, but also political treatises, prose tracts, plays, and romances. In all these texts, foreign settings were sometimes just an excuse for talking about domestic affairs; at other times, descriptions of foreign lands and people necessarily entailed cross-cultural comparisons and introspection about English identity. In his discussion of *The Tempest,* Hadfield reminds us that many critics of the play still tend to pit the colonial and the domestic as mutually exclusive spheres. Instead, he suggests that contemporary discussions about colonial hierarchies and inequities were also shaped by the inequalities within European societies: "the treatment of various underclasses within England was not necessarily better than the treatment of colonial subjects of European masters." To the play's vexed geographies—which, as recent criticism has shown span, interrelate but also superimpose North Africa, the Mediterranean, and the Americas—Hadfield adds a domestic, class dimension, a dimension that is largely neglected by discussions of the play's investments in colonialism. It is curious, however, that a scholar who has contributed so much to our understanding about colonization in Ireland should not address the Irish dimension in his discussion of *The Tempest* here, given that the early modern discourse on Ireland is often usefully linked to the question of class and "masterless men" in the play and in the culture at large. This absence is especially noticeable because Hadfield makes the far more unusual (but rewarding) suggestion that in *Othello,* Cyprus, being a borderland between Venetian civilization and Turkish barbarity, can be read as "analogous to Ireland," which was also seen as sort of liminal space (232).

In 1986, Peter Hulme's *Colonial Encounters* had masterfully demonstrated the ways in which the experiences of the New World generated a new vocabulary and practices, a new "Atlantic discourse" that in *The Tempest* could only be articulated through a "re-inscription" of an older "Mediterranean" vocabulary. Hadfield shows how an older domestic discourse of inequality is also reflected by this play: Caliban, Ariel, Stephano, Trinculo, and the Boatswain all indicate the percolation of Old World class relations into the new colonial context. But Hadfield goes much further and suggests that *The Tempest*

> can be read as a cynical play, exposing the hollow pretentions of Prospero without providing any viable alternative means of government. The circular structure of the plot indicates *that the voyage to the Utopian island teaches the characters nothing they did not already know or could not have learned from a European experience if they had only looked hard enough within the boundaries of their own states.* All have exported their perceptions and problems to a foreign destination, and the miraculous solution provided within the play does not, in the end, mean that all will change. Politics will continue to be worked out via the marriage alliances of the high and mighty. (252; emphasis added)

Such an assessment makes the colonial space merely a setting, a backdrop that does not fundamentally change previous concepts of governance or difference. Hadfield is interested in placing *The Tempest* in a tradition of writing about "others" inaugurated by Sir Thomas More's *Utopia,* which "deliberately juxtaposed the discovery of the New World with the problems of politics in the old" (253). But to fold *The Tempest* entirely within an earlier tradition in writing where foreign locales are merely excuses for self-examination (even if we agree that such was the case with texts like *Utopia*) is to undermine the ways in which the foreign (and especially the colonial) actively shapes perceptions of the domestic.

This is not to suggest that Hadfield registers no differences between various English inscriptions of foreign or colonial spaces. He contrasts Fletcher's *The Island Princess* (1619–22), a play based on Spanish and French histories of colonial rivalries in the Molucca islands, to *The Tempest:* Fletcher's play is "centrally concerned with the question of the relationship between European and non-European peoples, which is why it can be described as a colonial—or possibly, an anti-colonial—text in the broadest sense." Unlike *The Tempest,* this play "does not focus on the 'Utopian' problem of Europeans exporting their political obsessions to the locations in which they find themselves"; it suggests that "ill-considered projects would lead only to a self-perpetuating cycle whereby European and non-European cultures would view each other with mutual suspicion" (263). I think *The Tempest* can also be read as concerned with precisely these intercultural/interracial relations, even if these relations are colored by domestic European ideologies of glass or gender. On the other hand, I do not read, as Hadfield does, *The Island Princess* as critical of "the Manichean fantasies" of its central character, the Portuguese adventurer Armusia, who converts his lover, the Moluccan princess Quisara, to Christianity; rather it seems to me that the play endorses the colonial project by depicting the colonial relation as an interracial romance. The anticolonial Governor is cast as villainous and duplicitous, and Christianity is the secret weapon of the colonists that teaches the natives *not* to curse.

But my point here is not to insist upon different readings of *The Island Princess* or *The Tempest*, which are, like any other texts, open to multiple readings. Rather, I want to suggest that a more dialectical relationship between the colonial and the domestic needs to be traced in both cases. Both plays make sense of the colonial spaces they deal partly by inscribing them within a domestic vocabulary: Quisara is very much like a haughty lady of the European romances, flirting with and controlling her knights errant, just as Caliban and Ariel are like the working men of England, needing to be controlled because yearning to be masterless. On the other hand, in both plays, the colonial setting and concerns are not reducible to the domestic scene. To deny that in the case of *The Tempest* is to reduce Caliban to Prospero's creation and possession, and to ignore that element in Caliban that eludes and baffles Prospero, and for which he has not been prepared by his previous experiences in Milan. Equally, it is to suggest that Prospero is simply a European export, who behaves on the island as he would have at home and upon whom his colonial experience has little effect. Ironically, it has been suggested that it was the Americas that jolted Europe in a way that the East (the setting of *The Island Princess*) could not, partly because Eastern contact was both more extensive and had built up over centuries, whereas the impact of the New World was more radical.

I have discussed the last section of *Literature, Travel and Colonial Writing* (which also deals with Christopher Marlowe's *Massacre at Paris*) first, because it raises the question of the colonial/national interrelation most sharply and brings together the whole range of locales (Europe, Africa, America, and Asia) that are also dealt with in the first three chapters. Each of these earlier chapters considers different kinds of travel writing, and each goes over the entire period that Hadfield is interested in. Therefore, we revisit the same period four times through the lens of different kinds of travel texts. This is a clever way of indicating intertextual resonance and historical depth. For example, the opening chapter deals with English travelers in Western Europe, discussing how the writings of Thomas Starkely, William Thomas, Robert Dallington, Lewis Lewkenor, and Thomas Coryat used Venice and its liberal government as an ideal in order to critique increasing English authoritarianism. This discussion enriches the last chapter's suggestion that *Othello*'s Venice is a liberal city in which the Spanish Iago is the most illiberal and the most racist. Such a suggestion is also thickened by a previous discussion of English responses to the threat posed by the Spanish empire.

Hadfield suggests that Sir Thomas More's *Utopia* is a "foundational text of early modern English travel and writing" (11)—its blurring of the distinction between real and fictional settings, and its "union of the representation of a foreign culture with the vast generic category of the literature of counsel" beings its two most influential features. Hadfield's main argument is that writing about real and imagined foreign lands is often a way of participating in "current pressing debates about the nature of society, the limitations of the existing constitution, the means of representing the populace at large, the relative distribution of power within the body politic, fear of foreign influences undermining English/British independence, the need to combat the success of other rival nations, religious toleration and persecution, and the protection of individual liberty" (12). He wants to demonstrate that the "sphere of the political goes beyond that of the explicitly political" and is able to show this by charting the ways in which travel writing developed as "a nervously agreed forum for debate," and how a range of seemingly utopian fictions commented directly upon English politics. And yet, curiously for a book that wants to "follow through" the insights of the cultural materialist or new historicist tradition (15), *Literature, Travel and Colonial Writing* seems most interested in politics as modes of governance. For this reason, it does not achieve its aims—those of intervening in subversion versus containment debates that have marked critical approaches to the period, and of demonstrating the heterogeneity of power. For if power is largely understood as governance, then its heterogeneity is confined to factionalism or debate within a relatively narrow social sphere.

Even so, the book uncovers a dialogue between travel writers (largely English travelers to Europe), their patrons, royalty and the advocates of colonialization. James I's writings on the subject of governance, Hadfield suggests, seek to counter travel writings that applaud the liberalism of the Venetian state. Hadfield rightly distinguishes between travel writing and colonial writing: the latter, he shows, "became yet another public forum" for debating new ideas that were generated as a result of colonial contact as well as those opinions that were suppressed at home. Here, he concentrates on English publications that dealt with the Spanish colonization of the Americas, such as Richard Eden's translation of Peter Martyr's *Decades of the Newe Worlde,* the English translation of Las Casas's *Brevissima Relación,* Theodor De Bry's *America,* and Hakluyt's writings and collections, as well as those of Samuel Purchas. Hadfield astutely suggests that in Eden's text, the Spanish are constructed as "akin to one of the lowest elements of European society, the landless poor" (76), but such insights about class are not developed at length. Hadfield's main argument is that these texts suggest the ways in which a Protestant English colonization of the Americas will be both beneficial for the natives of these lands and ward off the threat of a Spanish tyranny over the rest of Europe: "As in so many other colonial texts, the focus is turned inwards, rather than outwards, the fear being that unless England is vigilant in both Europe and the Americas then their own fate could be that of the Indians" (99). This chapter suggests (and this is a point to which Scanlon's book returns in some detail) that for Eden and Hakluyt, "national renewal and the colonial enterprise were inter-related goals.... Just as Elizabeth would have to speculate in order to accumulate wealth, so would the nation have to expand in order to unify itself" (102–3). Here the relationship between nation and colony seems to be more dialectical than at some other points in the book. Hakluyt described idle Englishmen as cannibals, and feared that if they were not rejuvenated by colonialism, the English would become "man-eating savages similar to those which inhabit the Americas" (104). The descriptions of the Indians in these texts, Hadfield argues, are often indirect ways of discussing English identity.

The third chapter deals with prose narratives, certainly the least well known of the many kinds of writings this book is concerned with. Here, Hadfield returns to less openly colonial writings such as fictions set in apparently imaginary lands, arguing that Robert Greene's *Gurydonius, The Carde of Fancie* and Mary Wroth's *Urania* were coded allegories that dealt with potentially subversive materials that could not be openly discussed at home. William Baldwin's *A Marvelous Hystory Intetulede, Beware the Cat* is analyzed as an elaborate and subtle commentary upon English rule in Ireland. William Painter's *Palace of Pleasure* is read as critique of the high-handedness of rulers as well as the dangers of mob-rule. Hadfield admits that his readings are highly selective, and indeed given the sprawling nature of texts such as Painter's, that is understandable. Still, he sometimes bypasses aspects of the texts that seem important to their colonial dimensions: for example, he suggests that the famous story of Hyreenee, the beautiful Greek woman captured and killed by the Turkish emperor Mahomet, is "best read as [a] variation . . . on that of Lucrece" (155). But it is hard to ignore the anti-Turkish and anti-Muslim dimensions of the story, which was repeated as an example of Turkish cruelty and licentiousness (in Richard Knolles's *Historie of the Turkes* as well as several other narratives of the period) and which resonates with the story of Othello and Desdemona, and with contemporary tales of Christian maidens lost to the harems of Eastern potentates. (In fact, it was stories like this that prompted European counter-narratives of Muslim women marrying kind and gentle Christian men.) Similarly, Hadfield mentions that in Geoffrey Fenton's *Certain Tragicall Discourses of Bandello* "the threat to a decent way of life comes from the uneducated rabble and, most specifically, an alien Jew" (165), but he does not comment upon this Jewish element or how it might affect the novel's politics. In these ways, the "political" as well as the "colonial" are read somewhat more narrowly than one might expect, given that the book's aim is to widen the understanding of both these terms. However, this book covers a lot of ground, drawing attention to little-known texts and juxtaposing them with well-known ones to suggest the ways in which foreign spaces become mirrors for national concerns.

In *Colonial Writing and the New World 1583–1671*, Thomas Scanlan goes over some of the same ground as *Literature, Travel and Colonial Writing* but spends much more time reflecting upon his central thesis: that nationalism and colonialism were interrelated endeavors in the early modern period. The first chapter suggests that this relationship was best (or even necessarily) expressed through allegory: "Allegory, which I will suggest is the mode one turns to when the concept one is trying to articulate seems just out of reach—or conversely, hopelessly lost to the past—gave colonial writers (and their readers) a means of imagining and expressing the tremendous religious, ideological, and economic potential implicit in the colonial undertaking itself" (9). Scanlon approvingly quotes Claire McEachern's thesis in *The Poetics of English Nationhood*,

1590–1612 that "the nation is an ideal of community that is, by definition, either proleptic or passing, ever just beyond reach" and goes on to suggest that if this is the case "then we should be careful not to attribute to 'English-ness' during this period the status of a fully imagined or articulated national identity" (33). This is a necessary caution: as scholars concentrate on this period as one in which ideologies of nationhood were consolidated, it is possible for them to overlook the fissures, contradictions, internal debates, and sometimes even tentativeness that marked nation formation. Scanlon suggests that it is precisely because English identity was so fraught and vexed, "always in danger of dissolving in the ferment of social, political, religious and economic turmoil," that colonial enterprises were so important. Outward journeying and plantations were less the work of a secure and aggressive nationalism than the necessary means to the creation of an otherwise fumbling national identity:

> The world from which colonial writing sprung was one marked by social and economic dislocation, religious and political controversey, periodic famine, and devastating world war. It was, in other words, a world marked more by loss than by plenitude. And as such, it was a world ideally suited to the allegorical mode. (15)

Scanlon bolsters his argument by appropriating Benedict Anderson's insight that one of the catalysts of national ideologies in Europe was the decline of linguistic and religious communities that were pan-European in nature. "The idea of 'nation-ness,' therefore, becomes necessary at precisely the moment when older notions of imagined communities cease to function" (35). Scanlon appropriates this idea to discuss nation-ness "as a desire which, because it is never wholly or completely fulfilled, must exist at the level of fantasy," although he is careful to point out that such a fantasy cannot discussed entirely in psychoanalytical terms, both because it needs to be historicized more sharply than those terms will allow, and because, in the case of the writings he discusses, national identity is not just an unconscious desire, but often a fully articulated, even calculated, objective.

Las Casas's *Brevíssima relación,* with its graphic catalogues of Spanish cruelty in the Americas, was the foil against which the English fashioned their own colonial identity. Las Casas suggested that the Spanish ruled entirely by arousing native fear and terror, so the English offered their own colonial method as one that would include a "loving" relationship with the natives. This combination of love and fear, Scanlon suggests, is the formula revisited and revised repeatedly by Protestant ideologues, be they secular like Thomas Harriot, Richard Hakluyt, and Theodore DeBry, or clergymen such as Robert Gray, William Crashaw, and John Donne, or colonists such as Roger Williams and John Eliot. Therefore, where Hadfield reads *Utopia* as the ur-text for travel writing in England, Scanlon takes the English translation of Las Casas's *Brevíssima relación* as the book that was most central to England's fashioning of its colonial identity as a paternal Protestant presence that "privileged religious and spiritual purity" but also "allowed for the pursuit of economic gain and geopolitical dominance" (22). Such a thesis is not far removed from Hadfield's observations about colonial writing, nor is it entirely new, but Scanlon's strength is the focused way in which it is systematically addressed and demonstrated over the course of the whole book. Perhaps this is possible precisely because he is interested in one slice of the colonial spectrum, and in a limited set of English writings that consider only the New World: "colonial" ideology or indeed English nationalism is not understood as in any way complicated by England's relationship to Africa or Asia. But it would be unfair to single out Scanlon for this critique because scholars of early modern colonialism have yet to pay systematic attention to the ways in which "Eastern trade" and "Western Planting" (not to mention the traffic with Africa) were increasingly interrelated enterprises. In fact, Scanlon's account allows one to think beyond the immediate context he takes up precisely because it repeatedly places the local and textual details it examines within a larger argument of the place of desire and loss in national allegories in general.

Scanlon's discussion of Protestant preaching in America, for example, resonates with some features of the literature dealing with the East Indies. The Virginia divines suggested that the English lacked a coherent sense of national identity as well as lack of commitment to Protestantism: colonialism would allow both to be redressed. "In this sense, colonialism becomes not only a vehicle for carrying Englishness and Protestantism to the new world . . . but also the very means by which the English can re-affirm their identity as Protestants and as a nation" (94). These sermons, Scanlon shows, construct the colonial relation in the language of the marketplace, offering the natives conversion in exchange for commodities. The plays and pageants of the period that deal with the East (such as Fletcher's *Island Princess*) dramatize precisely such a scenario, where natives give their wealth willingly in exchange for Christianity. The mercantilism of the journeys to the East is usually pitted against the crusading rhetoric of the New World enterprises, and it is often suggested that Eastern trade was, at this time, free of colonial desire. But, as Scanlon shows, the languages of religion and of commerce mesh together in these New World sermons. In the East at this time there were no English missionary activities and no English colonies, which is why the same hybrid vocabulary shows up in literary texts rather than in more descriptive accounts. But the overlap reminds us that English planting in the West and trade in the East both emerged from the same well-spring of national desire (as well as doubt) back at home.

Scanlon traces not just the continuities but the important shifts within Protestant colonial rhetoric, showing how these sermons revise the earlier Protestant rhetoric of DeBry or Hakluyt by acknowledging more openly that colonialism could not be entirely "bloodless." The relationship of Ireland to the Americas is considered in an entire chapter devoted to Edmund Spenser, but here Scanlon challenges the view that England's Irish experience was simply duplicated in a more sophisticated manner in the Americas. He argues that Spenser's *View of the Present State of Ireland* offers us a "significant counter-example" to the pattern he outlines in the New World: instead of seeing colonial activity as a panacea for national ills and an anvil for forging an English Protestant identity, the tract regards the colonial space and the colonial enterprise as unfixing and unhinging that identity. All the Irish customs Irenius scrutinizes, "rather than revealing something specific about Irish identity, reveals the limits of, and poses challenges to, English surveillance of the Irish" (82). This is a persuasive argument, and Scanlon goes on to suggest that the "real challenge" facing Spenser was both "simple" and "insurmountable": "How could colonizers who don't behave like a nation colonize a people who *do* behave like a nation?" (86). Thus Spenser discovers, in a negative way, that "colonial-ness needs nation-ness," whereas the English divines understood the converse that "nation-ness needs colonial-ness" (92). Scanlon thus repeatedly draws attention to the give-and-take between colonial and national cultures. Scanlon's aim is also to take into account how portrayals of the natives shape these narratives. He differs with Stephen Greenblatt's reading of Harriot's *Briefe Report,* arguing that where Greenblatt sees a complete erasure of Indian cultures in the text, actually the emotions of the Indians are used by Harriot to describe "a conflict within himself and the English" or "an underlying ambivalence that permeated English attitudes both toward themselves and toward native populations . . . rather than functioning simply as Machiavellian quest for power, the fear and love of the native peoples also formed a crucial component in England's attempt to conceive of and represent itself as a colonizing nation" (58). Greenblatt's Foucaultian emphasis has been widely critiqued, but I am not sure that English ambivalence about their colonial project can be read as an argument against the coercive power of colonialism or its negative effect upon the Indians. After all, Greenblatt's point is precisely that even the potentially subversive elements of Harriot's account can be appropriated by the dominant ideological and material mechanisms. It may not be useful to pit "ambivalence" against "a Machiavellian quest for power," or indeed to read containment as "Machiavellian." The word "Machiavellian" might imply an entirely self-conscious agent of power, but of course no dominant regime can be understood along those lines. Contradictions, ambivalence, fraught uncertainties are found to mark even the most repressive colonial regimes. Ultimately, the material practices that accompanied such rhetoric must be brought into focus: Hadfield reminds us of the genocide that colonial America witnessed, and reminds us too that in many ways "such problems were overshadowed for early writers and readers by a whole host of self-absorbed concerns, moral, political, and national" (91). In that sense, Hadfield's argument is internally consistent: Indians were simply not there in any real sense in these materials, a point that Greenblatt has also made very eloquently. The colonial and the national sphere might shape each other, but within colonial representations the natives are certainly hard to find, except as mirrors for English identities.

Hadfield and Scanlon seem to agree that Indian culture in these texts emerges as a more childlike or simplified version of England's own bygone self. Scanlon's book traces the multiple ways in which they disappear in various Protestant texts. Thus, we learn that there is a real difference between DeBry's manipulation of early ethnographies, which makes the Indians less alien in order to suggest their relationship with England's own lost past or glorious childhood, and Harriot's view of the Indians as potentially disobedient children who need to be disciplined by fear more than by love. The chapter on Roger Williams's *Key into the Language of America* is especially useful in this regard because it shows how Williams's elaborate representations of Indians and their customs and languages were used by him to conduct a "devastating polemic" against his fellow colonists. By suggesting that other English colonists were terrorizing the Indians, Williams constructs himsewlf as the loving and true inheritor of the Protestant legacy. In his text, like DeBry's, the natives are both ready to be civilized and needy for governance, but whereas DeBry worked against the specter of Catholic Spain, Williams's battlefield is the Anglo-American colonial space. Finally, in its last chapter, the book suggests that John Eliot's *Indian Dialogues* shift the ground still further away from the original battle between Protestant England and Catholic Spain: they are fully colonial documents in as much as they speak to Eliot's fellow colonists rather than to people left behind in England.

In his discussion of Protestant ambivalence, Scanlon inverts Bhabha's notion of "colonial mimicry" to suggest that it describes the process by which colonial masters construct the natives as childlike or primitive versions of themselves. He writes that in Jean de Léry's *History of a Voyage to the Land of Brazil*, "even when he is identifying with the Brazilian native people, the Tupinamba natives. . . . Léry does not endow them with a fully operational human subjectivity. Thus, even within the process of identification itself, there is ambivalence. Homi Bhabha has called this phenomenon 'colonial mimicry. . . .'" (45). It seems to me that colonial mimicry refers to the *natives'* mimicry of their masters (even if Bhabha often discusses it via colonial representations of native desire rather than via native articulations of their own desires). Scanlon appropriates the concept for the colonists too smoothly. For all of us who work on colonial encounters in this period, it is genuinely very difficult to locate native presences, not only because of our own limited training and skills but also because of the very real archival problems in locating that which was erased by European writings on the subject. Still, postcolonial criticism has taught us to make conceptual space available even for those "subalterns" who "cannot speak."[1] When English colonists use descriptions of Indians to contemplate their own identities, they are not really mimicking the natives at all. Mimicry would involve their altering their own behavior and practices to bring them in line with the Indians (something that did happen when colonists "went native"), which does not seem to be the case here at all. Colonial mimicry is usually understood as a way of survival for the colonized: often the only way of affirming their humanity is to claim that they are like their masters. Such mimicry is often pathetic and tragic, but at other times can also be subversive or critical of colonial ideologies, as Mary Louise Pratt has discussed in relation to colonial America.

While in certain instances colonial masters may also have mimicked native cultures the two forms of mimicry cannot be conflated without erasing the difference in power between the colonized and the colonizers.

Scanlon certainly places the colonial space in a more dialectical relationship with the mother country than does Hadfield, but within this space Indians are understood as merely rhetorical devices for colonial dialogues. We do not hear, even in summary, the practices that accompanied such rhetoric. In what way did English colonialism really differ from that of the Spanish? Hadfield reminds us that the Black Legend flattened out disputes within Spain and helped establish a Protestant/Catholic dichotomy (94). It would have been useful to learn whether or not other (pro-colonial) Spanish accounts entered the English colonial debate, and whether or not English critiques of English colonialism shaped this debate. *Literature, Travel and Colonial Writing in the English Renaissance* interconnects a larger and much more diverse range of materials, while *Colonial Writing and the New World 1583–1671* reflects more deeply on the formation of the colonial nation. Both books will be enjoyable and useful for scholars in the field.

Notes

1. This strategy asks us to suppose a presence that at first cannot be found; Gayatri Spivak endorses it as the enabling fiction of the Subaltern school of Indian history, in "Subaltern Studies: Deconstructing Historiography," in *Subaltern Studies IV; Writings on South Asian History and Society,* ed. Ranajit Guha (Delhi: OUP, 1985).

The Polarisation of Elizabethan Politics: The Political Career of Robert Devereux, 2nd Earl of Essex, 1585–1597
By Paul E. J. Hammer
Cambridge University Press, 1999

Reviewer: Pauline Croft

The second earl of Essex was the single most dominating figure in Elizabethan politics between the death of his stepfather the earl of Leicester in 1588 and his own execution after an abortive rebellion in 1601. Yet Essex has never attracted a serious historical biographer until now, not least because of the daunting complexity of the multifarious and fragmented sources on which any study of his life must rely. This volume will form the first of a two-volume study continuing to Essex's death. The old view usually dismissed the earl as a political butterfly, colorful and dynamic but a lightweight, particularly when compared to his contemporaries Sir Robert Cecil and Lord Burghley. Instead, Essex emerges here as a man of vast energies and abilities, deeply committed to an ideology of classical virtue. He deliberately positioned himself as a warrior-leader of the godly Protestant cause against Spain. His self-image increasingly clashed with his position at court as the queen's young favorite, though it was this personal relationship that was the source of his influence.

Hammer traces Essex's formative years, beginning with the death in 1576 of his father, which left young Essex as a royal ward in the guardianship of Burghley and the earls of Huntingdon and Sussex. They jointly oversaw his upbringing. More significant was his godfather and stepfather Leicester, who secretly married the widowed Lady Essex in 1578. After coming to court in 1585, Essex quickly followed Leicester to the Low Countries, where the English were aiding the rebel Dutch against Spain. He was knighted for valor on the field at Zutphen, the battle in which his cousin by marriage, Sir Philip Sidney, was fatally wounded. Sidney cast a long shadow; Essex married his widow and henceforth strove to emulate and outdo his fame as the paragon of knightly honor.

After 1586, Essex was conditioned to see both domestic and foreign policy in moral and ideological terms. His rise to leadership in the conflict with Spain culminated in the successful Cadiz expedition of 1596, the disastrous Azores voyage of 1597, and what Hammer perceptively calls the "decidely hollow" triumph of being appointed England's earl marshal in the same year. This was an empty honor since his rival the lord admiral was created earl of Nottingham and given the credit for victory at Cadiz. Financially and mentally stretching himself to the limit, Essex made a wholly disproportionate contribution to the war effort, charismatically leading his men from the front, but receiving little by way of recognition or thanks from his sovereign. Blocked at home by the Cecils, father and son, Essex also alienated potential allies and eventually faced a coalition of privy councillors made uneasy by his aggressive war aims and his implacable hostility to any moves toward European peace.

Hammer follows recent scholarship in depicting the 1590s as a decade markedly different from the previous thirty years of Elizabeth's reign. He brings out the declining ability of the queen herself to control either her court or her policies; in wartime she was hampered both by her gender and her increasing age. The result was that her generals repeatedly ignored or modified her instructions. Essex was wholeheartedly committed by 1597 to the view that England faced a continued threat from Spain that required a massive pre-emptive strike, preferably by taking either Cadiz or Lisbon, or both, and holding them as English garrisons. This would shift the main theater of war to Spain itself, a grandiose vision that was at odds with the perceptions of the queen and Burghley; once England's own safety was assured after 1588, both grew more concerned about the Catholic revolt in Ireland than the threat posed by Spain in Europe. The disintegration of Essex's career followed between 1597 and 1601.

Although the prime focus of the book is naturally on Essex as politican and general, there is much that is illuminating on related areas. Essex was a master of using *imprese,* the shield-like combinations of motto and imagery beloved of Elizabethans in tournaments, which were later displayed at Whitehall. He spent heavily on his tiltyard appearances, where his striking appearance and martial abilities advanced and sustained his image as a great chivalric figure. The almost theatrical skills utilised in impressing his public can also be seen in his portraits. Except for Hilliard's famous miniature of the young man amidst the roses, almost certainly

Essex as a young favorite jealous of his then rival Sir Walter Ralegh, all the images depict him as a warrior. The Cadiz portrait became his definitive visual statement; the town burns in the background, waves crash on the rocks, and Essex stands grasping his sword and general's baton. He is dressed entirely in the queen's white, save for his Garter medal and an armored collar; the favorite as military victor. Similarly, Essex used the circulation of manuscript and printed material to forward his cause, including the text of the supper entertainment after his Accession Day tilt of 1595 (which was read as an attack on his enemies at court). The "True Relacion," his account of the Cadiz voyage, written on board ship during the return, sets out his strategy for winning England the maritime hegemony of the Atlantic.

The book is densely informative, and demands careful reading, but Hammer writes with the clarity and good judgment that comes from thorough familiarity with the sources. He provides a superb overview of the late Elizabethan regime, at the same time building on his earlier discussion of Essex's career at court in the symposium volume *The World of the Favourite* edited by Sir John Elliott and L. W. B. Brockliss (1999). Let us hope that the second volume, taking the story to the tragic and shocking denouement of 1601, will emerge as soon as possible.

The Romance of the New World: Gender and the Literary Formations of English Colonialism
By Joan Pong Linton
Cambridge: Cambridge University Press, 1998

Reviewer: Kim F. Hall

Feminism has been an outspoken presence in early modern English literary scholarship, yet it remains a relatively still voice when scholars of modern England turn to England's relationship to the New World. The formative and powerful books of individual feminists such as Annette Kolodny and Mary Louise Pratt that are so influential in American studies have no clear parallel in the literary study of New World materials. This absence becomes particularly notable as Shakespeare and early modern studies move towards a less localized and more global perspective. Joan Pong Linton's excellent *Romance of the New World* helps correct that absence and promises a more extended feminist, trans-Atlantic approach to English literature that brings England closer to its new world territories. It provocatively weaves together structures of gender, culture, race, class, and religion that produced English understandings of the New World.

The Romance of the New World examines the interplay between modes of romance in print culture and the contemporary circulation of New World narratives. Arguing that there is an "intergeneric" space between more overtly literary romance narratives and the texts of New World colonization, Linton excavates this space through thematic chapters that artfully juxtapose romance narratives with New World texts. In this interplay, the household becomes a key model "for a range of social exchanges in which the domestic gender hierarchy comes to underwrite other forms of cultural difference" (4). In addition to providing the narrative means for communicating the unfamiliar, the domestic contains threats posed by the unknown: "the trope of domesticity functions as a vehicle for transcending moments of crisis, thereby conferring upon travelers and colonists a degree of mastery in intercultural contact" (185).

Her first chapter prepares for the extended argument by mapping out a generic shift in romance, one that recuperates courtly values for adventurers on lower rungs of the social ladder: the open-ended (and potentially endless) efforts of chivalric knights in service of a distant lady that were the staple of romance mutates into travel and labor, with the specific goal of a marriage that will be productive both of children and of the prerogatives of increased social rank. This move, Linton argues, makes romance the site that simultaneously accommodates and interrogates the interests of a nascent capitalist economy. Moreover, this newly articulated vision makes romance "a vehicle for the translation of one set of social relations into another" (4) and thus a useful instrument for comprehending and mastering the novelty of the American experience. This new "family romance," in which adventurers eventually make their fortunes through marriage, generates a "new domestic masculinity" that shapes the ideals of English commercial and colonial adventurers abroad. Supported by the innovative work of Suzanne Hull,

Lorna Hutson, and Juliet Fleming, Linton sees through romances' putative appeal to women to argue that these texts naturalize a patriarchal gender hierarchy (with its newly capitalist interests) and thus best serve the interest of the male traveler/lover. Its assumption that female wandering betokens a female sexual errancy that must be domesticated "by male sexual prowess in marriage" reinvents the romance project for aspiring bourgeois males.

Reading Lodge's *A Margarite for America* against Spencer's *Faerie Queene* and Raleigh's *Voyage to Guiana* in chapter 2, Linton uses Lodge to demonstrate the distinctly Protestant nature of this vision. English aims for the New World are articulated in part as a response to Spanish advances in the Americas. Elizabeth I's and her colonizers' preference for plunder and piracy rather than settlement becomes understood as resistance to the motives and methods of Catholic Spain: New World narratives in particular rely on providentialist notions of a divinely ordained acquisition of land and commodities. Lodge's romance contains a self-conscious critique of the very tropes of New World/romance on which his narrative is based. Particularly compelling here is Linton's discussion of wonder. Lodge produces scenes of New World wonder and ironically reveals their illusory nature: "In these ludic moments, Lodge's text becomes the magician's book, encoding and dissolving its own power of illusion" (61). Such strategies are key to Lodge's mockery of the veil of romance often used to mystify the mercenary aims of English empire.

After mapping out this sense of the changing nature of romance, Linton moves to a more materialist focus on trade and objects. Chapter 3 examines the importance of cloth and cloth production as sites for cultivation of a new, bourgeois English manhood. Juxtaposing Deloney's *Jack of Newberry* with narratives of Sir Francis Drake in California, she contends that stories of cloth in both domestic and colonial narratives "are in fact stories of an ideal bourgeois manhood elaborated through the economics and politics of cloth-making" (62). This ideal of manhood is characterized by commercial skill, success at trade, and the proper exercise of domestic/national authority. *Jack of Newberry* marks a significant gendered shift in cloth production—the displacement of women weavers in a new, male-controlled cloth industry. Rather than the site of women's productive skilled labor as weavers, the home in this narrative becomes the place where male domestic mastery over women results in their unskilled support of an increasingly patriarchal economy. In a like manner, Drake narratives posit a primal moment of "clothing" the natives—and thus imaginatively create a market for English goods that universalizes this commercial sense of English male mastery. Although Linton is careful to point out that these narratives are allegorical and may redirect attention from actual frustration over attempts to create markets for cloth, her analysis leaves one wondering whether the narrative of triumphant English manhood also displaces a long mythic tradition that associates weaving with women's power.

Moving from production to consumption in chapter 4, Linton considers the symbolic significance of the "trifles" that circulate so promiscuously in travel narratives. She reads trifles within twinned discourses of eros and science that help create a specifically masculine English power. Through descriptions of exchange involving trifles, the early modern conception that profit for merchants must occur at the expense of the consumer becomes in the colonial arena an equation of commercial advantage with cultural superiority: "Englishwomen and Indians emerge as 'trifle-lovers' in the domestic and colonial arenas": both discourses help the English articulate developing conceptions of economy and consumerism for a colonial context (85). The ideal of the English provider who gives trifles (while holding onto valuables such as land, weapons, and gold) is produced through a magical sense of commercial manipulation in which the Englishman withholds desire—for goods and women—while exploiting the alleged desires of Indians and English women. Drawing on a range of print discourses, Linton sees the colonist, the peddler, and the romance writer generating an ideal consumer in whom they locate their projected desires even as they claim ideal knowledge of the Other's desires. While any reader in the period can recall countless domestic narratives that condemn and manipulate English women's putative love of finery as well as colonial discourses that proclaim English superiority in the face of the native's putative love of insignificant "baubles," Linton ends with a crucial counter narrative composed of resistant subjects who refuse complicity in this economy. Her readings of John Smith's attempts at manipulation/trade with Powhatan are nuanced accounts that demonstrate indigenous agency and resistance to manipulation. She likewise sees feminist writings such as *Jane Anger Her Protection for Women* as challenges to literary conventions and gendered fictions that construct women as consumers.

In recounting Columbus's landing on Hispaniola, Sebastian Münster's *Cosmographia* tells of an Indian woman who the Spanish capture, feed, and clothe before releasing her to join her people. According to this account, their generosity towards the woman makes the natives lose their fear (based on their mistaking European strangers for local cannibals) and initiate trade. Analyzing representations of this encounter within a reading of Serena's story in book 5 of *The Faerie Queene,* Linton produces a fascinating understanding of cannibals and voyeurs as culturally marked figures that represent different attitudes towards the vexed for trifles: "If the cannibal represents the commercial deficit of Indians, the voyeur stands for an English commercial sophistication in which Spenser . . . participates" (111). Women, in representation and in actuality, function as important mediators between ideals of male domestic/colonial mastery and concurrent fears of loss of masculinity and status through improper or excessive consumption. The numerous attacks on women as hyper-consumers of fashion addressed in the previous chapter are the most obvious manifestation of this. In chapter 5 she demonstrates how the highly gendered debate over tobacco negotiates English fears of losing identity on multiple levels when the English taste for this foreign "trifle" threatens the loss of the "civility," property and masculinity that constitute the proper English commercial subject. The drive to re/produce a domestic masculine ideal finds its material counterpart in a little-discussed phenomenon that should be fascinating for readers interested in women's history: the exchange of tobacco for wives in the Virginia colony. This exchange of an "object of cultural otherness for one of domestic propriety" (128) is a civilizing process that manages commercial and racial anxieties; however, as the case of one such woman, Jane Dickenson (held captive both by Amerindians and the Englishman who ransoms her from them) illustrates, once stripped of the veil of romance, the line between Englishmen and their allegedly uncivilized others may not be so clear.

In chapter 6, Linton uncovers an "intertextual nexus of travelers and false lovers" (132) between English constructions of inconstancy epitomized by *Troilus and Cressida* and problems of trade in the early Jamestown narratives. In *Troilus and Cressida,* warriors' self-valuations are affected by new market-generated values that produce the value of the self as endlessly negotiable. No longer a stable, heroic essence, the self becomes mutable, subject to a destabilizing, temporally stimulated market economy. Male anxiety over this instability becomes displaced as fear of female inconstancy: "Inconstancy is thus not fundamentally moral but economic: it reveals the unstable valuation of the self, male and female, amid the competitive exchanges of a market-oriented society" (133). The shift from this dynamic of female constancy in romance to the marketing of Virginia produces a narrative of competing modes of value/economic exchange that disturbs traditional notions of authority and the social self. Value operates on many levels here: on the corporate level, there was the problem of the failing Virginia enterprise, which not only did not secure returns for its investors, but failed to provide necessary supplies to its colonists. On the local level, the difficulties of acquiring and distributing food profoundly impact upon notions of leadership and authority in the colony. The lack of clear power to enforce policy made in the metropolis and the disruption of traditional conceptions of authority or rank meant that attempts to gain the desired im/balance of trade for food with the Powhatan tribes becomes mired in the competing methods and aims of the leaders, Smith and Newport. This competition is itself complicated by sailors' rogue attempts to profit from Indian trade. Both levels of value involve a crisis in fixing the masculine self that is resolved through narrative strategies of romance. In the former, promotional tracts substitute an erotics of colonial travel for actual evidence of a productive economy and investment; in the latter, allegations of Indian treachery translate Indian acumen in trade into a moral defect. Both scenarios mark the desired masculine control (conceived of as the power to fix value—of others and of objects) by the recuperation of economic advantage.

In chapter 7, two key tropes of husbandry—rape and education—converge in Chapman's *Memorable Masque* and Shakespeare's *The Tempest,* which were both performed at the marriage of James I's daughter, Elizabeth, to Frederick, the elector palatine. These texts offer different approaches to reproduction (both, however, still rely on similar ideas of erring femininity and feminized natives). Linton sees in these performances and in narratives written after the founding of Jamestown the articulation of a new Jacobean discourse of husbandry: the structures of family romance address the problems of cultural reproduction in ways that paradoxically circulate and efface crises of past and future indigenous resistance. "What emerges is a colonial hierarchy in which gender and race are mutually defining, and subordination to English husbandry is mediated through a feminine image of the native" (156). For example, the discursive play of "virgin/Virginia" aligns domestic and colonial discourses by linking natives with a virginity that needs proper male disposition. Resistance to English colonial husbandry is clearly gendered female: Indian religious leaders who resist claims of English mastery are feminized rhetorically; even Caliban's adversarial and threatening masculinity is bolstered by a claim to the island through a maternal genealogy. Moreover, husbandry and indigenous resistance are mutually engaged through "the thematics of magic" (164). In *The Tempest,* resistance is "temporalized"; that is, made distant through generational politics of the family romance. Desires to domesticate/assimilate Amerindian children through English education are haunted by the problem of resistance—native children (or allegedly childlike natives) who ideally would be easily assimilated into English cultural practices potentially become adult Calibans who find ammunition for resistance in their indigenous family inheritance.

The Romance of the New World is a complex and compelling book—a must-read for anyone interested in the literary aspects of cultural formation in England and the Americas. It provides careful analyses of its texts and a much-needed materialist rethinking of epistemologies and technologies of England in America. Linton's deft juxtaposition of canonical literary forms with colonial and other narratives leads the reader to a new understanding of more traditional literary forms, although I found some readings (such as the engagement with *The Fairie Queene* throughout the book) more compelling than others (the discussion of *Troilus and Cressida* with Jamestown promotional material seemed more jarring than the combinations in other chapters).

Paradoxically, Linton's attempts to draw attention to nonelite figures creates the desire for more insight into the heretofore marginal players in the colonial arena. For example, in her discussion of the trade for food in chapter 6, there appears little awareness of the role Amerindian women seem to have played in the cultivation, production, and distribution of food. Obviously, one is limited by the available resources, which themselves tend to marginalize certain figures. Linton herself points out that Pocahontas's "death in 1617 made possible her apotheosis as a cultural symbol behind which the Amerindian woman finally disappears" (130). However, this disappearance poses a crucial challenge as scholars trained in early modern cultural studies move to a more Atlantic view of Shakespeare and England: can we produce a criticism imaginative enough to delve behind this disappearance, to release the women "held hostage to romance" (186)?

Linton addresses this problem of the inadequate stories that survive colonial encounter in her coda, which fittingly concludes with the ultimate colonial family romance—the ever-evolving myth of Pocahontas (and the ultimate in corporate multiculturalism, Disney's *Pocahontas*). She issues a stirring call for a decolonizing pedagogy that, rather than trying to substitute some version of "truth" for fiction, "transforms students into makers of knowledge for themselves" (189). Within this framework, the idea of historical agency becomes more pressing and more expansive. One way to combat the blinding impact of national and corporate myth-making, Linton suggests, is to emphasize not only the agency of the dispossessed in history, but also the agency of students as producers of history and fiction themselves: "For it is in recognizing their own historical agency that inhabits their fiction-making that students make of their learning ways of living and acting in the world that are critically responsible to the legacies of the past as well as the possibilities of the future" (189).

Shakespeare and Social Dialogue: Dramatic Language and Elizabethan Letters
By Lynne Magnusson
Cambridge: Cambridge University Press, 1999

Reviewer: William H. Sherman

Lynne Magnusson suggests that studies of Shakespeare's language are at something of an impasse. Traditional close reading tended to isolate the linguistic from the social and historical; to look at individual passages for insights into the poetic genius of Shakespeare or the motivations of his characters. The "cultural poetics" of Greenblatt et al. tended to bring the social and historical back into play, but at the expense of the linguistic; to restore the cultural contexts of particular texts but to ignore the detailed workings of the language in which they are written. *Shakespeare and Social Dialogue* sets out to offer a sociolinguistic via media, using the discipline that focuses on language in its social context as a natural bridge between the poetic concerns of New Criticism and the political concerns of New Historicism.

In what it delivers and in what it doesn't, Magnusson's book draws much-needed attention to the difficult project of recovering the "socially situated verbal interaction" that informs Shakespeare's language. Such a project poses some challenging questions: Which sources can provide evidence of "social dialogue" in the past? How did Renaissance writers, readers, actors, and spectators mediate between spoken and written, or spontaneous and scripted, language? Which disciplines—traditional and emergent—can we turn to for help?

Magnusson brings three types of sources into play: the chapters move between passages from Shakespeare, "modern-day discourse analysis," and "the theory and practice of Elizabethan letter-writing." In chapter 1, Magnusson introduces her methodology by reading some key passages from *Henry VIII* in the terms provided by the "politeness model" of anthropologist Penelope Brown and linguist Stephen C. Levinson—an analysis of the strategies speakers use to minimize the risks to their position, credit, or self-esteem. The point here is to "demonstrate how much the complicated eloquence of characters . . . arises not as a matter of their individual expression but instead out of the contexts of their interactions" (11). Chapter 2 applies the model to Shakespeare's sonnet 58 and an epistolary exchange between Philip Sidney and his father's secretary. Following the lead of recent work by Frank Whigham, Jonathan Goldberg, Gary Waller, Judith Rice Henderson, and others, chapter 3 turns to the theory of Elizabethan letter-writing, describing the manuals of Erasmus and Angel Day. In chapter 4, Magnusson analyzes some early modern administrative letters, in order both to shed light on Shakespeare's dialogues and to make them a topic for literary criticism in their own right. The focus of chapter 5 shifts to *mercantile* interaction, setting two of the relevant epistolary handbooks (William Fulwood's *Enemie of Idlenesse* and John Browne's *Marchants Avizo*) alongside scenes from *Love's Labour's Lost, A Midsummer Night's Dream, The Merchant of Venice,* and *Timon of Athens.* The final two chapters return to sociolinguistic models and offer the most promising conjunction of linguistic and literary analysis. Chapter 6 draws on studies of how conversation works (especially those of Mikhail Bakhtin) to analyze the ways it does and does *not* work in *King Lear* and *Much Ado About Nothing.* And chapter 7 offers a reading of *Othello* that foregrounds the relations between gender, class, race, necessity, and rhetorical mastery, suggesting that Iago's verbal machinations can best be understood as a struggle for what Pierre Bourdieu has described as "linguistic capital."

In so far as Magnusson is interested in languages as a form of social interaction, a more accurate (and catchier) title might have been *Shakespearean Dialogics.* In Bakhtin's influential formulation of this concept, all utterances—spoken and written—are governed by rhetorical rules and social hierarchies, oriented toward future responses, and directed toward particular ends. Within Shakespeare studies, the turn from poetics to dialogics has traditionally been associated with the recovery of Renaissance rhetorical practices, and—in Magnusson's account—there is surprisingly little contact with this large and growing body of work. At its best, Magnusson's approach complements that of scholars such as Walter Ong, Marion Trousdale, Marc Shell, and many others, adding nuance and muscle to the study of specific tropes, and the general workings of social and economic power in Elizabethan language. It works especially well with scenes where the rules that govern linguistic exchange break down—failures of decorum in the early comedies, Shylock's alienation from the linguistic economy, and Cordelia's unwillingness to do the "housework" of conversation. In places, though, its reliance on linguistic models leads to readings that are more mechanical and less historical than those of New Criticism and New Historicism. I wondered, for instance, if we need Brown and Levinson's inventory of "positive and negative politeness strategies" to unpack messages that most readers will grasp intuitively, and which most scholars have preferred to study using the period's own terminology (e.g., "courtesy," "decorum," and "propriety").

Given that Magnusson puts so much weight on the conjunction of plays and letters (setting "Dramatic Language" and "Elizabethan Letters" alongside each other in her subtitle, her general argument, and half of her chapters), I would have expected a more explicit discussion of the kind of light they shed on each other. Magnusson turns to both types of text for important traces of "real-life" verbal interaction, but this is a notoriously elusive quarry and it needs to be explored rather than assumed. What makes dramatic language especially interesting, in ways that linguistics can surely help to explain, is that it depends on and allows for different kinds of play than the "real-life" contexts of letters and conversations. Recent work in the field of performance studies has been suggesting that a Renaissance play—in an important sense—does *not* represent real life; and Magnusson's characterizations of theatrical performance ("Actors in plays have scripted parts, which their characters appear to make up as they go along, for the benefit of an audience that overhears the conversation" [155]; or "the external forms of politeness may help to organize the psychology of real persons and its illusion in the presentation of dramatic characters" [27]) have more in common with modern than with early modern conventions.

As for letters, they are useful sources for a particular culture's, or group's, dialogics. They are strongly marked by the writer's social position, and combine both the live and the written—something which the advent of e-mail has brought into even sharper focus. But they are by no means the only or even "the main rhetorical texts which conceptualize interpersonal exchange in language" (3): others have been turning, with powerful results, to legal proceedings, and (again) to the rhetorical tools—including training in oratory, debate, and the use of commonplace books—which Renaissance writers and speakers were trained to use in generating discourse. Magnusson seems to favor letters not only because they are so clearly interactive but because of the extent to which they capture the "everyday language" of Elizabethan England. Day's letter-writing manual, for instance, is described as "a practical guide to the language of typical social relations, an Elizabethan's map of lived relations" (12). But Renaissance letters are not, necessarily, any more reliable than Renaissance plays as an unmediated record of what "face-to-face interaction" or "day-to-day conversation" was actually like. Magnusson provides a useful introduction to the verbal scripts that informed letters—and, presumably, dialogues in the street and on the stage—but needs to take fuller account of the ways they are shaped by the texts that record and transmit them. Her use of nineteenth-century editions of sixteenth-century letters is especially problematic, since the mediation by their editors is often as significant as in eighteenth-century editions of Shakespeare's plays.

Ultimately, I found myself asking whether Shakespeare himself is the best source for his period's dialogics. However rich his dialogues may be, as a playwright Shakespeare has always seemed less interested than (say) Dekker in the resources of "everyday language"; and he left behind only two letters (both of which are dedicatory epistles in printed works), whereas Jonson left records of his thoughts on language, his conversations with Drummond, and a considerable corpus of manuscript and printed letters, addressed to a diverse group of recipients and serving a wide range of rhetorical purposes. But that is part of a bigger conversation.

Islam in Britain 1558–1685
By Nabil Matar
Cambridge: Cambridge University Press, 1998

Turks, Moors, and Englishmen in the Age of Discovery
by Nabil Matar
New York: Columbia University Press, 1999

Reviewer: Charles Burnett

The reader would be forgiven in thinking that these two books, published within a year of each other, are on the same subject, especially since 'Turks' in the period concerned and 'Muslims' were almost synonymous, since, in the Mediterranean basin, only Morocco lay outside the Ottoman Empire. Nevertheless, although both books cover the same time and space, Professor Matar manages to avoid duplicating material. He does this in two ways: first of all, he writes what is essentially a series of extended essays on specific aspects of the relationship of Islam and 'Turks' to Great Britain, and distributes these essays between the two books. Secondly he sets up a different leitmotif for each book. In *Islam in Britain* the leitmotif is the consequences of the acknowledgment during this period that Muslims of the Mediterranean shore were both politically and culturally equals or even superiors to the Christian European States. The leitmotif of *Turks, Moors and Englishmen* is that European attitudes toward Muslims coloured their impressions of and dealings with the indigenous peoples of the New World, and that the imperialist policy that developed towards possessions in the New World, in turn, eventually determined European attitudes towards Muslims (this leitmotif is more clearly brought out in the title under which the second book is referred to in the first: *The Renaissance Triangle: Britons, Muslims, and American Indians*, which has survived as the title of a chapter within the book).

Of the individual chapters of the two books some exemplify the leitmotifs of the volumes more closely than others. In each, a thesis which could be applied to several countries of Europe, is demonstrated within the British context, and each chapter is virtually self-contained. In *Islam in Britain*, the topics covered are the historical examples of conversion to Islam, the depiction of conversation to Islam on the English stage, the knowledge and use of works of Arabic literature and theology (which includes a self-contained essay on coffee and coffee-houses), the conversation of Muslims to Christianity, and eschatological theories relating to the final defeat of Islam (especially those that involve the "Jewish restoration" to Palestine). The conversions (in both directions), the perception of the "renegade" in drama, the reception of Arabic literature, and the theological discussions, all illustrate how Englishmen engaged with the Turk as an equal, whether as an ally or (more often) as an opponent. This was inevitable, considering the importance of Islamic trade and piracy in the period. This background of the political and cultural might of the Turk is sketched in the wide-ranging Introduction.

The chapters of *Turks, Moors, and Englishmen* are devoted to Turks and Moors in England, and (contrariwise) Britons among the Muslims; then, after the central chapter on the significance of the contemporaneity of dealings with the Turks and Moors, and discovering the New World, come two essays, on the use of the terms "sodomy" and "Holy War" respectively, in relation to attacks on Muslims and on American Indians. This book, unlike the first, includes documentary appendices, providing a list of printed accounts of Englishmen's experiences as captives of Muslims, a summary of the first account of the New World written in Arabic, and a translation of an early seventeenth-century Muslim's discussion of the Islamic view on sodomy.

The first thesis, nowadays, is hardly controversial, though readers with an Anglo- or Eurocentric viewpoint still need to be reminded of it. Since at least the late tenth century, Europeans recognised the contribution that Arabic culture could make towards their own. The perceived cultural imbalance resulted in a surge of translations from Arabic into Latin and Spanish, which flowed unabated from the late eleventh to the end of the thirteenth century. But even when the cultural and scientific goods of Christendom and Islam appeared to have been brought to the same level, the riches of Islamic culture continued to attract Latin scholars. This was particularly true in the sixteenth century, when new manuscripts of Arabic texts were being sought in Istanbul, Damascus and Crete, new translations were made and published, and, eventually, with the Arabic printing press set up by Giovan Battista Raimondi under the aegis of the Medici in the 1580s, Arabic texts were published in Europe in their original language. Arabic studies continued to be pursued for the sake of the furtherance of knowledge in the seventeenth century, and may be said to have culminated in the publication of the Arabic astronomical tables of Ulugh Begh by Thomas Hyde in 1665 and the translation of the books of Appollonius's *Conics* that were lost in their Greek original by the English scholar, Edmund Halley in 1710. The European dimensions of this subject are being explored by a project in the University of Oklahoma on "Scientific exchanges between Islam and Europe: the making of the modern world 1300–1800." The English elements of the interest in Arabic learning have been investigated in two recent books to which Matar refers: the collection of essays edited by Gül Russell on *The 'Arabick' Interest of the Natural Philosophers in Seventeenth-Century England* (Leiden, 1994), and Gerald Toomer, *Eastern Wisdom and Learning: The Study of Arabic in Seventeenth-Century England* (Oxford, 1996). Emblematic of the importance of Arabic culture is the statement of John Selden in 1642 that "the liberal and correctly taught sciences were formerly for a long time called by us [English] 'the studies of the Arabs' . . . as if called from the race and the places where they were then alone seriously cultivated." Matar's study nicely complements these works by concentrating not on the scientific inheritance, but rather on three more popular cultural exchanges: the translation of the Muslim's "untranslatable" Holy Book, the Koran, into English, the Arabic (or alleged Arabic) element in the writings of the Rosicrucians, alchemists and astrologers, and the fortune of Ibn Tufayl's *Hayy al-Yaqzan* as an exemplification of natural theology. With good reason Matar calls the chapter in which these cultural exchanges are discussed "Arabia Britannica," quoting an appellation given to Great Britain by Thomas Decker in a pageant put on for King James I in 1604.

The thesis of *Turks, Moors, and Englishmen* is likely to be more controversial. While *Islam in Britain* shows implicitly that the "Orientalism" described in the notorious book by Edward Said (for a later period) is inapplicable to the situation in the sixteenth and seventeenth centuries, *Turks, Moors, and Englishmen* suggests a source for the "Orientalism" of more recent times. In the words of Matar (17–18): "If the orientalism of the late eighteenth century, as Edward Said defines it, is colonialism as a form of discourse, then what the Renaissance English writers produced was merely a discourse—without colonialism—that was generated by superimposing the discourse about the conquest of America on Islam. The Renaissance witnessed the birth of a British/European discourse of conquest that preceded the development of the other constituents of conquest, namely technological superiority and capitalism. Once the Ottoman and the North African Muslim dominions began their military and commercial decline in the eighteenth century, British and other European writers turned to their discourse about America and the Indians during the Age of Discovery and imposed it on Islam." The central chapter of the book, "The Renaissance Triangle," approaches this topic most directly, by pointing out the similarities between English descriptions of Muslims and those of American Indians, and the similarity of the accounts of Englishmen "going native" in both contexts. Matar rightly claims that such comparisons have been neglected, since most writers treat the English experience of North America as a completely different subject from that of North African affairs, in spite of the fact that most English voyages to the New World took in North Africa—forming a real geographical triangle. Matar's arguments are cogent and engaging, but must still remain speculative.

Even if the leitmotif of the second book is questioned, both books remain rich in information, and eminently readable. They are written in a style which is distinctive of modern English scholarship, and, as such, show great sensitivity to nuances of language, as one would expect of a professor of English. Matar, however, is able to draw upon his knowledge additionally of Arabic, not only in translating the passage from Ahmad bin Qasim on sodomy which forms Appendix C of *Turks, Moors, and Englishmen*, but also in putting forward the Islamic interpretations of the Koran and Traditions throughout the two books, where they differ from the meanings imposed on the Arabic material by Christian readers (e.g., in *Islam in Britain*, 151). Nevertheless, it would be helpful, especially for an Arabist or an Arab or Turkish reader of the book, to have more help in recognizing Arabic and Turkish equivalents. For example, in *Islam in Britain*, 142, one would like to know which Arabic word is translated as "Trust" and, on 149, the conventional Turkish transliteration of the office of "Chiou" could be given. Also (94) Matar wrongly identifies the astrologer "Haly" with "al-Majusti" (read: al-Majusi, the medical authority known in Latin as "Halyabbas"), rather than Ali ibn abi r-rijal or Ali ibn al-Ridhwan. Similarly, on the following page, he does not identify "Nassir Eddin," when it is of importance to know that he is Nasr ad-Din at-Tusi, the leading mathematician and astronomer at the Mongol observatory of Maragha. Moreover, for the eponymous hero of the novel celebrating natural theology, Hayy al-Yaqzan, it would be appropriate to give the translation of Yaqzan ("awake") as well as of Hayy ("alive"; 98).

History of Suicide: Voluntary Death in Western Culture
By Georges Minois, translated by Lydia G. Cochrane
London: Johns Hopkins University Press, 1999

Reviewer: Jonathan Dollimore

Georges Monois does not do with suicide what Foucault tried to do with madness or Baudrillard with death—namely, to offer an intellectual history of the phenomena that sought to radically alter our understanding of the societies in which they occurred. So the overall story is familiar: a gradual, uneven movement from unequivocal condemnation to greater tolerance. Throughout, church and state have condemned it as severely as was possible at the time. Philosophers have been in the vanguard of demystifying and helping to decriminalize suicide—showing, for example, that it is not evil, against nature or God's providence, and so forth. Regarded rationally, suicide might be a sensible option when things have gotten very bad. That said, most philosophers have been on the side of life, not advocating suicide but acknowledging it as a rational response to intolerable conditions.

Minois reminds us throughout that those who wrote in defence of suicide, cautiously or enthusiastically, rarely killed themselves:

"authentic philosophical suicides ... motivated by ... a sentiment of the absurdity and worthlessness of existence, were rare and dubious." Even Hamlet, the touchstone for Minois's study, doesn't kill himself. What Burton said of melancholy—that he wrote about it in order to avoid it in himself—Minois says of philosophers:

> To reflect on death, even to desire it, was a way of renouncing the temptation to kill oneself, because it was also a way to enjoy the essence of what it means to be human, which lies in thought about that very essence....

There's also just a suggestion of hypocrisy, a lingering suspicion that such writers on suicide are practicing a double standard; or, that they are enjoying a privileged and comfortable enough life that, on the one hand, makes it possible to reflect philosophically on suicide, and on the other, keeps them insulated from the brutal deprivations like poverty that drive the less fortunate to take their lives. And where it is, for instance, something like honor rather than poverty that is the cause of suicide, Minois seems to have a slight, half-aware admiration for its practitioners—"real" suicides are not word spinners but people of "action." Those who can kill themselves do, those who can't write about it.

But from Seneca onwards, the intellectual realization that one has the option of suicide is, paradoxically, a way of staying alive: to know one can "cancel" that praxis that is life at any time leads one to hang on in there for longer than one might otherwise do without that reassurance. But there have been notable exceptions. In 1700 an Oxford scholar, Thomas Creech, a translator of Lucretius, hanged himself. Voltaire reported that Creech had written on the margin of his translation "N.B. Must hang myself when I have finished." But finish he did.

The "philosophical suicides" of Seneca are well known. Minois records cases that are less so, but that readers may well find more compelling. For example, the London bookbinder Richard Smith and his wife, Bridget, who in 1732 killed their two-year-old daughter and then hanged themselves. Or the young French (and homosexual) soldiers who took their own lives in a room of an inn on Christmas Day 1773. In each case, the letters they left are poignant, courageous, and disturbing. The Smiths were escaping "Poverty and Rags: Evils that through a Train of unlucky Accidents were become inevitable." The soldiers wrote of wanting to escape "the pain of existing for a moment in order to cease being for an eternity."

One of the most interesting aspects of this book is its emphasis on class. It's obvious that those lower down the scale are more likely to suffer hardships great enough to make suicide seem the only way out. But also, time and again, it's these same people who get villified for taking their own lives. In earlier centuries, suicides were not only denied Christian burial, but their bodies were "punished," often by being hung by the feet, and their land was confiscated. Even in late-eighteenth-century France we read of a suicide whose punishment was that his memory be "extinguished and suppressed in perpetuity," his cadaver dragged through the streets, hanged from the feet, and then thrown on "the common refuse heap," and his property confiscated. The more wealthy often escaped these penalties. From quite early times, courts would exonerate the privileged of any criminal intent by finding them to be of unsound mind at the time of their suicide, or otherwise interpreting the death an accident. As Minois observes, the relative immunity of noble suicides is alluded to by one of Shakespeare's gravediggers when he says of Ophelia that had she not been a gentlewoman, she wouldn't have got a Christian burial. Class figured as well in the method of despatch: one eighteenth-century commentator warns that the rope and drowning are for the common lot; for the person of standing, "poison, steel or firepower are what is needed."

Consistently across the period that Minois mainly addresses—that is, from the sixteenth to the eighteenth centuries—it is in literature that dissident and transgressive attitudes to suicide are most fully explored. Given the consistent and emphatic condemnation of official culture, this is remarkable. Minois offers the safety-valve explanation: literary suicide is a "symbolic liberation for a troubled society"; literature plays "a therepautic role by helping a troubled generation get through difficult times and by limiting the number of real suicides" (110–11). One suspects though that even in literature where suicide is condemned, it has a more ambivalent fascination than this allows. And often, literature generates sympathy for and even glorifies suicide. In the English drama between 1580 and 1640 there are more than two hundred suicides in about one hundred plays; Shakespeare has no less than fifty-two. And, as Minois himself remarks, characters in eighteenth-century literature kill themselves by the hundreds with not a word of authorial reproach" (223). Goethe's *Sorrows of Young Werther* "inspired" actual suicides. The book was prohibited in some areas and denounced by many. Towards the end of his life, when the bishop of Derby reproached him for writing the work of such devastating influence,

Goethe apparently replied that politicians send millions of men to their deaths with a clear conscience.

Why is it that, Catholic or Protestant, the religious almost universally condemn suicide? Is it despite or because of the fact that religion itself articulates profound suicidal tendencies? Minois explores this in the seventeenth-century spiritual texts where the thirst for the annihilation of the self could be given full reign. Jansenists especially generated deep anxiety by prohibiting suicide while affirming an intense desire for death.

For church and state, theologians and most others on the side of authority, the "real" cause of suicide was despair generated by the active intervention of the devil. It was a diabolic act. So perhaps the main interest of John Donne's *Biathanatos* (written around 1610, published 1647) is not its tortuous rehabilitation of suicide so much as the fact that he arrives at his conclusions through recourse to Christian theology rather than the example of the ancients. Was not the death of Christ one of the noblest suicides? The suggestion that it might have been was also one of the most daring blasphemies.

For their part, philosophers have not been keen on the devil as a cause. They have tended to blame insanity, the climate, or too much thinking; in the case of the English, consumption, boredom, or moroseness; the Germans, their "metaphysical enthusiams." Montesquieu was more interesting than most, seeing suicide as the supreme act of self-love, a sacrifice of our being for the love of our being; the suicide is driven by a "natural and obscure instinct that makes us love ourselves more than our very life" (229). Madame de Staël in 1796 discerned one of the things underlying our fascination with the suicide when she remarked that "there is something sensitive or philosophical in the act of killing oneself that is completely foreign to a depraved being" (275).

Attitudes in England have tended to be the most liberal, and one is led to reflect again that it may be because and not in spite of this that it was the last to decriminalize suicide (in 1961). It has always been an issue where liberal, rational thinking has stood most fully at odds with church and state. In England, cadavers were still being punished in the early nineteenth century, and attempted suicides arrested for long after that.

Minois has the judiciousness of the trustworthy historian, carefully assessing all the evidence he has available and, for the most part, steering clear of speculative generailzation. He's especially good on using social-historical evidence of actual rates to counter the impressions people have had that suicide in their own time is on the increase. Even when the figures suggest that it was on the increase, this wasn't necessarily the case. For example, the figures rise quite noticeably in England during the sixteenth century. But the probable reason is new laws that gave coroners a payoff for all verdicts of self-murder. (The term "suicide" replaces "self-murder" shortly before 1700.)

Minois says of mysticism:

> At that profound level limits blur, the unconscious emerges into the conscious, the concrete blends with the abstract, prohibitions are consumed in the forge of desire, and the spirit levitates somewhere between heaven and earth, above barriers of morality and intellect. (165)

I sometimes wished that this kind of insight had been extended to the literary and philosophical explorations of suicide; for the most part, Minois remains helpfully descriptive. Regrettably, his book deals only briefly with the nineteenth and twentieth centuries, but he does rightly remark that the old contradictions persist unchanged: we admire suicides in literature, or the military suicide of a soldier who sticks to his post, or the member of the resistance who kills himself rather than risk giving information under torture, while at the same time regretting the increasing numbers of ordinary suicides whose motives do not seem noble enough. Minois concludes that in the last two centuries, we have stifled a debate on human liberty that flourished between the sixteenth and eighteenth centuries, and at the same have censored suicide as a fundamental human liberty.

Pegasus Shakespeare Bibliographies
General Editor, Richard L. Nochimson
Asheville, Pegasus Press, 1995 ff.

Reviewer: Tanya Pollard

The Pegasus Shakespeare Bibliographies series operates on an appealing premise. These compact and affordable paperbacks offer annotated bibliographies of Shakespeare scholarship, designed for a wide range of audiences: scholars, graduate and undergraduate students, college and high school teachers, and ordinary readers of Shakespeare. The goal of serving so many disparate audiences is ambitious, and at times the emphasis on a general readership may limit its uses for specialists. By and large, however, these slim and succinct volumes are surprisingly effective at having something for everyone. Selective, thorough, and clearly written, they offer a broad survey of significant contributions to Shakespeare scholarship. To have centuries of scholarship on a given play (or several) surveyed, prioritized, and set out succinctly by someone with a good sense of the field is hard to resist, especially for $10.95.

The first five volumes of this series are the subject of this review: *Love's Labors Lost, A Midsummer Night's Dream, and The Merchant of Venice*, edited by Clifford C. Huffman (1995); *King Lear and Macbeth*, edited by Rebecca W. Bushnell (1996); *Richard II, Henry IV, Parts I and II, and Henry V*, edited by Joseph Candido (1998); *Hamlet*, edited by Michael E. Mooney (1999); and *Shakespeare and the Renaissance Stage to 1616 and Shakespearean Stage History 1616–19998*, edited by Hugh M. Richmond (1999). As the distribution of titles suggests, the space accorded to individual plays is correlated to perceived significance or extent of critical attention. *Hamlet*, curiously, is the only play to have a volume all to itself, and not all of Shakespeare's plays will be included. The series, which is projected to include twelve volumes, will cover a total of twenty-five plays and one narrative poem. Forthcoming volumes will include one on Roman works: *The Rape of Lucrece, Titus Andronicus, Julius Caeser, Antony and Cleopatra, and Coriolanus*, edited by John W. Velz and Clifford C. Huffman; and one on romances: *Cymbeline, The Winter's Tale, and The Tempest*, edited by

John S. Mebane. As well as further volumes on additional plays, there will also be a volume on critical theory edited by Jean E. Howard. The editors hope that all volumes will be available by the end of 2003.

The volumes essentially follow the same structure, with modifications based on number and type of works covered. Each begins with an opening section that catalogues and describes editions of Shakespeare's plays and basic reference works. This section, which is the same in each volume, represents a coauthored effort; its annotations have been written by Jean E. Howard, Clifford C. Huffman, John S. Mebane, Richard L. Nochimson, Hugh M. Richmond, Barbara H. Traister, and John W. Velz. This opening section is divided into three parts. Part A analyzes four single-volume editions: David Bevington's *Complete Works, The Riverside Shakespeare, The Norton Shakespeare,* and *The Norton Facsimile: The First Folio of Shakespeare.* The discussions of these texts are extensive, approximately a page each; they explain the volumes' editorial aims and principles, with comments on special features, strengths, weaknesses, and the audiences for whom they might be most appropriate. Part B does the same with multivolume editions, describing in considerable detail the contents and attributes of the major series. These two parts will be particularly useful for teachers, at every level, in choosing texts for courses. They give a thorough inventory and appraisal of the sorts of contexts provided—historical and critical essays, textual apparatus, sources, and so on—as well as suggestions about who will find them the most helpful, and for what ends.

Part C of this opening section surveys basic reference works for Shakespeare studies. Including concordances, source books, collections of documents, glossaries, biographies, and historical works, this section provides a good overview of how to find various kinds of information related to Shakespeare and the plays. Most of these works will be familiar to scholars already working in the field; collecting them here may fill in gaps and offer reminders, but this section will primarily serve as a useful introduction to resources for students and readers newer to Shakespeare studies.

After this shared opening section, the volumes diverge somewhat, although they continue to share basic organizing principles. The four volumes covering Shakespeare's plays have sections, for each play, on editions; dating and textual studies; influences, sources, historical and intellectual backgrounds, and topicality; language and linguistics; criticism; stage history and performance criticism; and bibliographies. Some editions, though not all, offer additional sections on reception history, pedagogy, and collections of essays. Within each section, entries are organized alphabetically by author and described in about a paragraph. As in the first section, annotations are thorough, clear, and accurate; readers will find it easy both to get a sense of the range of approaches to the play, and to locate good references on subjects of their choice. Some aspects of the organization, however, can be frustrating. At times the distinctions between some of these sections seem tenuous: scholars of imagery such as Madeleine Doran and Caroline Spurgeon tread a fine line between "language and linguistics" and "criticism" (they are listed in the former), while Rosalie Colie's study of paradox stands separately from either, in "historical and intellectual backgrounds." Separating collections of essays from critical categories can also be a bit distracting, particularly when many of the individual essays in the collections are also cited in other sections. Perhaps most troublingly for specialists, the alphabetical rather than chronological arrangement of entries makes it harder to trace shifts and developments of critical approaches, and to look for criticism from a given period. Similarly, the emphasis on covering a range of different periods and approaches means that there is no more weight put on recent criticism than on that from earlier eras; this may usefully broaden many critical horizons, but will not directly help someone trying to engage with recent dialogues in the field.

Hugh M. Richmond's volume of Shakespearean stage history shares the general principles of the others, but has a necessarily different format. After the introductory section on editions and reference works, this volume has two primary sections: Shakespeare and the Renaissance Stage to 1616, and Shakespearean Stage History: 1616–1998. The earlier section lists and describes general studies of the Elizabethan theater; the physical characteristics of Elizabethan theaters (divided into background studies and Shakespeare's theaters), and Shakespeare and Elizabethan theatrical practices. The latter is divided largely by periods. After overviews (1616–1998), there are early performances: 1616–1642; the interregnum: 1660–1837 (divided into general studies, and individual managers and actors), and modern performances: 1837–1998, divided into general studies, Victorians and Edwardians, World War I to World War II, the contemporary period, and Shakespeare on film and video. The volume closes with a section on pedagogy. There is much valuable material here, organized in a clear and logical format. This volume will be extremely useful to everyone whose research or teaching draws on performance-related matters.

Given the small size of the volumes, and the ample space accorded to each entry, comprehensive coverage is not one of their goals. The prefaces to the volumes note that they are highly selective. While attempting to represent a range of different approaches and time periods (some reaching as far back as the sixteenth century), the editors have chosen work they considered to be of high quality and/or great influence. Accordingly, annotations emphasize description rather than evaluation. In terms of their uses for readers, this emphasis means that the bibliographies supply a broad introductory overview to the treatments of a certain work, rather than detailed coverage of particular schools of thought. For those who will want access to further material, other bibliographies are listed in the final sections.

The value of these volumes lies particularly in their selective but broad-ranging treatment of their subjects, their clarity, and the thoroughness of their descriptions of the works they cite. For these reasons, they should be particularly helpful for undergraduates doing research on Shakespeare, and the teachers helping to direct this research. Students should be able to take away both a well-informed sense of the history and breadth of writings about the plays and some specific recommendations for writings of good quality on topics and approaches pertinent to them. For college teachers, the straightforward and concise organization will make it easy to find readings to recommend in response to specific queries, and the detailed attention to the resources of different editions will be extremely useful for ordering texts. These same factors may apply for high school teachers as well. For graduate students and scholars, this series has strengths but also limitations. Again, their clarity and brevity will make it easy to identify works of immediate relevance. Their breadth will be useful for those who want to survey a range of approaches to the plays. As mentioned above, however, critics interested in tracing the historical development of approaches, or seeking to focus on dialogues among their peers, will not necessarily find the format and emphasis conducive to these particular goals. That said, the volumes in this series have many more advantages than disadvantages. The scope of the information they contain, combined with their ease of organization, and multiple indices, makes it easy for readers to take what they want from them without being burdened by the less pertinent sections. Their size, simplicity, and affordability make these attractions all the more accessible.

Gender and Literacy on Stage in Early Modern England
By Eve Rachele Sanders
Cambridge: Cambridge University Press, 1998

Reviewer: Margo Hendricks

In some ways, the title of Eve Sanders's commendable book is slightly misleading, as her analytical net is case far wider than the early modern English stage. As her readers quickly discover, *Gender and Literacy on the Stage in Early Modern England* deals with dramatic texts, conduct and instruction manuals, women's autobiographies, and epic poetry. In what proves to be a judicious and cogent reading of premodern and early modern literacy practices and ideologies, Sanders demonstrates the interlocking relations between the politics of gender and the politics of literacy.

Chapter 1 begins with a detailed account of humanist attitudes about female literacy. Women's access to literacy was both circumscribed and carefully monitored, according to Sanders: "not only did men and women acquire literacy at different rates during this period; the specific practices of expression and interpretation in which each was instructed were designed to form them as male and female subjects" differentiated by their sex (1). In the course of her analysis, Sanders draws upon a rich panoply of texts to frame her overview of women's reading practices, humanist theories about the spiritual and moral efficacy of reading only devotional matter, and the responsibilities of fathers and husbands to "mold" a woman's "character by regulating her reading" (8). This exploration of literacy practices and theories cogently sets the stage for Sanders's reading of Book 2 of *The Faerie Queene* and *Love's Labors Lost;* two texts, for Sanders, that privilege reading as a site for self-understanding through the construction of idealized male and female readers.

The book's remaining chapters examine more closely the gendered effects of humanist literacy practices on the English stage. Beginning with an analysis of Shakespeare's use of reading in *Hamlet* and concluding with a discussion of Grace Mildmay's autobiography, Sanders illuminates the competing and often oppositional models of the gendered reader, both male and female. As she notes with *Hamlet*, more often than not the gendered reader on the stage is rarely an unproblematized figure. Sanders' reading of this and other plays by Shakespeare provide familiar insight into his complex recalibration of humanist ideals about subjectivity. As Sanders rightly argues, Shakespeare's "readers" do not embrace, "in a straightforward manner, the male heroic or female iconic function that he or she are assigned" (58). On the contrary, throughout Shakespeare's canon, the humanist idea of learning from exemplum is thrown into question by complicated male dramatic subjectivities such as Richard II, Hamlet, or even the heroic figure Henry V.

Much of *Gender and Literacy on Stage in Early Modern England* rehearses familiar ground to critics and students of Renaissance and early modern English culture. The gender discourse of conduct and instruction manuals for men and women, exemplified in the writings of Vives, Castiglione, Braithwait, Elyot, and others has received much attention lately and thus is fairly well acknowledged. It is when Sanders turns her attention to women writers, such as Mary Sidney and Grace Mildmay, that her study offers new insight into the icon of reading woman. In a chapter titled "She Reads and Smiles," Sanders looks at Mary Sidney's cultivation of a dual public persona—"her persona as a reader" and "as a patron, editor, and author" (90). Sidney's translation of Robert Garnier's *Marc Antoine* becomes the focal point for Sanders's exploration of Sidney's engagement with the iconic figure of "reading" woman as "authorial" woman. Sidney's translation and publication of Garnier's play offers, in Sanders's view, a more complex representation of the Egyptian queen, Cleopatra. Adhering to Garnier's image of Cleopatra as a "multifaceted character—queen, lover, mother, wife, and classical hero—captivating for her courage as well as her constancy," Sidney refuses to acquiesce to normative humanist categorization of Cleopatra as an exemplum of female treachery.

"In *Antonius*," Sanders contends, "Sidney decoupled chastity from female virtue" (124). Importantly, in this chapter, Sanders highlights the profound effect reading has on the dramatic imagination. Had Mary Sidney not undertaken her translation of Garnier's tragedy, the Renaissance "reading" of Cleopatra might not have been as complex as it ultimately became. Furthermore, Sanders illustrates what effect a female authored text re-reading female subjectivity might have on future representations of women. Though Sidney's translation and intervention in Robert Garnier's *Marc An-*

tonie did not manifest an immediate cessation of misogynistic stage representations or the proliferation of gender-specific conduct and instruction manuals, the text's publication meant that, for the theater spectator and the reading woman, there was "an alternative model of Cleopatra and . . . an alternative model of virtue" (137).

Sanders's reading of Sidney's translation against its competitors, Samuel Daniel's *Tragedy of Cleopatra* (1594), Samuel Brandon's *Tragicomedy of the Virtuous Octavia* (1598), William Shakespeare's *Antony and Cleopatra* (1607), and Daniel's revised *Tragedy of Cleopatra* (1607), is a rich and informative treatment of this debate. Sidney's *Antonius: A Tragedy* (1592) generated dramatic tensions, not surprisingly along gendered lines. Daniel's Cleopatra, as he acknowledges, "would not be recognizable to [Sidney's] Antony" (117). Cleopatra, in each of the succeeding plays, is a "potent negative symbol" of femininity. For Samuel Brandon, the idea of a rehabilitated Cleopatra is unthinkable; "everything that distinguishes Cleopatra in Sidney's *Antonius* Brandon reassigns to the title character of his *Virtuous Octavia:* her [Cleopatra] regal aura, her claim to eloquence, her maternal love, her conjugal constancy, her courage to die" (122). While Sanders does not treat Shakespeare's play in great detail, it does become the performative link (in her analysis) between Sidney's text and Samuel Daniel's revision of his *Tragedy of Cleopatra.*

Sidney's translation, for Sanders, exemplifies Sidney's challenge of the "humanist model of the ideal woman as a figure of virtuous passivity, Chastity on a monument reading psalms, and valorized in its place a model of action not alabaster, Cleopatra toiling physically to raise the dying Antony to the top of a building for a last embrace, passion exemplified in a feat of heroic exertion" (92). In essence, with her assumption of the "anti-conventional role of writer-translator," Mary Sidney "took a public stance against the constriction of the exemplary woman to chastity icon and against the reduction of female literacy to chastity exercise" (92), This idea, of the resisting "female" reader/author, is the theme of Sanders's book and she concludes with a discussion of women's autobiography. It is with the autobiography, Sanders determines, that women came to "define themselves" yet still "according to prevailing models of sex-defined differences" (195). Even so, women (and men) "contested and transformed those models, documenting their struggles with each other and with themselves in writing, most vividly in works for the English public theatre" (195).

Despite its coverage of already familiar territory, *Gender and Lit-*

eracy on Stage in Early Modern England is a useful study for a number of reasons. First, Sanders does an excellent job of providing historical background to her analysis. Second, her discussion of Mary Sidney is an illuminating and insightful exploration of the interconnections between writing and reading as articulations of gendered notions of literacy and its purpose. In addition, Sanders guides her readers carefully through the maze of instruction and conduct manuals that flood Renaissance and early modern European cultures, and she does so with diligent attention to the differences produced by culturally specific texts. Sanders's attentive eye to the generic distinctions that need to be maintained between a literary work and a conduct manual makes her close readings of the literary works she studies, from *The Faerie Queene* to *King Lear*, persuasive. If *Gender and Literacy on Stage in Early Modern England* has any shortcomings, they are born of familiarity with her subject matter and the literary works she canvasses.

Bodies and Selves in Early Modern England: Physiology and Inwardness in Spenser, Shakespeare, Herbert, and Milton
By Michael C. Schoenfeldt
New York: Cambridge University Press, 1999

Reviewer: *Jonathan Gil Harris*

Michael C. Schoenfeldt's *Bodies and Selves in Early Modern England* makes an indispensable addition to the growing "corpus" of studies of the early modern English body. Like several literary and cultural critics before him, Schoenfeldt argues that the pre-Cartesian self was a thoroughly embodied one. But where Francis Barker and Jonathan Sawday have hunted for signs of the emergent interior self in the discourses of Renaissance anatomy, Schoenfeldt follows Gail Kern Paster in locating a constellation of experiences of inwardness within early modern discourses of humoral physiology. This is to understate the real originality of Schoenfeldt's book, however, which is noteworthy for the radical theoretical departure it makes from previous scholarship on early modern English bodies. The latter has tended to focus on issues of social control: Peter Stallybrass and Allon White's influential study of carnivalesque transgression and Paster's equally influential work on the humors, to name but two, situate the early modern body within shifting grids of power and techniques of domination. By contrast, Schoenfeldt attends to the body less to expose it as "a victim of the power that circulates through culture" than to illuminate a physiological self-mastery that "authorizes individuality" (11). Lest there be any doubt, though, this is certainly not the disembodied Romantic individuality of Harold Bloom's *Shakespeare: The Invention of the Human.* Although Schoenfeldt has no truck with the early Michel Foucault's emphasis on the self as an effect and instrument of power—an emphasis that has of course provided the theoretical heart of the new historicist project—it is because he embraces the later, mostly neglected Foucault's interest in the "care of the self." And in Schoenfeldt's early modern England, as in Foucault's classical Greece, the care of the self very much entails the care of the body.

Schoenfeldt's starting point is temperance, an ideal that demanded of its early modern practitioners an inwardness that was as much physiological as it was psychological. By cultivating an awareness of their bodies' internal functions, Renaissance English men and women attempted to temper the psychic turbulence stirred up by the disruptive corporeal phenomena of the passions, digestion, and humoral flux. Galenic theories of physiology placed a premium on the body's fungibility and its processes of ingestion and excretion; yet *pace* Paster's argument to the contrary, the humoral body bore little resemblance to the grotesque body of carnival described by Mikhail Bakhtin. Whereas the grotesque body found liberation in festive, scatologically explosive release, the humoral body privileged balance, moderation, and control, particularly of the appetitive and alimentary functions. To moderns who make a fetish of letting it all hang out, the humoral ideal of physiological self-control may sound like a repressive straitjacket. For the quartet of early modern poets Schoenfeldt examines, however, the construction of the self through the practice of bodily temperance represented a mode of liberation—liberation from slavery to one's appetites, and, in the case of Milton, liberation from political tyranny as well. As Schoenfeldt argues in his introduction, "the Renaissance seems to have imagined selves as differentiated not by their desires, which all more or less share, but by their capacity to control these desires" (17).

Chapters 2 and 3 attend specifically to two writers who sought to cultivate the "capacity to control" desires. In his reading of Spenser's Book of Temperance, Schoenfeldt takes issue with David Lee Miller's and Stephen Greenblatt's influential interpretations of Sperserian desire, each of which tends to "locate the self on the axis of genital eroticism" (53). Schoenfeldt argues that such approaches ignore how "other forms of somatic activity—including . . . the alimentary tract—assumed equal if not greater importance in the formation of identity" (62). The necessity of controlling the physiological processes of the body, especially digestion, is integral to the control of desire in the Book of Temperance; the enemies with which the Castle of Alma and Guyon have to reckon are, Schoenfeldt insists, external versions of the intemperate bodily forces that potentially lurk within each. Such forces are even more threatening in Shakespeare's sonnet sequence, which is the subject of Schoenfeldt's next chapter. Although the alimentary tract figures in Shakespearean physiology far less than it does in Spenser's, both writers "imagine the self as a fragile construction barely containing the physiological and psychological pressures of desire" (73). Many modern readers have recoiled from sonnet 94's praise of those who are "as stone, / Unmoved, cold, and to temptation slow" (lines 3–4). But as Schoenfeldt points out, the ideal of cold stoniness makes sense within a neo-Stoic physiological regime that is suspicious of overheated bodily states, especially those prompted by the fires of sexual desire and syphilitic infection to which the later sonnets allude: "far from indicating an inhuman dispassion, the coldness the sonnet counsels represents the victory of an unruffled reason over insurrectionary desire" (88).

Chapters 4 and 5 underscore the role played by food and the alimentary tract in the formation of early modern selves. In a particularly nuanced discussion, Schoenfeldt considers the importance of eating in the spiritual poetry of Herbert, especially *The Temple,* where "the inner self is constructed by regulating carefully the substances that enter and exit the physical body" (96). Schoenfeldt's analysis of diet and waste management in Milton's *Paradise Lost* unravels a similar entanglement of the spiritual and the alimentary. While Herbert views digestion as the physiological process by which humans morally discriminate "nourishment from dung" and "the pure from the impure" (107), it assumes for Milton an even greater ethical significance as the means by which humans can regain something of what was lost in the Fall. If Satan can find that Hell is within him, Milton insists that through temperate diet, postlapsarian humanity can similarly discover "Paradise is ultimately a moral and physiological state rather than a geographical location" (163).

Schoenfeldt persuasively demonstrates how anachronistic habits of thought have impoverished modern readings of Renaissance lyric verse. Our squeamishness with the alimentary and evacuative aspects of Spenser's Castle of Alma, our difficulty with Shakespeare's praise of unmoved cold stones, our tendency to erase the physiological register of Herbert's spiritual inwardness, and our etiolated understanding of the role played by food in Milton's ethics all emerge from uncritically held assumptions about the division between body and self that the four writers would not have shared, let alone understood. Schoenfeldt goes about puncturing these modern assumptions with considerable glee. He is at his most inventive and playful when he rematerializes the physiological within the otherwise disembodied language we use to talk about early modern subjects: "as their common etymology would suggest, the regulation of diet and the keeping of diaries are engaged in corollary forms of diurnal inwardness" (32); "Spenser's portrait of the temperate subject has more traffic with the conduct of the colon than with the suppressions of colonialism" (73); and "so intense and pervasive is Milton's concern with the material processes of existence that his Garden of Eden is in many ways a Garden of Eating" (139).

Given the breadth and depth of insight on display in Schoenfeldt's book, it may seem churlish to fault it for its omissions. The following are intended less as criticisms, therefore, than as possible points of departure for future discussions of Shakespearean and pre-Cartesian physiology. Most of my questions have to do with the primacy of Galenism in Schoenfeldt's analysis of early modern bodies and slaves. This primacy is hardly surprising; all four writers he examines resort extensively to the Galenic language of diet and the humors. As Schoenfeldt would doubtless concede, however, the alimentary tract was by no means the exclusive bodily location for early modern experiences of inwardness. In particular, the physiology of the passions—which Schoenfeldt often touches on yet never comprehensively dissects—frequently entailed a somewhat different bodily register. Shakespeare's plays offer glimpses of the latter: Hamlet's request that actors overcome the "whirlwind of . . . passion" and acquire "a temperance that may give it smoothness" (3.2.5–7), and even Othello's "shadowing passion . . . that shakes me thus" (4.1.40–41), suggest a more histrionic experience of the embodied self in which temperance is equated with control of the body's outward movements rather than its internal digestive processes. How, then, might the passions complicate as well as clarify the largely Galenic, alimentary physiology that Schoenfeldt sees as delimiting the conceptual horizons of Renaissance inwardness?

One might likewise ask whether non-Galenic pathological methods place pressure on the humoral framework within which Schoenfeldt situates Spenser's Book of Temperance. Even Spenser's seventeenth-century commentator, Kenelm Digby, saw Paracelsan elements in the structure of the Castle of Alma, as Schoenfeldt notes (56). Might other quasi-Paracelsan notions haunt book 2, such as the counter-Galenic theory that disease is located in an external invading seed rather than in a state of humoral imbalance? In the episode of Maleger, disease is glaringly a product of bodily invasion as much as of internal insurrection. To insist, as Schoenfeldt does, that Maleger simply represents the irruptive forces of the humors is to finesse the complexity of Spenserian pathology. "Part of the difficulty," Schoenfeldt argues, "is the way in which Spenser needs his allegory to find external correlatives for the largely internal activities that temperance entails" (66). This need, Schoenfeldt maintains, has created something of a red herring that has diverted Greenblatt and his ilk from the trail of Spenser's true intent: if Maleger is identified with Irish woodkerns, it's not because book 2 betrays the entanglement of Renaissance English desire with colonialist discourse but because such external threats are necessary to represent internal physiological processes. With a flick of his wand, then, Schoenfeldt depoliticizes Maleger's Irish attributes and recasts them as harmless Eliotian objective correlatives for inner corporeal turmoil—appropriately intemperate Gertrudes, in other words, occasioned by that within the Castle of Alma which passeth show. This is where I find Schoenfeldt's argument least convincing and most peremptory. Surely Spenser's displacement of "largely internal activities" onto "external correlatives" *does* have political consequences; just as importantly, it also has physiological consequences. To what extent might England's colonial contacts with foreign cultures, peoples, and hitherto unknown epidemic diseases such as syphilis have encouraged Spenser and his contemporaries to rethink, if only metaphorically, the hitherto purely endogenous pathologies of humoralism? How might the embodied English self in the age of colonialism begin to look different as a result?

A last and very different question is prompted by the chapter on Milton, which Schoenfeldt concludes with the observation that "the only revolution over which one finally has control is a revolution within, cultivating the individual liberty that emerges from the disciplined application of reason to one's desires" (166). Schoenfeldt is ventriloquizing the post-Restoration Milton; but one might also be tempted to hear in this assessment the voice of the politically demoralized North American academic at the millenium, writing in a culture for which collective political agency seems increasingly to have become a mirage, the body has emerged as the one remaining area in their lives over which many people believe themselves to have any meaningful control, and the gym or the nutritionist's clinic has supplanted the protest movement as the vehicle of change. Which raises the question: is this a history of bodies in early modern England, or a prehistory of bodies in postmodern North America? Schoenfeldt's afterword suggests that he regards it as both. The ghost he acknowledges in his title, that of the famous 1970 Women's Collective work *Our Bodies, Our Selves* (172), makes clear that he is engaging—and partly endorsing—a contemporary, if "alternative," tradition of understanding the body. In the process, his book offers fitful glimpses of the precarious balancing act that Michel de Certeau enjoined writers of history to perform between the past that is their object and the present that is the place of their practice.

The vicissitudes of that balancing act are responsible, though, for an intriguing vacillation. Throughout *Bodies and Selves in Early Modern England,* Schoenfeldt seems torn between insisting on the irrevocably alien nature of humoral physiology and pleading for its fundamental familiarity. He needs to adopt the first position to make the case that mainstream Western medical science and literary criticism have by and large lost touch with a materially embodied notion of the self; but he needs to uphold the second to suggest that this notion more closely approximates the "real," lived experiences of bodies and selves in the present. It is this desire to tease out points of continuity between Renaissance and modern bodies, I suspect, that leads Schoenfeldt to focus primarily on the humoral language of digestion and the alimentary tract—an aspect of early modern physiology that resonates with the gut experiences of our diet-obsessed age—yet shy away from sustained analysis of the far more alien and ornery physiology of the passions, whose murky materiality arguably presents a greater stumbling block to moderns. To be fair to Schoenfeldt, the passions are probably less explicitly embodied or anatomized in his chosen genre, the lyric, than they were on the Renaissance stage. The book on the early modern passions is still to be written, and I imagine that once it is, the drama of Shakespeare and his contemporaries will figure prominently in its purview. For the time being, though, Schoenfeldt's magnificent study will provide the benchmark against which subsequent scholarship on Renaissance physiology and psychology must be measured.

The Drama of Landscape: Land, Property, and Social Relations on the Early Modern Stage
By Garrett A. Sullivan
Stanford University Press: Stanford, 1998

Reviewer: John Gillies

How can so irresistibly visual a category as "landscape" be fruitfully taken as a topic of early modern English drama when that drama is so famously vocal rather than visual? Garrett Sullivan suggests that we take "landscape" in a broader, more dialectical, sense than is allowed by the perspective-bound aesthetic of "the landscape arts" and the advances of early modern cartographic science. The problem with both these aspects of the early seventeenth century invention of "landscape," Sullivan argues, is to have locked the land into a set of practices and an ideology that—while historically irresistible—were hotly contested in the period and interrogated by the drama. "Landscape," in other words, was and remains not the whole story about "land." Painted landscapes tend to be restful rather than agonized, pastoral rather than historical. Maps and surveys, on the other hand, tend to be affectless. There is no emotional or moral room in either for the agonized histories of dispossession, enclosure, rack-renting, eviction, and vagrancy upon which such paintings (particularly estate views) are materially predicated.

Such histories are, Sullivan suggests, present in the drama under a coded rubric of "absolute property," "stewardship," and "custom." Absolute property—the ideological concomitant of "landscape" as a cultural invention—signifies a landscape removed from entailment in a network of wider (predominantly feudal) social obligation; removed that is to say, from duties of "stewardship." Like the landscape of stewardship, the landscape of custom is one of traditional observance and significance, presupposing and championing "a land-based moral order" (12). Unlike it, however, the landscape of custom tends to be oriented towards the experience of the tenant rather than the lord, placing the tenant "under specific obligations" but also conferring "certain rights." If, for Sullivan, these three types of "landscape" represent three orders of early modern narrative about land, the long view of history reads a "transition from precapitalist to capitalist conceptions of property" where land is conceptualized "not as a site of customary relations but as a fungible 'plot'" (14). The word "plot"—signifying both "map" and parcel of land—nicely catches the complicity of the new cartography in the new commoditization of land. That in turn is a world removed from traditional land observances such as the Rogationtide ceremony (in which the land is perambulated by the community in an assertion of local identity).

The first text in which Sullivan traces the "agon" between these different conceptions of land is *Arden of Faversham* (1592), a tragedy perhaps better thought of as "material" than "domestic" in light of the sensitivity with it registers changes of contemporary material culture. Where the play understands land in terms of an ethic of stewardship, Arden himself represents the new kind of landlord more concerned with surveying and commoditizing his property than negotiating the social network he inherits by virtue of that property. Like estate surveys or maps, whereby (according to a farmer-figure in John Norden's *The Surueyor's Dialogue* (1607) "customes are altred, broken, and sometimes peruerted or taken away" (41), Arden's idea of land carries no entail of "social meaning" (51). The map, according to a contemporary *topos,* allowed the landlord to "see" his land and holdings while "sitting in his chayre" (42). That in turn allowed the landlord to absent himself from the estate (that chair might just as well be in the town). Arden is an absentee landlord. Physically and emotionally absent from the land, he is equally so from his wife, whom he treats purely as an item of property. When he is finally murdered, it is not by "the usual suspects" (here "Black Will" and "Shakebag") but by "friends, family, and members of the household" (53).

In the anonymous *Woodstock* (c. 1594), the commoditized estate engulfs the nation itself. The King becomes an absentee landlord, "farming out" the kingdom for a flat fee to rapacious favorites who ruthlessly rack-rent the inhabitants (now tenants). Notoriously in this play, Richard disseminates "blank charters" throughout the kingdom—pieces of paper signed by individual property owners before being made out (to its own advantage) by the Crown. Sullivan points to a revealing disparity between the attention lavished on this device in the play and the thinness of the historical evidence on which it is based (in Holinshed it is merely a rumour). What, if not the history itself, is behind the play's obsession with this theme? Sullivan compellingly argues that the motive is really to be sought in contemporary developments in land survey and land traffic. The crown itself was at the centre of these developments initially facilitating the then novel idea of *selling* land. In the first place, this was managed only by a jerry-rigged legal fiction whereby the buyer and seller pretended to be engaged in a legal suit "that resulted in the purchaser's being fined in the amount of the purchase price. . . . The more abstract concept of capital value had yet to be invented" (64). To be traded however, land also needed to be surveyed: the more searching the survey, the higher the value. "Concealment hunting" was one contemporary result: the divulging of land which had been notionally "concealed" from notice—possibly by forms of traditional obligation which found no expression in (and were once disabled by) the beady eye of the surveyor. Such practices quickly gave surveying a bad name and, Sullivan argues, are behind *Woodstock*'s "blank charters." This play is also remarkable for the way it shows survey shading into surveillance. Surveying not only suppresses precapitalist spatial practices in the interests of a capitalist "production of space," but intrudes upon the social life of the market town when conversations, ballads and other voice-based knowledges are written down as "evidence" against individual citizens. By such means is the market place—as well as the land—brought within the purview of the landlord's chair, and public forms of social being reduced to monosocial control. Sullivan compellingly demonstrates how this thematic underwrites the scene (late in the play) when a map if produced as a tool for dividing the kingdom into allotments. Emphatically in this play, the Saxtonian nation map is not taken at its own valuation as a glory of early modern English culture.

What does Shakespeare make of the generic nation map? In *1 Henry IV,* Hotspur and his rebel associates produce a map in order to divide the kingdom. If, on one level the map functions as mischievously as that in *Woodstock,* on another it is purely comic. Hotspur balks at the equity of the division, but instead of redrawing the lines speaks wildly of altering the geographic boundary itself by rechannelling the river Trent. Such was their contemporary credence, that maps could be taken as transparent images of the land rather than contingent projections of it, as was Saxton's map of Pembrokeshire which, because drawn on a more generous scale than the other Welsh counties, was on one occasion taxed by Elizabethan councillors at a greater rate. The map in *King Lear* is used to more ominous effect. Again, a map is used to divide the kingdom. But this map gives its user (Lear) the sense that the land is as unpopulated, unregionalised, univalent and untroubled as the rural expanse (the landscape of "ideal emptiness") which England appears to be on the surface of Saxton's map. While no map as such is produced in *Richard II,* Sullivan finds here the "most sustained and most elliptical of all Shakespearean explorations of the meaning of early modern maps" (109). John of Gaunt's apostrophe of England as an island is read as "map enabled" both in the sense of explicitly echoing *Woodstock*'s image of the nation as farm, and in the sense of creating an opposing image of the country as a "blessed plot" (117). Gaunt's speech is also plausibly shown to anticipate the later emblem of the garden, "showing, as in a model, our firm estate" (118). All three of Shakespeare's maps are shown as indebted to *Woodstock*'s critique of a "landscape of sovereignty," but as less interested than that play is in respecting "the customary life of particular regions" (122).

While property and estate represented one motive of cartography in the period, another is represented by the needs of travel and communication. In perhaps the cleverest of his Shakespeare discussions, Sullivan reads *Cymbeline* against the road atlasses of John Nordern and John Ogilby. Imogen's question, "how far it is / To this same blessed Milford", serves as point of departure to a fascinating discussion of the meaning of distance. Nordern's 1625 *Guyde for English Travailers* contains the distances between towns and places. But curiously, these distances take no account of "hills, dales, woods, and other impediments," or "the curuing crookednes, and other difficulties of the wayes" (129)—all which should have been far more significant to the early modern traveller than distance considered in the abstract. Why then does Nordern compute distance "as the crow flies," and why did the "statute mile" of 1593 supplant the various forms of customary miles to be found in various parts of a highly regionalised country? The answer is both imperial (the statute mile was originally local to London) and related to an "encyclopedic impulse." The atlasses were less traveller's aids than part of "a larger empiricist project" (132). Again, they attested to the primacy of vision (distance computed visually from station to station) rather than by actual perambulation or local custom. The fixation on Milford Haven in *Cymbeline* is thus seen as transcending the Tudor significance by which it was justified by an earlier generation of critics. Both as a port offering harbour to an invasion fleet and as an elusive destination within the "wild" landscape of Wales, Milford represents that paradox of closeness and otherness, familiarity and inaccessibility, that Wales itself presented to England in the period. In terms of vision it was close (as close as Milford had seemed to Imogen from a hilltop). In terms of custom, language and geography however, it was remote. If the play might be seen as celebrating British independence from Rome, it more deeply celebrates the Roman penetration of Britain as a type of England's own Jacobean claim on Wales or indeed of Nordern's championship of a uniform road measure.

Friction existed between highway and estate—right of way and right of ownership (absolute property)—contributing towards the key early modern phenomenon of vagabondage. Excavation of this three-way relationship provides wonderful conceptual access to the perplexing oddness of Brome's *A Jovial Crew* (1641). Not only does Brome ask his audience to believe in a squire (Oldrents) so addicted to hospitality as to quarter a crew of beggars on his estate every winter, but also in a conscientious estate steward (Springlove) so addicted to the roving life as to join the beggars every summer in their "stroll-all-the-land-over." What is the material ground of these unlikely propositions (Pepys thought the play "the most innocent . . . that ever I saw")? Sullivan begins by exploring the early modern highway, a space "overdetermined" by "negative associations" of violence and vagabondage (164–65). Effectively the highway was less a materially consistent site than "a perpetual *right of passage* in the sovereign" (a form of easement) over the subject's property (165). If this was one source of resentment, another was that the upkeep fell to local proprietors and communities. Lawlessness resulted as unpaid road workers—"the King's Hiwaymen"—took to beggary and pestering travellers. For their part, travellers would simply blaze their way over property if a section of road proved unusable (for which angry landowners might extort payment). The tension between Springlove the steward and the vagabondage to which he is addicted was thus extreme, not least because the rise of the estate steward (to replace absentee landlords) was one of several signs of the increasing privatising of the estate. If the steward guarded the portals of an emergent capitalist subjectivity, the vagabond—neither knowing his place nor known by any place—stood outside any of the existing structures of identity formation. Meanwhile hospitality passed from being an aristocratic ethic to becoming a grudging institutional duty. The beggars then "are perched not only between freedom and constraint, anonymity and identity, but between hospitality and the poor laws that modify and replace it" (191). Absurd though it seems then, Brome's play puts highly fraught material changes into dialogue—siding, as did so much of the drama, with a nostalgic attachment to the rapidly obsolescing customary worlds.

Space itself is reprised in Sullivan's final chapter exploring "the beleaguered city" theme in Thomas Heywood's *1 Edward IV* (c. 1599) where London is defined in terms of the historical threat of invasion posed by the bastard Falconbridge. But what can this myth of civic preservation—what can civic space itself—mean to the modern critic? Sullivan seeks to augment the justly influential "ceremonial" and "ritual" account of London in Stephen Mullaney's *The Place of the Stage* with a more materially focused account. Yet one that is not quite so material as Henri Lefebvre's in *The Production of Space.* Accordingly, Sullivan modifies Lefebvre's materialist anatomy of space into "representations of space" (space as scientifically modelled or projected in maps), "spatial practice" (sociospatial networks and material formations), and "representational spaces" ("space as directly *lived* through its associated images and symbols"). Where Lefebvre thinks of *lived* (and dreamed) space as a passive or second-order phenomenon, Sullivan rightly insists that it is just as active and "productive" as the former two categories. "Landscape" indeed—at once representational, model-based and material—is the perfect instance. Turning then to *Edward,* Sullivan notes a disparity between the play's valorisation of the city wall and the obsolescence of the wall within contemporary spatial practice. While the wall was valorised in contemporary polemic against the lawlessness of the suburbs, it was negated by a growing dependance on the suburbs as industrial sites beyond the regulation of the obsolescing Guild structures which still prevailed within the "City" proper. In this sense, Heywood's play is as nostalgic as Brome's or indeed *Woodstock.* In dramatising Edward's own encroachment on the city however—his sexual assault on Jane Shore, wife of the honest citizen Matthew Shore—Heywood is surprisingly contemporary. The assault can be read "partly as the symbolic displacement of anxiety regarding relations between the Crown and the city's masculinized mercantile economy" (219)—an anxiety focussed particularly on the Crown's evasion of the Guild structure by the awarding of monopolies. By comparison, Shakespeare pictures the beleaguered city in *3 Henry VI* merely as a stage for aristocratic agency.

This book is important for its informational wealth and its analytic subtlety—affording a truly bountiful array of insights into early modern spatial production and imagining. This is a genuine work of exploration. Many of Sullivan's texts the reader (even the informed reader) may encounter for the first time; certainly in the context of such searching analyses. It is this readers' feeling that—his reading of *Cymbeline* aside—Sullivan is at his best with the less well-known texts. The book is exemplary for the way in which it poses theatrical and imaginative texts against cartographic and "material" texts. While influenced predominantly by Lefebvre's materialist conception of space, Sullivan never falls into the trap of "materialising" the play-texts he deals with, of seeing them as mere extensions of (effectively of "mapping" them onto) a set of material substructures. Sullivan's willingness to allow theatre its own agency, its own thickness, is alike independent of the old "humanist" reverence for art as it is of the materialist irreverence for it. In no small part this dialectical openness is expressed in the structure. One does not find the analyses of texts following obediently in the trail of theoretical exposition or historical analysis. Instead, the analyses of aesthetic and material texts proceed hand in hand, dialectically. Very occasionally one finds oneself wanting to quibble—I am not entirely convinced that Gaunt's speech in *Richard II* is map-based for instance—but for much the greater part one is both convinced and compelled by this fine book.

Catholicism, Controversy, and the English Literary Imagination, 1558–1660
By Alison Shell
Cambridge University Press, 1999

Reviewer: Lowell Gallagher

Alison Shell has undertaken an important, timely, and ambitious project. Her book maps a history of the interrelated literary, social, and political aspects of English Catholic experience at a critical juncture in English history, the period between Elizabeth I's Act of Uniformity and the Restoration. The particular value of Shell's handling of this topic owes a good deal to her intuition of the broad stakes in what happened to the very notion of the English Catholic during the period that saw the consolidation of England's sense of itself as a nominally Protestant nation and cultural entity. What gives this book its argumentative heft is its double agenda. Not only does it follow the trail of English Catholics' marginalization in a variety of cultural spheres, it argues that such marginalization has left blind spots in received notions of English literary and social history, as well as in current critical assessments of the poetics and aesthetics of Tudor-Stuart culture. Overall, the most significant contribution of Shell's book is its suggestive depiction of the need to assemble (and reassemble) both early modern textual matter and current critical methodologies for locating and assessing the encrypted role of a specifically English Catholic presence in the making of English literary tradition and culture.

The sheer scale of the topic, which is undoubtedly one of the book's chief assets, makes it perhaps inevitable that the book does not entirely fulfill the promise of its revisionist claims. It should be said at the outset, then, that the shortcomings apparent to me in Shell's particular approach are also, in part, a measure of the difficulty the book's interdisciplinary ambition faces. The project calls for a disciplinary and methodological eclecticism, which Shell engages powerfully on occasion, but does not take on board as a matter of principle. This discrepancy ultimately diminishes the force of the book's project to assess the scope of what has become, in effect, a phantom presence of an early modern "catacomb culture"

(p. 16): the Catholic component to an English "literary imagination," as encoded not only in canonical literary history but also in the critical vocabularies used to address the poetics of early modern culture.

That said, the book's overarching scheme is lucidly laid out. In brief, the argument establishes four interlocking areas of inquiry, addressing two general topics: canonicity and loyalism. Under the rubric of canonicity, Shell first examines the exemplary place of Webster and Middleton in English literary history. Shell argues that the genre these playwrights helped to consolidate, Jacobean revenge tragedy, produced a configuration of decadence driven by a specific anti-Catholic animus, one which, having become the stuff of cliché rather quickly, further metamorphosed into a condition of virtual invisibility. Virtual invisibility, Shell points out, remains legible in the apparent ease with which the critical history of Jacobean revenge tragedy has helped perpetuate an "unconscious association of Catholicism with evil" (18) within a nominally secular or agnostic critical practice. Shell's interest in the camouflaging of the contingent polemics that animated Webster's and Middleton's poetics of evil establishes an important part of the book's larger project, which is to refocus critical attention on the impact of a cultivated misrecognition concerning what could be called the "Catholic problem" in the formation not only of a literary canon but of a canonical hermeneutic as well. The second phase of Shell's argument amplifies this double perspective. By orchestrating principles of archival evidence, historiographical scholarship, and a literary critic's ear for subtext, Shell reevaluates the stature of the devotional poetry and poetics of Robert Southwell and Richard Crashaw in English literary history, demonstrating both the critical contributions of each and their virtual displacement into the corridors of literary history by their own contemporaries. Of particular interest here is Shell's conjectural recuperation of polemical voices that the historical dominance of the Sidney-Spenser genealogy has cast into virtual oblivion: the intervention of Catholic poets in the widespread and protracted debate over the proper calibration of biblical and secular tropes in the emerging vernacular devotional lyric. Shell suggests, convincingly, that the significance of the poetry of Catholic converts like William Alabaster and Thomas Lodge in this polemic has been underestimated and needs to be reassessed, as does the poetic component to the very notion of conversion.

The second topic, which addresses the problem of Catholic loyalism, identifies the dynamics of erasure and misrecognition in a broader field of inquiry, one which addresses more squarely the difficult, changing interface of literary and political conceptions of boundary-marking in Elizabethan, Jacobean, and Caroline cultures. Two subtopics provide the nominal frame for this phase of the argument: the useful claim that scholars need to shelve the notion of a single (however fraught) English Catholic community, and should think instead of several coexistent English Catholic communities; and the equally useful claim that a similar diversity to the experience and "politicised" use of exile, "Catholic homesickness," and nostalgia needs to be explored (109).

The claims are more than promissory notes, in the sense that the last half of the book sets up a striking counterpoint of familiar and less familiar documents and cultural scenes, giving a satisfying taste of the range of domestic and expatriate English Catholic communities, together with their polemical and poetic idioms. Perhaps inevitably, pride of place is given to the vexed role of Mary Stuart in the simmering loyalism debates in Eizabethan literary and political cultures. Pride of place, however, turns out to be preamble. Observing the rival status of Mary Stuart and Elizabeth Tudor as objects of royal panegyric across the confessional divide, Shell focuses her attention on two less well known cultural instances of vexed and tactically ambiguous loyalty, the Petrarchan verse of Elizabethan diplomat and Catholic poet Henry Constable, and the *imprese* designed by secular priest and emblematist Thomas Wright for the Earl of Essex's presentation at the 1595 Accession Day tilts.

Shell's juxtaposition of these two cases is illuminating, on several fronts. Brief but careful readings of a handful of Constable's poems demonstrate how a perceived need for political discretion on the topic of Catholic loyalism was met by the poet's deft play on a range of topical and allegorical associations of Marian-influenced praise to a Virgin Queen. What Shell's assessment of Constable's poetry does not make clear—the uncertain reception his negotiatory idiom could expect to find in various communities of readership (both Catholic and Protestant)—appears vividly in her discussion of Thomas Wright's career in the entourage of Essex. Shell's reading of the extant copies of Wright's *imprese* shows real discernment, conveying probable points of guarded accord and private irony in the nominal collaboration between two "loose cannons" in the courtly world, the loyalist priest and the ambitious political pragmatist. More provocatively, Shell pays attention to recalcitrant aspects of the historical record, notably the apparent absence of evidence that Wright's *imprese* were in fact used. For Shell, the discrepancy between extant textual production and excluded social performance functions like a symptom of a blind spot in the cultural scene itself. That is, the discrepancy becomes a gauge of the incompatibility of different alignments of communal identity: Essex's pragmatic interest in cultivating the support of Catholic loyalists versus his equally pragmatic interest in dispelling gossip, at a critical juncture in his career, about his own "crypto-popery" (133). In these pages, which are among the most compelling in the book, Shell engages an interpretive practice seemingly constituted not so much by a desire to read against the grain of the historical record, as by a willingness to give apparent lacunae an eloquence that speaks to the aporias produced by the specific historicity of the artifacts under Shell's cautious speculation.

To varying degrees, the book's subsequent topics display a similar balance of archival reconstruction, historical synthesis, and interpretive entrepreneurship. The Constable-Wright pairing, for example, is braced by an illuminating, though brief, discussion of turn-of-the-century verse romances like Anthony Copley's *A Fig for Fortune* (1596) and R. C.'s *Palestina* (1600). Shell indicates how these romances fused traits of Spenserian allegory and an apocalypticism specific to the Catholic loyalist imaginary, in a quixotic attempt to secure the loyalist cause within the parameters of a providentially informed English nationhood. The unusual texture, if it can be called that, of the Catholic presence in Stuart literary and court cultures—its combination of prominence and elusiveness—is conveyed first by Shell's insightful (though, again, brief) account of the career of polymath John Barclay, whose novels *Euphormio* and *Argenis* infused the conventions of Heliodoran romance with controversial topical subtexts on the dangers posed to monarchical absolutism by Jesuits as well as Puritans and Huguenots. More substantial coverage is given to topics that, unlike Barclay, have been promoted from specialist to canonical status: the masque cultures of Henrietta Maria's court and Elizabeth Cary's biblical drama *Mariam*.

A different cost-benefit analysis might have resulted in more ample coverage of Barclay, whose political as well as literary importance is parsimoniously handled here. On the other hand, there is a certain tactical advantage to Shell's emphasis on the respective careers of Henrietta Maria and Elizabeth Cary. The scholarly currency of these figures' particular social and literary contexts has given rise to a set of dominant critical perceptions of the ideological work that the masques and the play perform on the loyalty question. Shell constructs an interventionist response, based on what her own book helps make clear: the complex tissue of loyalties and competing ideological positions that characterized the identity and the perception of English Catholics (and Catholics in England) in the period. Shell makes a useful adjustment to Erica Veevers' important analysis of Henrietta Maria's masques, by proposing, contra Veevers, that the masques' fusion of neo-Platonic and Marian imagery is both more and less than a proto-feminist assertion of female power or a mark of pro-Catholic resistance.[1] Reading the masques with an eye to their unstable place in the syntax governing the French Catholic queen's range of movement in the English court, Shell enjoins us to consider how the masques "externalise Henrietta Maria's particular loyalist obligations, as stratagems of deference towards a husband who was also a monarch," producing a "form of chaste conversation coupled with fear" (151, 155). Shell's assessment exemplifies an important ramification of the book's well-documented general assumption: being English Catholic, or Catholic in England, rarely meant one thing, for at least two reasons. First, there were multiple ways of identifying oneself as Catholic. Second, being Catholic did not, and could not, erase other habits or marks of group and personal identification. As with her treatment of Constable's poetry and Wright's *imprese,* Shell's approach to the literary and social texts summoned here to address the question of English Catholic identity and loyalty, as it was broached in the Caroline court, helps locate a textual chiaroscuro-effect that corresponds to the competing requirements of social and political discretion and assertion at large in the culture.

A similar habit of mind informs Shell's discussion of Cary's *Mariam*. Shell suggests, plausibly, that *Mariam* is neither a straightforward autobiographical rendering of Cary's confessional and domestic difficulties, nor an abstract of a theoretical collusion of political and domestic economies, but something else: an imaginative "experimentation with Catholicism," as well as a projection of a "genuine contemporary ambiguity" in the kinds of congress that mixed marriages required (157). Here Shell recalls her earlier discussion of the hermeneutic difficulties posed by the uncertain boundaries of conversion-experiences, as represented by the radically different cases of William Alabaster, Richard Crashaw, and Thomas Lodge. Like other poetic articulations of the dynamics of conversion, Cary's play, Shell suggests, should be considered an "autodidactic" rather than autobiographical enterprise (157). That is, the play constituted a form of "imaginative role-playing" (93) in which degrees or aspects of what might be called confessional otherness could be provisionally inhabited for reasons that would become intelligible only retrospectively, after a subsequent point of conviction (or after a sequence of contingent events). The notion of a poetics of autodidacticism is one of the most fertile areas of inquiry that the book proposes, though it must be said that the notion does not rise to the level of a genuine concept or methodological tool in these pages. (In footnotes the author indicates that future work will pursue the topic.)

Allusively, however, the notion continues to resonate in the final section of the book. This section addresses, appropriately, cross-sections of the social condition and poetic idiom of English Catholic communities in exile—communities transported or "converted" into nominally parenthetical spaces. The treatment of what the author calls the "subject of exile" in the last two chapters constitutes one of the book's major accomplishments. Snapshots of English Catholics of the move, in the ranks of itinerant virtuosi across the Channel, frame an interesting discussion of Catholic and baroque implementations of lamentation and complaint genres and a corresponding investment in the trope of tears and the figure of "weeping England." Like the treatment of Mary Stuart, this sketch serves as introduction to a more sustained examination of juxtaposed cultural scenes. The fascinating story of the adventures of a cult object in Spanish Marian veneration is paired with the rise of polemical and didactic Jesuit dramas in seminaries and colleges across Europe. In brief, a statue of the Virgin and Child was desecrated by English troops under Essex during the sack of Cadiz in 1596; eventually the object, now converted into a "unique combination of statue and relic" (201), ended up at the College of Valladolid. From there, Shell argues, the so-called Madonna Vulnerata began its career as emblem of the exiled English Catholic communities. Together with the tropes of tears and weeping, the Madonna Vulnerata became a resource for polemical allusion and didactic allegory in Jesuit dramas. These tropes furnished a vocabulary for a militant as well as therapeutic representation of a specifically Catholic experience of wounded, "disfigured" subjectivity and community. Shell's brief accounts of politically spiced Jesuit dramas, like *Captiva Religio* (Rome, 1614) and *St. Thomas Cantuar* (Rome, 1613) suggest a further axis. The poetics of disfigurement could also be applied to a revisionist cause, in which divisive events in

English political and religious history were revisited and reclaimed, in order to promote a viable Catholic imaginary—what Shell calls a condition of "mental impregnability" against current and future encroachments of a "dominant" protestantizing culture in England. In essence, Shell's survey of this marginalized dramatic genre assembles the central rhetorical and ideological tools for what could be called, after Matteo Ricci, a new kind of "memory palace," a mental fortress in which to dwell while anticipating the reconquest of a lost land.

These are the main contours of Shell's book. A few final observations. One feature this book shares with other contributions of its kind to cultural studies is that its greatest strength is also its weakness. The book's encyclopedic range is warranted by the author's thorough grounding in a historiographical enterprise that until recently has remained on the periphery of early modern cultural studies: the archival recuperation of recusant and, more broadly, English Catholic history. The advances and changing ideological positions within this field since the nineteenth century make for an absorbing story, one that Shell tells well early in the book, presumably in order to situate the constellation of topics she advances. As the discussion of the Catholic "literary imagination" unfolds, however, Shell's broad canvas of topics and texts presents an increasingly conspicuous tactical problem (one not entirely due to the current exigencies of the book publishing trade, which dictate the feasible length of monographs). Because a high proportion of the literary documents and relevant contxts cannot be assumed to be readily familiar to many readers, the language of paraphrase or summary often prevails over analysis. Critical perceptions are indeed spelled out, but they often need to be taken on the basis of textual instances whose exemplarity cannot be gauged.

This feature is not by itself disabling, primarily because Shell shows such an impressive command of the historical fund. Yet the book's critical orientation is both less and more than what it appears to be at the outset. Early chapters suggest that the author's command owes something to a scrupulous, quasi-positivist historiographical ethos, without which, of course, the very field of recusant studies would not have achieved respectability (in view of its hagiographical component). It is also clear, early on, that this ethos is here coupled with a generalized new-historical and cultural-materialist feel for the involutions to be traced in a cultural poetics. Such elasticity of approach is precisely what enables the book to read "through" the archives and the literary-historical truisms relating to the English Catholic presence in the culture. It is therefore unfortunate that Shell did not sacrifice some of the achieved breadth of coverage to lay out more clearly the hermeneutic and critical assumptions that appear to underpin some of the book's most illuminating and provocative gestures (as in the Constable-Wright pairing). At a minimum, such a frame would help explain how certain formal techniques reminiscent of a new-historical hermeneutic can be used to identify elements of an encrypted English Catholic poetics. Crucially, a more explicit metacritical discussion would also help establish links between otherwise isolated, hastily characterized, yet strategically prominent terms punctuating Shell's argument. Discussions of the "illiberal act of perpetuating" anti-Catholic "prejudice" (p. 56) and self-indulgent "anachronism" (p. 50) in the critical reception of Jacobean revenge tragedy, for example, seem to conflate ethical and hermeneutic notions of prejudice uncritically, and to ignore the evidence from Shell's own argument that the complex temporality of conversion includes a tactical use of anachronism. (On a different topic, Shell seems to acknowledge such use, when she appreciatively paraphrases Paul Tabori's insight that the exile lives "in the present and the past simultaneously," 194.).[2] A moment's pause to qualify the argumentative stance here (against Jonathan Dollimore's "camp" reading of Webster, as it happens) would have helped Shell avoid the unwarranted, and I think unintended, impression that critical uses of anachronism (as can be found in queer studies, for example) are somehow fundamentally "irresponsible" (50). Finally, if the book's brief excursions into the relations between the English Catholic literature of diaspora and English "baroque" poetics were integrated with the absorbing discussions of conversion as a mode of imaginative role-playing, the book would be in a position to give more substance to its claim that the traits of a specific English Catholic "literary imagination" can be identified. Much of the content of that "imagination" can be found in this book. So can a good deal of its form or poetics, though these elements remain, ironically enough, dispersed.

None of the concerns I have raised, however, diminishes the importance of this book. Shell has made a significant contribution to early modern religious and cultural studies, by presenting what will likely become an indispensable map of the diverse English Catholic itineraries in the early modern world, and by establishing an impressive range of new issues and questions for fellow scholars to explore with her.

Notes

1. Erica Veevers, *Images of Love and Religion: Queen Henrietta Maria and Court Entertainments* (Cambridge University Press, 1989).
2. Paul Tabori, *The Anatomy of Exile: A Semantic and Historical Study* (London: Harrap, 1972), 32ff.

Index

Akrigg, G. P. V., 132
Alabaster, William, 266, 269
Anderson, Benedict, 217
Anderson, Judith H., 165–69
Anna of Denmark, Queen, 136, 140, 151, 156
Anzai, Tetsuo, 185
Aquinas, Thomas, 52
Ascham, Roger, 123

Bahar, Nazife, 77
Bakhtin, M. M., 36–37, 233–35, 253
Baldwin, William, 215
Bamborough, J. B., 19
Barclay, John, 268
Barker, Deborah E., 63
Barker, Francis, 252
Barnes, Barnabe, 29, 31, 33
Barroll, Leeds, 132–62
Barry, Philippa, 180–84
Bartels, Emily, 85, 120
Barthes, Roland, 186
Baskins, Cristelle, 97–98
Beale, Simon Russell, 41
Beaumont, Francis, 29, 30, 31, 32, 198
Behn, Aphra, 207–9
Belsey, Catherine, 169–73
Bergeron, David, 173–79
Bevington, David, 246
Bishop, Elizabeth, 200
Blau, Herbert, 54
Blayney, Peter, 197
Bloom, Harold, 253
Blount, Charles, 143, 145
Boccaccio, 93–108
Booke of Sir Thomas More, 109–31
Bothwell, Earl of, 143
Bourdieu, Pierre, 36–37
Bowers, Fredson, 110
Brahe, Tycho, 152

Brandon, Samuel, 251
Bredbeck, Gregory, 65
Bristol, Michael, 203–7
Brome, Richard, 29, 30, 198
Brown, John Russell, 184–89
Brown, Kathleen, 208
Brown, Penelope, 233
Browne, John, 233
Bruce, Edward, 139, 144
Bruno, Giordano, 181
Bry, Théodore de, 210, 215, 218, 221
Burbage, Richard, 27
Burnett, Charles, 236
Burton, Robert, 241
Bushnell, Rebecca, 245
Butler, Judith, 21

Callaghan, Dympna, 23, 25, 64, 68–71, 190–95
Candido, Joseph, 245
Carlino, Andrea, 21
Carr, Robert, 173
Cary, Elizabeth, 268–70
Cave, Terence, 168
Cecil, Edward, 153
Cecil, Robert, 135, 136, 139, 140, 141, 149, 223–25
Cecil, Thomas, 140
Cecil, William, 143, 223–25
Chambers, E. K.., 116
Chamberlain, John, 154
Chapman, George, 29, 230
Charnes, Linda, 204
Chaucer, Geoffrey, 96–108
Chettle, Henry, 100
Chikamatsu, 185
Cibber, Colley, 38–42
Cochrane, Lydia, 240–45
Coeffeteau, Nicholas, 52
Colie, Rosalie, 247

Index

Constable, Henry, 267
Cooper, Helen, 169–73
Copley, Anthony, 268
Cornwallis, Sir William, 19
Coryat, Thomas, 214
Crashaw, Robert, 266, 269
Crashaw, William, 218
Creech, Thomas, 241
Croft, Pauline, 223–25
Crooke, Helkiah, 21
Cunningham, Karen, 84, 85
Cunningham, William, 60

Dallington, Robert, 214
Daniel, Samuel, 251
Davenport, Robert, 31, 32
Day, Angel, 233, 235
Dekker, Thomas, 29, 30, 31, 32, 33, 34, 100, 198, 207, 235, 238
Deloney, Thomas, 227
Derrida, Jacques, 180
Descartes, René, 44
Dessen, Alan, 23, 24, 27–35, 196–99
Detmer-Goebel, Emily, 75–92
Deutsch, Niklaus, 172
Devereaux, Robert, 142, 223–25
DiGangi, Mario, 177
Digby, Kenelm, 256
Dollimore, Jonathan, 240–45, 272
Donne, John, 20, 59–60, 70, 132, 218, 243
Doran, Madeleine, 247
Drake, Francis, 227–28
Dubois, Claude-Gilbert, 168
Dubrow, Heather, 199–203

Eden, Richard, 215
Elam, Kier, 36
Eliot, John, 218
Eliot, T. S., 20
Erasmus, 233
Erskine, Sir Thomas, 139, 149

Falco, Raphael, 203–7
Fawcett, Mary, 85
Fenton, Geoffrey, 216
Ficino, Marsilio, 49
Field, Nathan, 30, 190
Flaubert, Gustave, 37
Fleming, Juliet, 227

Fletcher, John, 29, 30, 31, 33, 34, 114, 120, 198, 212–22
Ford, John, 28, 29, 33, 55–56, 196
Foucault, Michel, 23, 209, 220, 253
Freud, Sigmund, 20, 173, 180–84
Frye, Northrup, 172
Frye, Roland, 172
Frye, Susan, 207–9
Fugita, Minoru, 185
Fulwood, William, 233
Fuss, Diana, 114

Gabrieli, Vittorio, 110
Gaines, Barry, 196–99
Gallagher, Lowell, 265–73
Garnet, Henry, 154
Garnier, Robert, 250–52
Garrick, David, 39, 41
Geertz, Clifford, 23
Genest, John, 39
Gillies, John, 24–25, 57–62, 258–64
Goethe, J. W., 58, 242
Goldberg, Jonathan, 65, 115, 122, 173, 233
Gosson, Stephen, 52
Gray, Robert, 218
Grazia, Margreta de, 116
Greenblatt, Stephen, 23, 116, 219–20, 232, 253, 256
Greene, Robert, 30, 33, 215
Greg, W. W., 11
Griselda, 93–108

Hackluyt, Richard 215, 218
Hadfield, Andrew, 209–22
Hall, Kim F., 225–32
Hammer, Paul, 223–25
Hapgood, Robert, 189
Harington, Sir John, 145
Harriot, Thomas, 210, 218, 219
Harris, Jonathan Gil, 252–58
Haughton, William, 100
Hazlitt, William, 39–42
Heidegger, Martin, 34, 166, 167
Helms, Lorraine, 77
Hemming, William, 30
Henderson, Judith Rice, 233
Hendricks, Margo, 208–9, 249–52
Henrietta Maria, Queen, 268–70
Henslowe, Philip, 27

Index

Herbert, George, 252–58
Herbert, Mary Sidney, 144, 250–52
Herbert, William, 146–48
Herodotus, 58
Heywood, Thomas, 29, 31, 32, 34, 77, 263
Hibbard, G. R., 46, 49
Hilliard, Thomas, 224
Hillman, David, 21
Hinman, Charlton, 114
Hippocrates, 58
Hodgdon, Barbara, 36
Home, George, 149
Hopkins, Lisa, 207–9
Hosley, Richard, 197
Howard, Lord Henry, 135–62
Howard, Jean, 180, 208, 246
Howard, Philip, 138
Howard, Lord Thomas, 137, 149
Howard, William, 138
Hoy, Cyrus, 110
Huffman, Clifford, 245, 246
Hull, Suzanne, 226
Hunt, Leigh, 39
Hutson, Lorna, 227
Hyde, Thomas, 238

Irigaray, Luce, 181–83
Irving, Henry, 40, 41

James, Henry, 40
Jaster, Margaret Rose, 93–108
Johnson, Geordie, 205
Johnson, Nora, 190–95
Jones, Inigo, 132
Jonson, Ben, 20, 29, 32, 33, 70, 132, 152, 153, 166, 207, 235
Jordan, Constance, 204–5
Josselin, Ralph, 46

Kahn, Coppélia, 81, 180
Kamps, Ivo, 63
Kean, Edmund, 39–42
Keats, John, 20
Kendall, Gillian, 83
Kennedy, Dennis, 186
Killigrew, Henry, 198
Kishi, Tetsuo, 189
Klapisch-Zuber, Christiane, 93–94
Knight, Joseph, 40

Kolodny, Annette, 225–32
Kott, Jan, 38
Kristeva, Julia, 181–83
Kuriyama, Shigehisa, 44
Kyd, Thomas, 28, 31, 33, 122, 259
Kyle, Barry, 189

Lacan, Jacques, 20, 171
Lacqueur, Thomas, 21
Lake, Sir Thomas, 150, 155
Lanyer, Amelia, 207
Lecercle, Anne, 165–69
Lefebvre, Henri, 58
Levinson, Stephen, 233, 234
Lewkenor, Lewis, 214
Linton, Joan Pong, 225–32
Lodge, Thomas, 28, 227, 266, 269
Loomba, Ania, 209–22

Macrobius, 58
Magnusson, Lynne, 232–36
Makin, Bathsua, 207
Manners, Roger, 143, 145
Marlowe, Christopher, 29, 31, 32, 68, 122, 205, 212
Marshall, Cynthia, 23, 24, 51–56, 180–84
Marston, John, 29, 30, 33, 34
Martyr, Peter, 215
Marx, Karl, 69
Massinger, Philip, 30, 31, 32, 33, 120
Masten, Jeffrey, 109–31
Matar, Nabil, 236–40
Mattes, Edmund, 19
Mazzio, Carla, 21
McEachern, Claire, 216–17
McGann, Jerome, 116
McKenzie, D. F., 114
McMillin, Scott, 110, 115, 122
Mebane, John, 246
Melchiori, Giorgio, 110
Mendes, Sam, 41
Merleau-Ponty, Maurice, 53, 55
Middleton, Thomas, 29, 30, 32, 77, 266
Mikalacki, Jodi, 207
Mildmay, Grace, 249–52
Miller, David Lee, 254
Milton, John, 206, 252–58
Minois, Georges, 240–45
Momose, Izumi, 185

More, Sir Thomas, 212–22
Mornay, Philippe de, 20
Mullaney, Stephen, 263
Mulryne, J. R., 184
Munday, Anthony, 20
Munster, Sebastian, 228–29

Nashe, Thomas, 32
Neely, Carol Thomas, 63
Neill, Michael, 172, 181
Nietzsche, F., 205
Ninagawa, Yukio, 189
Noble, Adrian, 189
Nochimson, Richard L., 245
Noda, Hideki, 185, 186
Nordern, John, 259, 261

Ogilby, John, 261
Olivier, Laurence, 41
Ong, Walter, 234
Orgel, Stephen, 65, 186
Ovid, 76, 85–86, 88

Painter, William, 216
Parker, Patricia, 181, 183
Paster, Gail Kern, 21, 22, 24, 44–50, 60, 68, 252
Peele, George, 33, 142
Percy, Charles, 136
Petrarch, 96–108
Phillips, John, 99–108
Pollard, Alfred, 111
Pollard, Tanya, 245–49
Potter, Lois, 184–89
Powell, Brian, 185
Pratt, Mary Louise, 225
Primrose, Diana, 207
Prynne, William, 24, 51–52

Rabelais, F., 168
Rackin, Phyllis, 180
Radel, Nicholas, 173–79
Raimondi, Giovan Battista, 238
Rainolds, John, 24, 51–52
Ralegh, Elizabeth, 207
Ralegh, Sir William, 135, 139
Ricci, Matteo, 271
Rich, Penelope, 143
Richmond, Hugh, 245, 246
Rimer, J. Thomas, 186

Roach, Joseph, 36
Robertson, Karen, 207–9
Roos, Lady, 155
Rowley, William, 77
Ruggles, George, 153–54
Russell, Edward, 143
Russell, Gull, 238

Said, Edward, 209–10, 238–39
Sanders, Eve, 249–52
Sasayama, Takashi, 184
Sawday, Jonathan, 252
Scanlon, Thomas J., 209–22
Scarry, Elaine, 54
Schoenfeldt, Michael, 22, 66, 252–58
Scholz, Susanne, 23
Seldon, John, 238
Senda, Akihiko, 185
Senda, Koreya, 185, 186
Seneca, 241
Shakespeare, William: Plays: *Antony and Cleopatra*, 28, 31, 186, 245, 251; *As You Like It*, 52–53; *Comedy of Errors*, 152; *Coriolanus*, 33, 206; *Cymbeline*, 189, 245, 261, 262, 264; *Edward III*, 109; *Hamlet*, 20, 24, 27, 30, 31, 37–38, 45–50, 169, 171, 182–83, 198, 204, 206, 241, 249, 250, 255; *1 Henry IV*, 245, 260; *2 Henry IV*, 51, 245; *Henry V*, 152, 245, 250; *1 Henry VI*, 33; *2 Henry VI*, 34; *3 Henry VI*, 31, 32, 198, 264; *Henry VIII*, 29, 32, 110, 233; *Julius Caesar*, 21, 27, 245; *King Lear*, 33, 54, 109, 171, 180, 182–83, 185, 187, 233, 245; *Love's Labour's Lost*, 152, 233, 245, 249; *Macbeth*, 171, 183, 245; *Measure for Measure*, 152, 155; *Merchant of Venice*, 121, 153, 154, 180, 233, 234, 245; *Merry Wives of Windsor*, 29, 152, 185; *Midsummer Night's Dream*, 34, 201, 233, 245; *Much Ado about Nothing*, 171, 233; *Othello*, 45, 64, 79, 152, 171, 182, 183, 194–95, 206, 233, 242; *Pericles*, 110, 200; *Richard II*, 30, 205, 206, 250, 261, 264; *Richard III*, 24, 28, 30, 38–42, 204; *Romeo and Juliet*, 29, 181–82; *Taming of the Shrew*, 93–108; *Tempest*, 34, 64, 185, 189, 192–95, 211–22, 230–31, 245; *Timon of*

Athens, 181, 233; *Titus Andronicus*, 28, 32, 33, 55, 75–92, 245; *Troilus and Cressida*, 229–31; *Twelfth Night*, 186, 195; *Two Noble Kinsmen*, 32, 109–10, 189; *Winter's Tale*, 54, 99, 170, 172, 198, 245
Shapiro, James, 120, 121
Shaw, G. B., 38, 41
Shell, Alison, 265–73
Shell, Marc, 234
Sherman, William, 232–36
Shewring, Margaret, 184–89
Sidney, Elizabeth, 143
Sidney, Sir Philip, 142, 144, 146, 222, 233
Sidney, Robert, 143
Siemon, James, 24, 36–43
Singh, Jyotsna, 23, 25, 63–67
Siraisi, Nancy, 21
Smith, Bridget, 241
Smith, Bruce R., 19–26, 176, 177
Smith, John, 228
Smith, Richard, 241
Somerset, Thomas, 136
Southwell, Robert, 266
Spenser, Edmund, 219–20, 227, 229, 231, 249, 252–58
Sprague, A. C., 38
Spurgeon, Caroline, 247
Stallybrass, Peter, 115, 116, 253
Starkely, Thomas, 214
Stewart, Alan, 177
Strong, Roy, 132
Struever, Nancy, 178
Stuart, Esmé, 149, 173–79
Stuart, King James, 132–62, 173–79
Stuart, Queen Mary, 138–39, 267
Sullivan, Garrett, 258–64
Suzuki, Tadashi, 185

Takahashi, Yasunari, 185
Takakuwa, Yoko, 186
Taylor, Gary, 113
Teskey, Gordon, 199–203
Thomas, William, 214
Thompson, E. M., 111
Thomson, Leslie, 24, 196–99
Tomer, Gerald, 238
Tomkis, Thomas, 153
Tourneur, Cyril, 31
Traister, Barbara, 246
Trousdale, Marion, 234
Tsubouchi, Shoyo, 185
Tudor, Queen Elizabeth, 135, 142, 267

Unwin, George, 120

Velz, John, 245, 246
Villiers, George, 173–79

Wack, Mary, 208
Waller, Gary, 233
Walsingham, Frances, 142
Wayne, Valerie, 208
Weber, Max, 203–4
Webster, John, 28, 32, 207, 266
Werstine, Paul, 111
Whigham, Frank, 233
White, Allon, 253
White, John, 210
Williams, Raymond, 115
Williams, Roger, 218, 220
Worthen, W. B., 36
Wright, Thomas, 46, 60, 267–68
Wriothesley, Henry, 143, 145
Wroth, Mary, 215

Yarington, Robert, 31
Yokota-Murakami, Gerry, 185, 186